Portrait by Sargent

THE COMPLETE WORKS

OF

JAMES WHITCOMB RILEY

IN WHICH THE POEMS, INCLUDING A NUMBER HERETOFORE UNPUBLISHED,
ARE ARRANGED IN THE ORDER IN WHICH THEY WERE WRITTEN,
TOGETHER WITH PHOTOGRAPHS, BIBLIOGRAPHIC NOTES
AND A LIFE SKETCH OF THE AUTHOR

COLLECTED AND EDITED BY

EDMUND HENRY EITEL

BIOGRAPHICAL EDITION

VOLUME ONE

INDIANAPOLIS
THE BOBBS-MERRILL COMPANY
PUBLISHERS

PRESS OF
BRAUNWORTH & CO.
BOOKBINDERS AND PRINTERS
BROOKLYN, N. Y.

TO
MY FATHER AND MOTHER

ACKNOWLEDGMENT

For the hearty and generous assistance of Mr. Riley's friends and kinsmen in the preparation of this edition, the publishers wish to make grateful acknowledgment. To Mrs. Charles Cox, Mrs. Benj. S. Parker, Mr. George C. Hitt, to Mrs. Julia A. Riley and to Mr. Henry Eitel especial thanks are due for material furnished and time freely given; to Mr. D. S. Alexander and Mr. Charles Vergil Tevis for permission to use excerpts from various interviews; to Miss Ora Williams, Mr. W. H. Cathcart and Mr. Frank G. Darlington for information for the bibliography; to Charles Scribner's Sons and The Century Company for permission to include poems originally published by them, and to Mr. Will D. Howe for editorial counsel.

CONTENTS

1870   PAGE
A Backward Look 1
Philiper Flash 4
The Same Old Story 8
To a Boy Whistling 10

1871
An Old Friend 11
What Smith Knew About Farming . . . 12

1872
A Poet's Wooing 18
Man's Devotion 20
A Ballad 23
The Old Times Were the Best 27

1873
A Summer Afternoon 28

1874
At Last 30
Farmer Whipple—Bachelor 32
My Jolly Friend's Secret 40
The Speeding of the King's Spite . . . 43
Job Work 49
Private Theatricals 51
Plain Sermons 53
"Tradin' Joe" 54
Dot Leedle Boy 59

1875
I Smoke My Pipe 64
Red Riding Hood 66
If I Knew What Poets Know 67

CONTENTS

	PAGE
An Old Sweetheart of Mine	68
Squire Hawkins's Story	73
A Country Pathway	85

1876

The Old Guitar	90
"Friday Afternoon"	92
"Johnson's Boy"	97
Her Beautiful Hands	99
Natural Perversities	101
The Silent Victors	104
Scraps	110
August	112
Dead in Sight of Fame	114
In the Dark	116
The Iron Horse	118
Dead Leaves	121
Over the Eyes of Gladness	123
Only a Dream	125
Our Little Girl	127
The Funny Little Fellow	128

1877

Song of the New Year	131
A Letter to a Friend	133
Lines for an Album	134
To Annie	135
Fame	136
An Empty Nest	139
My Father's Halls	140
The Harp of the Minstrel	141
Honey Dripping From the Comb	143
John Walsh	144
Orlie Wilde	146
That Other Maud Muller	154
A Man of Many Parts	156
The Frog	158
Dead Selves	160

CONTENTS

	PAGE
A Dream of Long Ago	163
Craqueodoom	166
June	168
Wash Lowry's Reminiscence	169
The Ancient Printerman	173
Prior to Miss Belle's Appearance	175
When Mother Combed My Hair	178
A Wrangdillion	180
George Mullen's Confession	182
"Tired Out"	191
Harlie	192
Say Something to Me	193
Leonainie	194
A Test of Love	196
Father William	198
What the Wind Said	200
Morton	207
An Autumnal Extravaganza	209
The Rose	211
The Merman	213
The Rainy Morning	215
We Are Not Always Glad When We Smile	216
A Summer Sunrise	218
Das Krist Kindel	220

1878

An Old Year's Address	225
A New Year's Plaint	227
Luther Benson	230
Dream	232
When Evening Shadows Fall	234
Ylladmar	236
A Fantasy	238
A Dream	242
Dreamer, Say	244
Bryant	246
Babyhood	247

CONTENTS

	PAGE
LIBERTY	249
TOM VAN ARDEN	259
T. C. PHILIPS	263
A DREAM UNFINISHED	264
A CHILD'S HOME LONG AGO	267
THE FLYING ISLANDS OF THE NIGHT	279
JAMES WHITCOMB RILEY—A SKETCH	367
NOTES	391

THE COMPLETE WORKS

OF

JAMES WHITCOMB RILEY

IN SIX VOLUMES

A BACKWARD LOOK

AS I sat smoking, alone, yesterday,
   And lazily leaning back in my chair,
Enjoying myself in a general way—
Allowing my thoughts a holiday
   From weariness, toil and care,—
My fancies—doubtless, for ventilation—
   Left ajar the gates of my mind,—
And Memory, seeing the situation,
   Slipped out in the street of "Auld Lang Syne"—

Wandering ever with tireless feet
   Through scenes of silence, and jubilee
Of long-hushed voices; and faces sweet
Were thronging the shadowy side of the street
   As far as the eye could see;
Dreaming again, in anticipation,
   The same old dreams of our boyhood's days
That never come true, from the vague sensation
   Of walking asleep in the world's strange ways.

Away to the house where I was born!
    And there was the selfsame clock that ticked
From the close of dusk to the burst of morn,
When life-warm hands plucked the golden corn
    And helped when the apples were picked.
And the "chany dog" on the mantel-shelf,
    With the gilded collar and yellow eyes,
Looked just as at first, when I hugged myself
    Sound asleep with the dear surprise.

And down to the swing in the locust-tree,
    Where the grass was worn from the trampled
        ground,
And where "Eck" Skinner, "Old" Carr, and three
Or four such other boys used to be
    "Doin' sky-scrapers," or "whirlin' round":
And again Bob climbed for the bluebird's nest,
    And again "had shows" in the buggy-shed
Of Guymon's barn, where still, unguessed,
    The old ghosts romp through the best days dead!

And again I gazed from the old schoolroom
    With a wistful look, of a long June day,
When on my cheek was the hectic bloom
Caught of Mischief, as I presume—
    He had such a "partial" way,
It seemed, toward me.—And again I thought
    Of a probable likelihood to be
Kept in after school—for a girl was caught
    Catching a note from me.

And down through the woods to the swimming-
    hole—
  Where the big, white, hollow old sycamore
    grows,—
And we never cared when the water was cold,
And always "ducked" the boy that told
  On the fellow that tied the clothes.—
When life went so like a dreamy rhyme,
  That it seems to me now that then
The world was having a jollier time
  Than it ever will have again.

PHILIPER FLASH

YOUNG Philiper Flash was a promising lad,
   His intentions were good—but oh, how sad
      For a person to think
      How the veriest pink
And bloom of perfection may turn out bad.
Old Flash himself was a moral man,
And prided himself on a moral plan,
      Of a maxim as old
      As the calf of gold,
Of making that boy do what he was told.

And such a good mother had Philiper Flash;
Her voice was as soft as the creamy plash
      Of the milky wave
      With its musical lave
That gushed through the holes of her patent churn-
            dash;—
And the excellent woman loved Philiper so,
She could cry sometimes when he stumped his toe,—
      And she stroked his hair
      With such motherly care
When the dear little angel learned to swear.

Old Flash himself would sometimes say
That his wife had "such a ridiculous way,—
   She'd humor that child
   Till he'd soon be sp'iled,
And then there'd be the devil to pay!"
And the excellent wife, with a martyr's look,
Would tell old Flash himself "he took
   No notice at all
   Of the bright-eyed doll
Unless when he spanked him for getting a fall!"

Young Philiper Flash, as time passed by,
Grew into "a boy with a roguish eye":
   He could smoke a cigar,
   And seemed by far
The most promising youth.—"He's powerful sly,"
Old Flash himself once told a friend,
"Every copper he gets he's sure to spend—
   And," said he, "don't you know
   If he keeps on so
What a crop of wild oats the boy will grow!"

But his dear good mother knew Philiper's ways
So—well, she managed the money to raise;
   And old Flash himself
   Was "laid on the shelf,"
(In the manner of speaking we have nowadays).
For "gracious knows, her darling child,
If he went without money he'd soon grow wild."
   So Philiper Flash

With a regular dash
"Swung on to the reins," and went "slingin' the
          cash."

As old Flash himself, in his office one day,
Was shaving notes in a barberous way,
     At the hour of four
     Death entered the door
And shaved the note on his life, they say.
And he had for his grave a magnificent tomb,
Though the venturous finger that pointed "Gone
          Home,"
     Looked white and cold
     From being so bold,
As it feared that a popular lie was told.

Young Philiper Flash was a man of style
When he first began unpacking the pile
     Of the dollars and dimes
     Whose jingling chimes
Had chinked to the tune of his father's smile;
And he strewed his wealth with such lavish hand,
His rakish ways were the talk of the land,
     And gossipers wise
     Sat winking their eyes,
(A certain foreboding of fresh surprise).

A "fast young man" was Philiper Flash,
And wore "loud clothes" and a weak mustache,
     And "done the Park,"

For an "afternoon lark,"
With a very fast horse of "remarkable dash."
And Philiper handled a billiard-cue
About as well as the best he knew,
  And used to say
  "He could make it pay
By playing two or three games a day."

And Philiper Flash was his mother's joy,
He seemed to her the magic alloy
  That made her glad,
  When her heart was sad,
With the thought that "she lived for her darling
      boy."
His dear good mother wasn't aware
How her darling boy relished a "tare."—
  She said "one night
  He gave her a fright
By coming home late and *acting* tight."

Young Philiper Flash, on a winterish day,
Was published a bankrupt, so they say—
  And as far as I know
  I suppose it was so,
For matters went on in a singular way;
His excellent mother, I think I was told,
Died from exposure and want and cold;
  And Philiper Flash,
  With a horrible slash,
Whacked his jugular open and went to smash.

THE SAME OLD STORY

THE same old story told again—
   The maiden droops her head,
The ripening glow of her crimson cheek
   Is answering in her stead.
The pleading tone of a trembling voice
   Is telling her the way
He loved her when his heart was young
   In Youth's sunshiny day:
The trembling tongue, the longing tone,
   Imploringly ask why
They can not be as happy now
   As in the days gone by.
And two more hearts, tumultuous
   With overflowing joy,
Are dancing to the music
   Which that dear, provoking boy
Is twanging on his bowstring,
   As, fluttering his wings,
He sends his love-charged arrows
   While merrily he sings:

"Ho! ho! my dainty maiden,
   It surely can not be
You are thinking you are master
   Of your heart, when it is me."
And another gleaming arrow
   Does the little god's behest,
And the dainty little maiden
   Falls upon her lover's breast.
"The same old story told again,"
   And listened o'er and o'er,
Will still be new, and pleasing, too,
   Till "Time shall be no more."

TO A BOY WHISTLING

THE smiling face of a happy boy
  With its enchanted key
  Is now unlocking in memory
My store of heartiest joy.

And my lost life again to-day,
  In pleasant colors all aglow,
  From rainbow tints, to pure white snow,
Is a panorama sliding away.

The whistled air of a simple tune
  Eddies and whirls my thoughts around,
  As fairy balloons of thistle-down
Sail through the air of June.

O happy boy with untaught grace!
  What is there in the world to give
  That can buy one hour of the life you live
Or the trivial cause of your smiling face!

AN OLD FRIEND

HEY, Old Midsummer! are you here again,
  With all your harvest-store of olden joys,—
Vast overhanging meadow-lands of rain,
And drowsy dawns, and noons when golden grain
  Nods in the sun, and lazy truant boys
Drift ever listlessly adown the day,
Too full of joy to rest, and dreams to play.

The same old Summer, with the same old smile
  Beaming upon us in the same old way
We knew in childhood! Though a weary while
Since that far time, yet memories reconcile
  The heart with odorous breaths of clover hay;
And again I hear the doves, and the sun streams
          through
The old barn door just as it used to do.

And so it seems like welcoming a friend—
  An old, *old* friend, upon his coming home
From some far country—coming home to spend
Long, loitering days with me: And I extend
  My hand in rapturous glee:—And so you've
          come!—
Ho, I'm so glad! Come in and take a chair:
Well, this is just like *old* times, I declare!

WHAT SMITH KNEW ABOUT FARMING

THERE wasn't two purtier farms in the state
   Than the couple of which I'm about to relate;—
Jinin' each other—belongin' to Brown,
And jest at the edge of a flourishin' town.
Brown was a man, as I understand,
That allus had handled a good 'eal o' land,
And was sharp as a tack in drivin' a trade—
For that's the way most of his money was made.
And all the grounds and the orchards about
His two pet farms was all tricked out
With poppies and posies
And sweet-smellin' rosies;
And hundreds o' kinds
Of all sorts o' vines,
To tickle the most horticultural minds;
And little dwarf trees not as thick as your wrist
With ripe apples on 'em as big as your fist:
And peaches,—Siberian crabs and pears,
And quinces—Well! *any* fruit *any* tree bears;
And the purtiest stream—jest a-swimmin' with fish,
And—*jest a'most everything heart could wish!*
The purtiest orch'rds—I wish you could see
How purty they was, for I know it 'ud be
A regular treat!—but I'll go ahead with
My story! A man by the name o' Smith—

(A bad name to rhyme,
But I reckon that I'm
Not goin' back on a Smith! nary time!)
'At hadn't a soul of kin nor kith,
And more money than he knowed what to do with,—
So he comes a-ridin' along one day,
And *he* says to Brown, in his offhand way—
Who was trainin' some newfangled vines round a
        bay-
Winder—"Howdy-do—look-a-here—say:
What'll you take for this property here?—
I'm talkin' o' leavin' the city this year,
And I want to be
Where the air is free,
And I'll *buy* this place, if it ain't too dear!"—
Well—they grumbled and jawed aroun'—
"I don't like to part with the place," says Brown;
"Well," says Smith, a-jerkin' his head,
"That house yonder—bricks painted red—
Jest like this'n—a *purtier view*—
Who is it owns *it?*" "That's mine too,"
Says Brown, as he winked at a hole in his shoe,
"But I'll tell you right here jest what I *kin* do:—
If you'll pay the figgers I'll sell *it* to you."
Smith went over and looked at the place—
Badgered with Brown, and argied the case—
Thought that Brown's figgers was rather too tall,
But, findin' that Brown wasn't goin' to fall,
In final agreed,
So they drawed up the deed

For the farm and the fixtures—the live stock an' all.
And so Smith moved from the city as soon
As he possibly could—But "the man in the moon"
Knowed more'n Smith o' farmin' pursuits,
And jest to convince you, and have no disputes,
How little he knowed,
I'll tell you his "mode,"
As he called it, o' raisin' "the best that growed,"
In the way o' potatoes—
Cucumbers—tomatoes,
And squashes as lengthy as young alligators.
'Twas allus a curious thing to me
How big a fool a feller kin be
When he gits on a farm after leavin' a town!—
Expectin' to raise himself up to renown,
And reap for himself agricultural fame,
By growin' of squashes—*without any shame*—
As useless and long as a technical name.
To make the soil pure,
And certainly sure,
He plastered the ground with patent manure.
He had cultivators, and double-hoss plows,
And patent machines for milkin' his cows;
And patent hay-forks—patent measures and
          weights,
And new patent back-action hinges for gates,
And barn locks and latches, and such little dribs,
And patents to keep the rats out o' the cribs—
Reapers and mowers,
And patent grain sowers;

And drillers
And tillers
And cucumber hillers,
And harriers ;—and had patent rollers and scrapers,
And took about ten agricultural papers.
So you can imagine how matters turned out:
But *Brown* didn't have not a shadder o' doubt
That Smith didn't know what he was about
When he said that "the *old* way to farm was played
    out."
But Smith worked ahead,
And when any one said
That the *old* way o' workin' was better instead
O' his "modern idees," he allus turned red,
And wanted to know
What made people so
Infernally anxious to hear theirselves crow?
And guessed that he'd manage to hoe his own row.
Brown he come onc't and leant over the fence,
And told Smith that he couldn't see any sense
In goin' to such a tremendous expense
For the sake o' such no-account experiments :—
"That'll never make corn!
As shore's you're born
It'll come out the leetlest end of the horn!"
Says Brown, as he pulled off a big roastin'-ear
From a stalk of his own
That had tribble outgrown
Smith's poor yaller shoots, and says he, "Looky
    here!

This corn was raised in the old-fashioned way,
And I rather imagine that *this* corn'll pay
Expenses fer *raisin'* it!—What do you say?"
Brown got him then to look over his crop.—
His luck that season had been tip-top!
And you may surmise
Smith opened his eyes
And let out a look o' the wildest surprise
When Brown showed him punkins as big as the lies
He was stuffin' him with—about offers he's had
For his farm: "I don't want to sell very bad,"
He says, but says he,
"Mr. Smith, you kin see
For yourself how matters is standin' with me,
I understand farmin' and I'd better stay,
You know, on my farm;—I'm a-makin' it pay—
I oughtn't to grumble!—I reckon I'll clear
Away over four thousand dollars this year."
And that was the reason, he made it appear,
Why he didn't care about sellin' his farm,
And hinted at his havin' done himself harm
In sellin' the other, and wanted to know
If Smith wouldn't sell back ag'in to him.—So
Smith took the bait, and says he, "Mr. Brown,
I wouldn't *sell* out but we might swap aroun'—
How'll you trade your place for mine?"
(Purty sharp way o' comin' the shine
Over Smith! Wasn't it?) Well, sir, this Brown
Played out his hand and brought Smithy down—
Traded with him an', workin' it cute,

Raked in two thousand dollars to boot
As slick as a whistle, an' that wasn't all,—
He managed to trade back again the next fall,—
And the next—and the next—as long as Smith
     stayed
He reaped with his harvests an annual trade.—
Why, I reckon that Brown must 'a' easily made—
On an *average*—nearly two thousand a year—
Together he made over seven thousand—clear.—
Till Mr. Smith found he was losin' his health
In as big a proportion, almost, as his wealth;
So at last he concluded to move back to town,
And sold back his farm to this same Mr. Brown
At very low figgers, by gittin' it down.
Further'n this I have nothin' to say
Than merely advisin' the Smiths fer to stay
In their grocery stores in flourishin' towns
And leave agriculture alone—and the Browns.

A POET'S WOOING

I woo'd a woman once,
But she was sharper than an eastern wind.

—TENNYSON.

"WHAT may I do to make you glad,
　　To make you glad and free,
　　Till your light smiles glance
　　And your bright eyes dance
Like sunbeams on the sea?
　　　Read some rhyme that is blithe and gay
　　　Of a bright May morn and a marriage day?"
And she sighed in a listless way she had,—
"Do not read—it will make me sad!"

"What shall I do to make you glad—
　　To make you glad and gay,
　　Till your eyes gleam bright
　　As the stars at night
When as light as the light of day?—
　　　Sing some song as I twang the strings
　　　Of my sweet guitar through its wanderings?"
And she sighed in the weary way she had,—
"Do not sing—it will make me sad!"

18

"What can I do to make you glad—
 As glad as glad can be,
   Till your clear eyes seem
   Like the rays that gleam
 And glint through a dew-decked tree?—
   Will it please you, dear, that I now begin
   A grand old air on my violin?"
 And she spoke again in the following way,—
   "Yes, oh yes, it would please me, sir;
 I would be so glad you'd play
   Some grand old march—in character,—
 And then as you march away
I will no longer thus be sad,
But oh, so glad—so glad—so glad!"

MAN'S DEVOTION

A LOVER said, "O Maiden, love me well,
For I must go away:
And should *another* ever come to tell
Of love—What *will* you say?"

And she let fall a royal robe of hair
That folded on his arm
And made a golden pillow for her there;
Her face—as bright a charm

As ever setting held in kingly crown—
Made answer with a look,
And reading it, the lover bended down,
And, trusting, "kissed the book."

He took a fond farewell and went away.
And slow the time went by—
So weary—dreary was it, day by day
To love, and wait, and sigh.

20

She kissed his pictured face sometimes, and
    said:
  "Oh! Lips, so cold and dumb,
I would that you would tell me, if not dead,
    Why, why do you not come?"

The picture, smiling, stared her in the face
    Unmoved—e'en with the touch
Of tear-drops—*hers*—bejeweling the case—
    'Twas plain—she loved him much.

And, thus she grew to think of him as gay
    And joyous all the while,
And *she* was sorrowing—"Ah, welladay!"
    But pictures *always* smile!

And years—dull years—in dull monotony
    As ever went and came,
Still weaving changes on unceasingly,
    And changing, changed her name.

Was she untrue?—She oftentimes was glad
    And happy as a wife;
But *one* remembrance oftentimes made sad
    Her matrimonial life.—

Though its few years were hardly noted, when
    Again her path was strown
With thorns—the roses swept away again,
    And she again alone!

And then—alas! ah *then!*—her lover came:
  "I come to claim you now—
My Darling, for I know *you* are the same,
  And I have kept *my* vow

Through these long, long, long years, and now
    no more
  Shall we asundered be!"
She staggered back and, sinking to the floor,
  Cried in her agony:

"I have been false!" she moaned, "*I* am not
    true—
  I am not worthy now,
Nor ever can I be a wife to *you*—
  For I have broke my vow!"

And as she kneeled there, sobbing at his feet,
  He calmly spoke—no sign
Betrayed his inward agony—"I count you meet
  To be a wife of mine!"

And raised her up forgiven, though untrue;
  As fond he gazed on her,
She sighed,—"*So happy!*" And she never
    knew
  He was a *widower.*

A BALLAD

CROWD about me, little children—
  Come and cluster 'round my knee
While I tell a little story
  That happened once with me.

My father he had gone away
  A-sailing on the foam,
Leaving me—the merest infant—
  And my mother dear at home;

For my father was a sailor,
  And he sailed the ocean o'er
For full five years ere yet again
  He reached his native shore.

And I had grown up rugged
  And healthy day by day,
Though I was but a puny babe
  When father went away.

Poor mother she would kiss me
  And look at me and sigh
So strangely, oft I wondered
  And would ask the reason why.

23

And she would answer sadly,
   Between her sobs and tears,—
"You look so like your father,
   Far away so many years!"

And then she would caress me
   And brush my hair away,
And tell me not to question,
   But to run about my play.

Thus I went playing thoughtfully—
   For that my mother said,—
"You look so like your father!"
   Kept ringing in my head.

So, ranging once the golden sands
   That looked out on the sea,
I called aloud, "My father dear,
   Come back to ma and me!"

Then I saw a glancing shadow
   On the sand, and heard the shriek
Of a sea-gull flying seaward,
   And I heard a gruff voice speak:—

"Ay, ay, my little shipmate,
   I thought I heard you hail;
Were you trumpeting that sea-gull,
   Or do you see a sail?"

And as rough and gruff a sailor
　　As ever sailed the sea
Was standing near grotesquely
　　And leering dreadfully.

I replied, though I was frightened,—
　　"It was my father dear
I was calling for across the sea—
　　I think he didn't hear."

And then the sailor leered again
　　In such a frightful way,
And made so many faces
　　I was little loath to stay:

But he started fiercely toward me—
　　Then made a sudden halt
And roared, "*I* think he heard you!"
　　And turned a somersault.

Then a wild fear overcame me,
　　And I flew off like the wind,
Shrieking *"Mother!"*—and the sailor
　　Just a little way behind!

And then my mother heard me,
　　And I saw her shade her eyes,
Looking toward me from the doorway,
　　Transfixed with pale surprise

For a moment—then her features
  Glowed with all their wonted charms
As the sailor overtook me,
  And I fainted in her arms.

When I awoke to reason
  I shuddered with affright
Till I felt my mother's presence
  With a thrill of wild delight—

Till, amid a shower of kisses
  Falling glad as summer rain,
A muffled thunder rumbled,—
  "Is he coming 'round again?"

Then I shrieked and clung unto her,
  While her features flushed and burned
As she told me it was father
  From a foreign land returned.

. . . .

I said—when I was calm again,
  And thoughtfully once more
Had dwelt upon my mother's words
  Of just the day before,—

"I *don't* look like my father,
  As you told me yesterday—
I know I don't—or father
  Would have run the other way."

THE OLD TIMES WERE THE BEST

FRIENDS, my heart is half aweary
  Of its happiness to-night:
Though your songs are gay and cheery,
  And your spirits feather-light,
There's a ghostly music haunting
  Still the heart of every guest
And a voiceless chorus chanting
  That the Old Times were the best.

CHORUS

All about is bright and pleasant
  With the sound of song and jest,
Yet a feeling's ever present
  That the Old Times were the best.

A SUMMER AFTERNOON

A LANGUID atmosphere, a lazy breeze,
   With labored respiration, moves the wheat
From distant reaches, till the golden seas
   Break in crisp whispers at my feet.

My book, neglected of an idle mind,
   Hides for a moment from the eyes of men;
Or, lightly opened by a critic wind,
   Affrightedly reviews itself again.

Off through the haze that dances in the shine
   The warm sun showers in the open glade,
The forest lies, a silhouette design
   Dimmed through and through with shade

A dreamy day; and tranquilly I lie
   At anchor from all storms of mental strain;
With absent vision, gazing at the sky,
   "Like one that hears it rain."

The Katydid, so boisterous last night,
  Clinging, inverted, in uneasy poise,
Beneath a wheat-blade, has forgotten quite
  If "Katy *did* or *didn't*" make a noise.

The twitter, sometimes, of a wayward bird
  That checks the song abruptly at the sound,
And mildly, chiding echoes that have stirred,
  Sink into silence, all the more profound.

And drowsily I hear the plaintive strain
  Of some poor dove . . . Why, I can
      scarcely keep
My heavy eyelids—there it is again—
  "Coo-coo!"—I mustn't—"Coo-coo!"—fall
      asleep!

AT LAST

A DARK, tempestuous night; the stars shut in
  With shrouds of fog; an inky, jet-black blot
The firmament; and where the moon has been
  An hour agone seems like the darkest spot.
The weird wind—furious at its demon game—
Rattles one's fancy like a window-frame.

A care-worn face peers out into the dark,
  And childish faces—frightened at the gloom—
Grow awed and vacant as they turn to mark
  The father's as he passes through the room:
The gate latch clatters, and wee baby Bess
Whispers, "The doctor's tummin' now, I dess!"

The father turns; a sharp, swift flash of pain
  Flits o'er his face: "Amanda, child! I said
A moment since—I see I must *again*—
  Go take your little sisters off to bed!
There, Effie, Rose, and *Clara mustn't cry!*"
"I tan't he'p it—I'm fyaid 'at mama'll die!"

Captain Reuben A. Riley—the poet's father

What are his feelings, when this man alone
   Sits in the silence, glaring in the grate
That sobs and sighs on in an undertone
   As stoical—immovable as Fate,
While muffled voices from the sick one's room
Come in like heralds of a dreaded doom?

The door-latch jingles: in the doorway stands
   The doctor, while the draft puffs in a breath—
The dead coals leap to life, and clap their hands,
   The flames flash up. A face as pale as death
Turns slowly—teeth tight clenched, and with a look
The doctor, through his specs, reads like a book.

"Come, brace up, Major!"—"Let me know the
         worst!"
   "W'y you're the biggest fool I ever saw—
Here, Major—take a little brandy first—
   There! She's a *boy*—I mean *he* is—hurrah!"
"Wake up the other girls—and shout for joy—
Eureka is his name—I've found A BOY!"

FARMER WHIPPLE—BACHELOR

IT'S a mystery to see me—a man o' fifty-four,
Who's lived a cross old bachelor fer thirty year'
    and more—
A-lookin' glad and smilin'! And they's none o' you
    can say
That you can guess the reason why I feel so good
    to-day!

I must tell you all about it! But I'll have to deviate
A little in beginnin', so's to set the matter straight
As to how it comes to happen that I never took a
    wife—
Kindo' "crawfish" from the Present to the Spring-
    time of my life!

I was brought up in the country: Of a family of
    five—
Three brothers and a sister—I'm the only one
    alive,—
Fer they all died little babies; and 'twas one o'
    Mother's ways,
You know, to want a daughter; so she took a girl
    to raise.

The sweetest little thing she was, with rosy cheeks,
    and fat—
We was little chunks o' shavers then about as high
    as that!
But someway we sort o' *suited*-like! and Mother
    she'd declare
She never laid her eyes on a more lovin' pair

Than *we* was! So we growed up side by side fer
    thirteen year',
And every hour of it she growed to me more
    dear!—
W'y, even Father's dyin', as he did, I do believe
Warn't more affectin' to me than it was to see her
    grieve!

I was then a lad o' twenty; and I felt a flash o'
    pride
In thinkin' all depended on *me* now to pervide
Fer Mother and fer Mary; and I went about the
    place
With sleeves rolled up—and workin', with a mighty
    smilin' face.—

Fer *somepin' else* was workin'! but not a word I said
Of a certain sort o' notion that was runnin' through
    my head,—
"Some day I'd maybe marry, and a *brother's* love
    was one
Thing—a *lover's* was another!" was the way the
    notion run!

I remember onc't in harvest, when the "cradle-in'"
    was done,
(When the harvest of my summers mounted up to
    twenty-one),
I was ridin' home with Mary at the closin' o' the
    day—
A-chawin' straws and thinkin', in a lover's lazy
    way!

And Mary's cheeks was burnin' like the sunset
    down the lane:
I noticed she was thinkin', too, and ast her to
    explain.
Well—when she turned and *kissed* me, *with her
    arms around me—law!*
I'd a bigger load o' Heaven than I had a load o'
    straw!

I don't p'tend to learnin', but I'll tell you what's a
    fac',
They's a mighty truthful sayin' somers in a'
    almanac—
Er *somers*—'bout "puore happiness"—perhaps
    some folks'll laugh
At the idy—"only lastin' jest two seconds and a
    half."—

But it's jest as true as preachin'!—fer that was a
    sister's kiss,
And a sister's lovin' confidence a-tellin' to me
    this:—

"She was happy, *bein' promised to the son o'*
    Farmer Brown."—
And my feelin's struck a pardnership with sunset
    and went down!

I don't know *how* I acted, and I don't know *what*
    I said,—
Fer my heart seemed jest a-turnin' to an ice-cold
    lump o' lead;
And the hosses kind o' glimmered before me in the
    road,
And the lines fell from my fingers—And that was
    all I knowed—

Fer—well, I don't know *how* long—They's a dim
    rememberence
Of a sound o' snortin' horses, and a stake-and-
    ridered fence
A-whizzin' past, and wheat-sheaves a-dancin' in the
    air,
And Mary screamin' "Murder!" and a-runnin' up
    to where

I was layin' by the roadside, and the wagon upside
    down
A-leanin' on the gate-post, with the wheels
    a-whirlin' roun'!
And I tried to raise and meet her, but I couldn't,
    with a vague
Sort o' notion comin' to me that I had a broken leg.

Well, the women nussed me through it; but many a
  time I'd sigh
As I'd keep a-gittin' better instid o' goin' to die,
And wonder what was left *me* worth livin' fer
  below,
When the girl I loved was married to another,
  don't you know!

And my thoughts was as rebellious as the folks
  was good and kind
When Brown and Mary married—Railly must 'a'
  been my *mind*
Was kind o' out o' kilter!—fer I hated Brown, you
  see,
Worse'n *pizen*—and the feller whittled crutches out
  fer *me*—

And done a thousand little ac's o' kindness and
  respec'—
And me a-wishin' all the time that I could break his
  neck!
My relief was like a mourner's when the funeral is
  done
When they moved to Illinois in the Fall o' Forty-
  one.

Then I went to work in airnest—I had nothin' much
  in view
But to drownd out rickollections—and it kep' me
  busy, too!

But I slowly thrived and prospered, tel Mother used
    to say
She expected yit to see me a wealthy man some day.

Then I'd think how little *money* was, compared to
    happiness—
And who'd be left to use it when I died I couldn't
    guess!
But I've still kep' speculatin' and a-gainin' year by
    year,
Tel I'm payin' half the taxes in the county, mighty
    near!

Well!—A year ago er better, a letter comes to hand
Astin' how I'd like to dicker fer some Illinois land—
"The feller that had owned it," it went ahead to
    state,
"Had jest deceased, insolvent, leavin' chance to
    speculate,"—

And then it closed by sayin' that I'd "better come
    and see."—
I'd never been West, anyhow—a'most too wild fer
    me,
I'd allus had a notion; but a lawyer here in town
Said I'd find myself mistakend when I come to look
    around.

So I bids good-by to Mother, and I jumps aboard
    the train,
A-thinkin' what I'd bring her when I come back
    home again—

And ef she'd had an idy what the present was to be,
I think it's more'n likely she'd 'a' went along with
    me!

Cars is awful tejus ridin', fer all they go so fast!
But finally they called out my stoppin'-place at last:
And that night, at the tavern, I dreamp' I was a
    train
O' cars, and *skeered* at somepin', runnin' down a
    country lane!

Well, in the morning airly—after huntin' up the
    man—
The lawyer who was wantin' to swap the piece o'
    land—
We started fer the country; and I ast the history
Of the farm—its former owner—and so forth,
    etcetery!

And—well—it was inter*est*in'—I su'prised him, I
    suppose,
By the loud and frequent manner in which I blowed
    my nose!—
But his su'prise was greater, and it made him won-
    der more,
When I kissed and hugged the widder when she
    met us at the door!—

It was Mary: . . . They's a feelin' a-hidin' down in
    here—
Of course I can't explain it, ner ever make it
    clear.—
It was with us in that meetin', I don't want you to
    fergit!
And it makes me kind o' nervous when I think about
    it yit!

I *bought* that farm, and *deeded* it, afore I left the
    town,
With "title clear to mansions in the skies," to Mary
    Brown!
And fu'thermore, I took her and the *childern*—fer
    you see,
They'd never seed their Grandma—and I fetched
    'em home with me.

So *now* you've got an idy why a man o' fifty-four,
Who's lived a cross old bachelor fer thirty year' and
    more,
Is a-lookin' glad and smilin'!—And I've jest come
    into town
To git a pair o' license fer to *marry* Mary Brown.

MY JOLLY FRIEND'S SECRET

AH, friend of mine, how goes it
   Since you've taken you a mate?—
Your smile, though, plainly shows it
   Is a very happy state!
Dan Cupid's necromancy!
   You must sit you down and dine,
And lubricate your fancy
   With a glass or two of wine.

And as you have "deserted,"
   As my other chums have done,
While I laugh alone diverted,
   As you drop off one by one—
And I've remained unwedded,
   Till—you see—look here—that I'm,
In a manner, "snatched bald-headed"
   By the sportive hand of Time!

I'm an "old 'un!" yes, but wrinkles
   Are not so plenty, quite,
As to cover up the twinkles
   Of the *boy*—ain't I right?

Yet, there are ghosts of kisses
　Under this mustache of mine
My mem'ry only misses
　When I drowned 'em out with wine.

From acknowledgment so ample,
　You would hardly take me for
What I am—a perfect sample
　Of a "jolly bachelor";
Not a bachelor has being
　When he laughs at married life
But his heart and soul's agreeing
　That he ought to have a wife!

Ah, ha! old chum, this claret,
　Like Fatima, holds the key
Of the old Blue-Beardish garret
　Of my hidden mystery!
Did you say you'd like to listen?
　Ah, my boy! the *"Sad No More!"*
And the tear-drops that will glisten—
　Turn the catch upon the door,

And sit you down beside me,
　And put yourself at ease—
I'll trouble you to slide me
　That wine decanter, please;
The path is kind o' mazy
　Where my fancies have to go,
And my heart gets sort o' lazy
　On the journey—don't you know?

Let me see—when I was twenty—
   It's a lordly age, my boy,
When a fellow's money's plenty,
   And the leisure to enjoy—
And a girl—with hair as golden
   As—*that;* and lips—well—quite
As red as *this* I'm holdin'
   Between you and the light.

And eyes and a complexion—
   Ah, heavens!—le'-me-see—
Well,—just in this connection,—
   Did you lock that door for me?
Did I start in recitation
   My past life to recall?
Well, *that's* an indication
   I am purty tight—that's all!

THE SPEEDING OF THE KING'S SPITE

A KING—estranged from his loving Queen
    By a foolish royal whim—
Tired and sick of the dull routine
    Of matters surrounding him—
Issued a mandate in this wise:—
    "The dower of my daughter's hand
I will give to him who holds this prize,
    The strangest thing in the land."

But the King, sad sooth! in this grim decree
    Had a motive low and mean;—
'Twas a royal piece of chicanery
    To harry and spite the Queen;
For King though he was, and beyond compare,
    He had ruled all things save one—
Then blamed the Queen that his only heir
    Was a daughter—not a son.

The girl had grown, in the mother's care,
    Like a bud in the shine and shower
That drinks of the wine of the balmy air
    Till it blooms into matchless flower;

Her waist was the rose's stem that bore
    The flower—and the flower's perfume—
That ripens on till it bulges o'er
    With its wealth of bud and bloom.

And she had a lover—lowly sprung,—
    But a purer, nobler heart
Never spake in a courtlier tongue
    Or wooed with a dearer art:
And the fair pair paled at the King's decree;
    But the smiling Fates contrived
To have them wed, in a secrecy
    That the Queen *herself* connived—

While the grim King's heralds scoured the land
    And the countries roundabout,
Shouting aloud, at the King's command,
    A challenge to knave or lout,
Prince or peasant,—"The mighty King
    Would have ye understand
That he who shows him the strangest thing
    Shall have his daughter's hand!"

And thousands flocked to the royal throne,
    Bringing a thousand things
Strange and curious;—One, a bone—
    The hinge of a fairy's wings;
And one, the glass of a mermaid queen,
    Gemmed with a diamond dew,
Where, down in its reflex, dimly seen,
    Her face smiled out at you.

One brought a cluster of some strange date,
  With a subtle and searching tang
That seemed, as you tasted, to penetrate
  The heart like a serpent's fang;
And back you fell for a spell entranced,
  As cold as a corpse of stone,
And heard your brains, as they laughed and
      danced
  And talked in an undertone.

One brought a bird that could whistle a tune
  So piercingly pure and sweet,
That tears would fall from the eyes of the moon
  In dewdrops at its feet;
And the winds would sigh at the sweet refrain,
  Till they swooned in an ecstacy,
To waken again in a hurricane
  Of riot and jubilee.

One brought a lute that was wrought of a shell
  Luminous as the shine
Of a new-born star in a dewy dell,—
  And its strings were strands of wine
That sprayed at the Fancy's touch and fused,
  As your listening spirit leant
Drunken through with the airs that oozed
  From the o'ersweet instrument.

One brought a tablet of ivory
  Whereon no thing was writ,—
But, at night—and the dazzled eyes would see
  Flickering lines o'er it,—

And each, as you read from the magic tome,
  Lightened and died in flame,
And the memory held but a golden poem
  Too beautiful to name.

Till it seemed all marvels that ever were known
  Or dreamed of under the sun
Were brought and displayed at the royal throne,
  And put by, one by one;—
Till a graybeard monster came to the King—
  Haggard and wrinkled and old—
And spread to his gaze this wondrous thing,—
  A gossamer veil of gold.—

Strangely marvelous—mocking the gaze
  Like a tangle of bright sunshine,
Dipping a million glittering rays
  In a baptism divine:
And a maiden, sheened in this gauze attire—
  Sifting a glance of her eye—
Dazzled men's souls with a fierce desire
  To kiss and caress her and—die.

And the grim King swore by his royal beard
  That the veil had won the prize,
While the gray old monster blinked and leered
  With his lashless, red-rimmed eyes,
As the fainting form of the princess fell,
  And the mother's heart went wild,
Throbbing and swelling a muffled knell
  For the dead hopes of her child.

But her clouded face with a faint smile shone,
  As suddenly, through the throng,
Pushing his way to the royal throne,
  A fair youth strode along,
· While a strange smile hovered about his eyes,
  As he said to the grim old King :—
"The veil of gold must lose the prize;
  For *I* have a stranger thing."

He bent and whispered a sentence brief ;
  But the monarch shook his head,
With a look expressive of unbelief—
  "It can't be so," he said ;
"Or give me proof ; and I, the King,
  Give you my daughter's hand,—
For certes THAT *is* a stranger thing—
  The strangest thing in the land!"

Then the fair youth, turning, caught the Queen
  In a rapturous caress,
While his lithe form towered in lordly mien,
  As he said in a brief address :—
"My fair bride's mother is this ; and, lo,
  As you stare in your royal awe,
By this pure kiss do I proudly show
  A love for a mother-in-law!"

Then a thaw set in the old King's mood,
  And a sweet Spring freshet came
Into his eyes, and his heart renewed
  Its love for the favored dame:

But often he has been heard to declare
   That "he never could clearly see
How, in the deuce, such a strange affair
   Could have ended so happily!"

JOB WORK

"WRITE me a rhyme of the present time":
    And the poet took his pen
And wrote such lines as the miser minds
    Hide in the hearts of men.

He grew enthused, as the poets used
    When their fingers kissed the strings
Of some sweet lyre, and caught the fire
    True inspiration brings,

And sang the song of a nation's wrong—
    Of the patriot's galling chain,
And the glad release that the angel, Peace,
    Has given him again.

He sang the lay of religion's sway,
    Where a hundred creeds clasp hands
And shout in glee such a symphony
    That the whole world understands.

He struck the key of monopoly,
  And sang of her swift decay,
And traveled the track of the railway back
  With a blithesome roundelay—

Of the tranquil bliss of a true love kiss;
  And painted the picture, too,
Of the wedded life, and the patient wife,
  And the husband fond and true;

And sang the joy that a noble boy
  Brings to a father's soul,
Who lets the wine as a mocker shine
  Stagnated in the bowl.

And he stabbed his pen in the ink again,
  And wrote, with a writhing frown,
"This is the end." "And now, my friend,
  You may print it—upside down!"

PRIVATE THEATRICALS

A QUITE convincing axiom
  Is, "Life is like a play";
For, turning back its pages some
  Few dog-eared years away,
    I find where I
    Committed my
Love-tale—with brackets where to sigh.

I feel an idle interest
  To read again the page;
I enter, as a lover dressed,
  At twenty years of age,
    And play the part
    With throbbing heart,
And all an actor's glowing art.

And she who plays my Lady-love
  Excels!—Her loving glance
Has power her audience to move—
  I am her audience—
    Her acting tact,
    To tell the fact,
"Brings down the house" in every act.

And often we defy the curse
   Of storms and thunder-showers,
To meet together and rehearse
   This little play of ours—
     I think, when she
     "Makes love" to me,
She kisses very naturally!

    .   .   .   .   .   .

Yes; it's convincing—rather—
   That "Life is like a play":
I am playing "Heavy Father"
   In a "Screaming Farce" to-day,
     That so "brings down
     The house," I frown,
And fain would "ring the curtain down."

PLAIN SERMONS

I SAW a man—and envied him beside—
  Because of this world's goods he had great
    store;
But even as I envied him, he died,
  And left me envious of him no more.

I saw another man—and envied still—
  Because he was content with frugal lot;
But as I envied him, the rich man's will
  Bequeathed him all, and envy I forgot.

Yet still another man I saw, and he
  I envied for a calm and tranquil mind
That nothing fretted in the least degree—
  Until, alas! I found that he was blind.

What vanity is envy! for I find
  I have been rich in dross of thought, and poor
In that I was a fool, and lastly blind—
  For never having seen myself before!

"TRADIN' JOE"

I'M one o' these cur'ous kind o' chaps
    You think you know when you don't,
        perhaps!
I hain't no fool—ner I don't p'tend
To be so smart I could rickommend
Myself fer a *congerssman,* my friend!—
But I'm kind o' betwixt-and-between, you
        know,—
One o' these fellers 'at folks call "slow."
And I'll say jest here I'm kind o' queer
Regardin' things 'at I *see* and *hear,*—
Fer I'm *thick* o' hearin' *sometimes,* and
It's hard to git me to understand;
But other times it hain't, you bet!
Fer I don't sleep with both eyes shet!

I've swapped a power in stock, and so
The neighbers calls me "Tradin' Joe"—
And I'm goin' to tell you 'bout a trade,—
And one o' the best I ever made:

Folks has gone so fur's to say
'At I'm well fixed, in a *worldly* way,
And *bein'* so, and a *widower,*
It's not su'prisin', as you'll infer,
I'm purty handy among the sect—

54

Widders especially, rickollect!
And I won't deny that along o' late
I've hankered a heap fer the married state—
But some way o' 'nother the longer we wait
The harder it is to discover a mate.

Marshall Thomas,—a friend o' mine,
Doin' some in the tradin' line,
But a'most too *young* to know it all—
On'y at *picnics* er some *ball!*—
Says to me, in a banterin' way,
As we was a-loadin' stock one day,—
"You're a-huntin' a wife, and I want you to see
My girl's mother, at Kankakee!—
She hain't over forty—good-lookin' and spry,
And jest the woman to fill your eye!
And I'm a-goin' there Sund'y,—and now,"
          says he,
"I want to take you along with *me;*
And you marry *her,* and," he says, "by 'shaw!
You'll hev me fer yer son-in-law!"
I studied a while, and says I, "Well, I'll
First have to see ef she suits my style;
And ef she does, you kin bet your life
Your mother-in-law will be my wife!"

Well, Sund'y come; and I fixed up some—
Putt on a collar—I did, by gum!—
Got down my "plug," and my satin vest—
(You wouldn't know me to see me dressed!—

But any one knows ef you got the clothes
You kin go in the crowd wher' the best of 'em
       goes!)
And I greeced my boots, and combed my hair
Keerfully over the bald place there;
And Marshall Thomas and me that day
Eat our dinners with Widder Gray
And her girl Han'! * * *

            Well, jest a glance
O' the widder's smilin' countenance,
A-cuttin' up chicken and big pot-pies,
Would make a man hungry in Paradise!
And passin' p'serves and jelly and cake
'At would make an *angel's* appetite *ache!*—
Pourin' out coffee as yaller as gold—
Twic't as much as the cup could hold—
La! it was rich!—And then she'd say,
"Take some o' *this!*" in her coaxin' way,
Tell ef I'd been a hoss I'd 'a' *foundered,* shore,
And jest dropped dead on her white-oak floor!

Well, the way I talked would 'a' done you good,
Ef you'd 'a' been there to 'a' understood;
Tel I noticed Hanner and Marshall, they
Was a-noticin' me in a cur'ous way;
So I says to myse'f, says I, "Now, Joe,
The best thing fer you is to jest go slow!"
And I simmered down, and let them do
The bulk o' the talkin' the evening through.

And Marshall was still in a talkative gait
When he left, that evening—tolable late.
"How do you like her?" he says to me;
Says I, "She suits, to a 't-y-*Tee*'!"
And then I ast how matters stood
With him in the *opposite* neighberhood?
"Bully!" he says; "I ruther guess
I'll finally git her to say the 'yes.'
I named it to her to-night, and she
Kind o' smiled, and said *'she'd see'*—
And that's a purty good sign!" says he:
"Yes," says I, "you're ahead o' *me!*"
And then he laughed, and said, *"Go in!"*
And patted me on the shoulder ag'in.

Well, ever sense then I've been ridin' a good
Deal through the Kankakee neighberhood;
And I make it convenient sometimes to stop
And hitch a few minutes, and kind o' drop
In at the widder's, and talk o' the crop
And one thing o' 'nother. And week afore last
The notion struck me, as I drove past,
I'd stop at the place and state my case—
Might as well do it at first as last!

I felt first-rate; so I hitched at the gate,
And went up to the house; and, strange to
          relate,
Marshall Thomas had dropped in, *too.*—
"Glad to see you, sir, how do you do?"
He says, says he! Well—it *sounded queer;*

And when Han' told me to take a cheer,
Marshall got up and putt out o' the room—
And motioned his hand fer the *widder* to come.
I didn't say nothin' fer quite a spell,
But thinks I to myse'f, "There's a dog in the
    well!"
And Han' *she* smiled so cur'ous at me—
Says I, "What's up?" And she says, says she,
"Marshall's been at me to marry ag'in,
And I told him 'no,' jest as you come in."
Well, somepin' o' 'nother in that girl's voice
Says to me, "Joseph, here's your choice!"
And another minute her guileless breast
Was lovin'ly throbbin' ag'in my vest!—
And then I kissed her, and heerd a smack
Come like a' echo a-flutterin' back,
And we looked around, and in full view
Marshall was kissin' the widder, too!
Well, we all of us laughed, in our glad su'prise,
Tel the tears come *a-streamin'* out of our eyes!
And when Marsh said " 'Twas the squarest
    trade
That ever me and him had made,"
We both shuck hands, 'y jucks! and swore
We'd stick together ferevermore.
And old Squire Chipman tuck us the trip:
And Marshall and me's in pardnership!

DOT LEEDLE BOY

OT'S a leedle Gristmas story
  Dot I told der leedle folks—
Und I vant you stop dot laughin'
  Und grackin' funny jokes!—
So help me Peter-Moses!
  Ot's no time for monkey-shine,
Ober I vast told you somedings
  Of dot leedle boy of mine!

Ot vas von cold Vinter vedder,
  Ven der snow vas all about—
Dot you have to chop der hatchet
  Eef you got der sauerkraut!
Und der cheekens on der hind leg
  Vas standin' in der shine
Der sun shmile out dot morning
  On dot leedle boy of mine.

He vas yoost a leedle baby
  Not bigger as a doll
Dot time I got acquaintet—
  Ach! you ought to heard 'im squall!—

59

I grackys! dot's der moosic
   Ot make me feel so fine
Ven first I vas been marriet—
   Oh, dot leedle boy of mine!

He look yoost like his fader!—
   So, ven der vimmen said,
"Vot a purty leedle baby!"
   Katrina shake der head. . . .
I dink she must 'a' notice
   Dot der baby vas a-gryin',
Und she cover up der blankets
   Of dot leedle boy of mine.

Vel, ven he vas got bigger,
   Dot he grawl und bump his nose,
Und make der table over,
   Und molasses on his glothes—
Dot make 'im all der sveeter,—
   So I say to my Katrine,
"Better you vas quit a-shpankin'
   Dot leedle boy of mine!"

No more he vas older
   As about a dozen months
He speak der English language
   Und der German—bote at vonce!
Und he dringk his glass of lager
   Like a Londsman fon der Rhine—
Und I klingk my glass togeder
   Mit dot leedle boy of mine!

I vish you could 'a' seen id—
   Ven he glimb up on der chair
Und shmash der lookin'-glasses
   Ven he try to comb his hair
Mit a hammer!—Und Katrina
   Say, "Dot's an ugly sign!"
But I laugh und vink my fingers
   At dot leedle boy of mine.

But vonce, dot Vinter morning,
   He shlip out in der snow
Mitout no stockin's on 'im.—
   He say he "vant to go
Und fly some mit der birdies!"
   Und ve give 'im medi-cine
Ven he catch der "parrygoric"—
   Dot leedle boy of mine!

Und so I set und nurse 'im,
   Vile der Gristmas vas come roun',
Und I told 'im 'bout "Kriss Kringle,"
   How he come der chimbly down:
Und I ask 'im eef he love 'im
   Eef he bring 'im someding fine?
"Nicht besser as mein fader,"
   Say dot leedle boy of mine.—

Und he put his arms aroun' me
   Und hug so close und tight,
I hear der gclock a-tickin'
   All der balance of der night! . . .

Someding make me feel so funny
  Ven I say to my Katrine,
"Let us go und fill der stockin's
  Of dot leedle boy of mine."

Vell.—Ve buyed a leedle horses
  Dot you pull 'im mit a shtring,
Und a leedle fancy jay-bird—
  Eef you vant to hear 'im sing
You took 'im by der topknot
  Und yoost blow in behine—
Und dot make much *spectakel*
  For dot leedle boy of mine!

Und gandies, nuts und raizens—
  Und I buy a leedle drum
Dot I vant to hear 'im rattle
  Ven der Gristmas morning come!
Und a leedle shmall tin rooster
  Dot vould crow so loud und fine
Ven he sqveeze 'im in der morning,
  Dot leedle boy of mine!

Und—vile ve vas a-fixin'—
  Dot leedle boy vake out!
I t'ought he been a-dreamin'
  "Kriss Kringle" vas about,—
For he say—"*Dot's him!—I see 'im
  Mit der shtars dot make der shine!*"
Und he yoost keep on a-gryin'—
  Dot leedle boy of mine,—

Und gottin' vorse und vorser—
  Und tumble on der bed!
So—ven der doctor seen id,
  He kindo' shake his head,
Und feel his pulse—und visper,
  "Der boy is a-dyin'."
You dink I could *believe* id?—
  Dot leedle boy of mine?

I told you, friends—dot's someding,
  Der last time dot he speak
Und say, *"Goot-by, Kriss Kringle!"*
  —Dot make me feel so veak
I yoost kneel down und drimble,
  Und bur-sed out a-gryin',
"Mein Gott, mein Gott in Himmel!—
  Dot leedle boy of mine!"

.   .   .   .

Der sun don't shine *dot* Gristmas!
  . . . Eef dot leedle boy vould *liff'd*—
No deefer-en'! for *Heaven* vas
  His leedle Gristmas gift!
Und der *rooster,* und der *gandy,*
  Und me—und my Katrine—
Und der jay-bird—is a-vaiting
  For dot leedle boy of mine.

I SMOKE MY PIPE

I CAN'T extend to every friend
  In need a helping hand—
No matter though I wish it so,
  'Tis not as Fortune planned;
But haply may I fancy they
  Are men of different stripe
Than others think who hint and wink,—
  And so—I smoke my pipe!

A golden coal to crown the bowl—
  My pipe and I alone,—
I sit and muse with idler views
  Perchance than I should own:—
It might be worse to own the purse
  Whose glutted bowels gripe
In little qualms of stinted alms;
  And so I smoke my pipe.

And if inclined to moor my mind
  And cast the anchor Hope,
A puff of breath will put to death
  The morbid misanthrope

That lurks inside—as errors hide
  In standing forms of type
To mar at birth some line of worth;
  And so I smoke my pipe.

The subtle stings misfortune flings
  Can give me little pain
When my narcotic spell has wrought
  This quiet in my brain:
When I can waste the past in taste
  So luscious and so ripe
That like an elf I hug myself;
  And so I smoke my pipe.

And wrapped in shrouds of drifting clouds
  I watch the phantom's flight,
Till alien eyes from Paradise
  Smile on me as I write:
And I forgive the wrongs that live,
  As lightly as I wipe
Away the tear that rises here;
  And so I smoke my pipe.

RED RIDING-HOOD

SWEET little myth of the nursery story—
    Earliest love of mine infantile breast,
Be something tangible, bloom in thy glory
    Into existence, as thou art addressed!
Hasten! appear to me, guileless and good—
Thou are so dear to me, Red Riding-Hood!

Azure-blue eyes, in a marvel of wonder,
    Over the dawn of a blush breaking out;
Sensitive nose, with a little smile under
    Trying to hide in a blossoming pout—
Couldn't be serious, try as you would,
Little mysterious Red Riding-Hood!

Hah! little girl, it is desolate, lonely,
    Out in this gloomy old forest of Life!—
Here are not pansies and buttercups only—
    Brambles and briers as keen as a knife;
And a Heart, ravenous, trails in the wood
For the meal have he must,—Red Riding-
        Hood!

IF I KNEW WHAT POETS KNOW.

If I knew what poets know
Would I write a rhyme
Of the buds that never blow
In the summer-time?
Would I sing of golden seeds
Springing up in ironweeds —
And of raindrops turned to snow
If I knew what poets know?

Did I know what poets do
Would I sing a song
Sadder than the pigeon's coo
When the days are long?
Where I found a heart that bled,
I would make it bloom instead,
And the false should be the true
Did I know what poets do.

IF I KNEW WHAT POETS KNOW

IF I knew what poets know,
  Would I write a rhyme
Of the buds that never blow
  In the summer-time?
Would I sing of golden seeds
Springing up in ironweeds?
And of rain-drops turned to snow,
If I knew what poets know?

Did I know what poets do,
  Would I sing a song
Sadder than the pigeon's coo
  When the days are long?
Where I found a heart in pain,
I would make it glad again;
And the false should be the true,
Did I know what poets do.

If I knew what poets know,
  I would find a theme
Sweeter than the placid flow
  Of the fairest dream:
I would sing of love that lives
On the errors it forgives;
And the world would better grow
If I knew what poets know.

AN OLD SWEETHEART OF MINE

AN old sweetheart of mine!—Is this her presence
    here with me,
Or but a vain creation of a lover's memory?
A fair, illusive vision that would vanish into air
Dared I even touch the silence with the whisper of
    a prayer?

Nay, let me then believe in all the blended false and
    true—
The semblance of the *old* love and the substance of
    the *new,*—
The *then* of changeless sunny days—the *now* of
    shower and shine—
But Love forever smiling—as that old sweetheart
    of mine.

This ever-restful sense of *home,* though shouts ring
    in the hall.—
The easy chair—the old book-shelves and prints
    along the wall;
The rare *Habanas* in their box, or gaunt church-
    warden-stem
That often wags, above the jar, derisively at them.

As one who cons at evening o'er an album, all alone,
And muses on the faces of the friends that he has
    known,

So I turn the leaves of Fancy, till, in shadowy de-
    sign,
I find the smiling features of an old sweetheart of
    mine.

The lamplight seems to glimmer with a flicker of
    surprise,
As I turn it low—to rest me of the dazzle in my
    eyes,
And light my pipe in silence, save a sigh that seems
    to yoke
Its fate with my tobacco and to vanish with the
    smoke.

'Tis a *fragrant* retrospection,—for the loving
    thoughts that start
Into being are like perfume from the blossom of the
    heart;
And to dream the old dreams over is a luxury di-
    vine—
When my truant fancies wander with that old
    sweetheart of mine.

Though I hear beneath my study, like a fluttering of
    wings,
The voices of my children and the mother as she
    sings—
I feel no twinge of conscience to deny me any
    theme
When Care has cast her anchor in the harbor of a
    dream—

In fact, to speak in earnest, I believe it adds a
    charm
To spice the good a trifle with a little dust of
    harm,—
For I find an extra flavor in Memory's mellow
    wine
That makes me drink the deeper to that old sweet-
    heart of mine.

O Childhood-days enchanted! O the magic of the
    Spring!—
With all green boughs to blossom white, and all
    bluebirds to sing!
When all the air, to toss and quaff, made life a
    jubilee
And changed the children's song and laugh to
    shrieks of ecstasy.

With eyes half closed in clouds that ooze from lips
    that taste, as well,
The peppermint and cinnamon, I hear the old
    School bell,
And from "Recess" romp in again from "Black-
    man's" broken line,
To smile, behind my "lesson," at that old sweet-
    heart of mine.

A face of lily-beauty, with a form of airy grace,
Floats out of my tobacco as the Genii from the vase;

And I thrill beneath the glances of a pair of azure
  eyes
As glowing as the summer and as tender as the
  skies.

I can see the pink sunbonnet and the little checkered
  dress
She wore when first I kissed her and she answered
  the caress
With the written declaration that, "as surely as the
  vine
Grew 'round the stump," she loved me—that old
  sweetheart of mine.

Again I made her presents, in a really helpless
  way,—
The big "Rhode Island Greening"—I was hungry,
  too, that day!—
But I follow her from Spelling, with her hand behind her—so—
And I slip the apple in it—and the Teacher doesn't
  know!

I give my *treasures* to her—all,—my pencil—blue-
  and-red;—
And, if little girls played marbles, *mine* should all
  be *hers,* instead!
But *she* gave me her *photograph,* and printed "Ever
  Thine"
Across the back—in blue-and-red—that old sweet-
  heart of mine!

And again I feel the pressure of her slender little
    hand,
As we used to talk together of the future we had
    planned,—
When I should be a poet, and with nothing else
    to do
But write the tender verses that she set the music
    to . . .

When we should live together in a cozy little cot
Hid in a nest of roses, with a fairy garden-spot,
Where the vines were ever fruited, and the weather
    ever fine,
And the birds were ever singing for that old sweet-
    heart of mine.

When I should be her lover forever and a day,
And she my faithful sweetheart till the golden hair
    was gray;
And we should be so happy that when either's lips
    were dumb
They would not smile in Heaven till the other's kiss
    had come.

But, ah! my dream is broken by a step upon the
    stair,
And the door is softly opened, and—my wife is
    standing there:
Yet with eagerness and rapture all my visions I
    resign,—
To greet the *living* presence of that old sweetheart
    of mine.

SQUIRE HAWKINS'S STORY

I HAIN'T no hand at tellin' tales,
  Er spinnin' yarns, as the sailors say;
Someway o' 'nother, language fails
To slide fer me in the oily way
That *lawyers* has; and I wisht it would,
Fer I've got somepin' that I call good;
But bein' only a country squire,
I've learned to listen and admire,
Ruther preferrin' to be addressed
Than talk myse'f—but I'll do my best:—

Old Jeff Thompson—well, I'll say,
Was the clos'test man I ever saw!—
Rich as cream, but the porest pay,
And the meanest man to work fer—La!
I've knowed that man to work one "hand"—
Fer little er nothin', you understand—
From four o'clock in the morning light
Tel eight and nine o'clock at night,
And then find fault with his appetite!
He'd drive all over the neighberhood

73

To miss the place where a toll-gate stood,
And slip in town, by some old road
That no two men in the county knowed,
With a jag o' wood, and a sack o' wheat,
That wouldn't burn and you couldn't eat!
And the trades he'd make, 'll I jest de-clare,
Was enough to make a preacher swear!
And then he'd hitch, and hang about
Tel the lights in the toll-gate was blowed out,
And then the turnpike he'd turn in
And sneak his way back home ag'in!

Some folks hint, and I make no doubt,
That that's what wore his old wife out—
Toilin' away from day to day
And year to year, through heat and cold,
Uncomplainin'—the same old way
The martyrs died in the days of old;
And a-clingin', too, as the martyrs done,
To one fixed faith, and her *only* one,—
Little Patience, the sweetest child
That ever wept unrickonciled,
Er felt the pain and the ache and sting
That only a mother's death can bring.

Patience Thompson!—I think that name
Must 'a' come from a power above,
Fer it seemed to fit her jest the same
As a *gaiter* would, er a fine kid glove!
And to see that girl, with all the care

Of the household on her—I de-clare
It was *oudacious,* the work she'd do,
And the thousand plans that she'd putt
    through;
And sing like a medder-lark all day long,
And drowned her cares in the joys o' song;
And *laugh* sometimes tel the farmer's "hand,"
Away fur off in the fields, would stand
A-listenin', with the plow half drawn,
Tel the coaxin' echoes called him on;
And the furries seemed, in his dreamy eyes,
Like foot-paths a-leadin' to Paradise,
As off through the hazy atmosphere
The call fer dinner reached his ear.

Now *love's* as cunnin' a little thing
As a hummin'-bird upon the wing,
And as liable to poke his nose
Jest where folks would least suppose,—
And more'n likely build his nest
Right in the heart you'd leave unguessed,
And live and thrive at your expense—
At least, that's *my* experience.
And old Jeff Thompson often thought,
In his se'fish way, that the quiet John
Was a stiddy chap, as a farm-hand *ought*
To always be,—fer the airliest dawn
Found John busy—and *"easy,"* too,
Whenever his *wages* would fall due!—
To sum him up with a final touch,

He *eat* so little and *worked* so much,
That old Jeff laughed to hisse'f and said,
"He makes *me* money and airns his bread!"

But John, fer all of his quietude,
Would sometimes drap a word er so
That none but *Patience* understood,
And none but her was *meant* to know!—
Maybe at meal-times John would say,
As the sugar-bowl come down his way,
"Thanky, no; *my* coffee's sweet
Enough fer *me!*" with sich conceit,
She'd know at once, without no doubt,
He meant because *she* poured it out;
And smile and blush, and all sich stuff,
And ast ef it was *"strong* enough?"
And git the answer, neat and trim,
"It *couldn't* be too 'strong' fer *him!*"

And so things went fer 'bout a year,
Tel John, at last, found pluck to go
And pour his tale in the old man's ear—
And ef it had been *hot lead,* I know
It couldn't 'a' raised a louder fuss,
Ner 'a' riled the old man's temper wuss!
He jest *lit* in, and cussed and swore,
And lunged and rared, and ripped and tore,
And told John jest to leave his door,
And not to darken it no more!
But Patience cried, with eyes all wet,
"Remember, John, and don't ferget,

Whatever comes, I love you yet!"
But the old man thought, in his se'fish way,
"I'll see her married rich some day;
And *that,*" thinks he, "is money fer *me*—
And my will's *law,* as it ought to be!"

So when, in the course of a month er so,
A *widower,* with a farm er two,
Comes to Jeff's, w'y, the folks, you know,
Had to *talk*—as the folks'll do:
It was the talk of the neighberhood—
Patience and *John,* and *their* affairs;—
And this old chap with a few gray hairs
Had "cut John out," it was understood.
And some folks reckoned "Patience, too,
Knowed what *she* was a-goin' to do—
It was *like* her—la! indeed!—
All *she* loved was *dollars* and *cents*—
Like old *Jeff*—and they saw no need
Fer *John* to pine at *her* negligence!"

But others said, in a *kinder* way,
They missed the songs she used to sing—
They missed the smiles that used to play
Over her face, and the laughin' ring
Of her glad voice—that *every*thing
Of her *old* se'f seemed dead and gone,
And this was the ghost that they gazed on!

Tel finally it was noised about
There was a *weddin'* soon to be

Down at Jeff's; and the "cat was out"
Shore enough!—'Ll the *Jee-mun-nee!*
It *riled* me when John told me so,—
Fer *I* was a *friend o' John's,* you know;
And his trimblin' voice jest broke in two—
As a feller's voice'll sometimes do.—
And I says, says I, "Ef I know my biz—
And I think I know what *jestice* is,—
I've read *some* law—and I'd advise
A man like you to wipe his eyes
And square his jaws and start *ag'in,*
Fer jestice is a-goin' to win!"
And it wasn't long tel his eyes had cleared
As blue as the skies, and the *sun* appeared
In the shape of a good old-fashioned smile
That I hadn't seen fer a long, long while.

So we talked on fer a' hour er more,
And sunned ourselves in the open door,—
Tel a hoss-and-buggy down the road
Come a-drivin' up, that I guess John *knowed,*—
Fer he winked and says, "I'll dessappear—
They'd smell a mice ef they saw *me* here!"
And he thumbed his nose at the old gray mare,
And hid hisse'f in the house somewhere.

Well.—The rig drove up: and I raised my head
As old Jeff hollered to me and said
That "him and his old friend there had come
To see ef the squire was at home."
. . . I told 'em "I was; and I *aimed* to be

At every chance of a weddin'-fee!"
And then I laughed—and they laughed, too,—
Fer that was the object they had in view.
"Would I be on hands at eight that night?"
They ast; and 's-I, "You're mighty right,
I'll be on hand!" And then I *bu'st*
Out a-laughin' my very wu'st,—
And so did they, as they wheeled away
And drove to'rds town in a cloud o' dust.
Then I shet the door, and me and John
Laughed and *laughed,* and jest *laughed* on,
Tel Mother drapped her specs, and *by*
Jeewhillikers! I thought she'd *die!*—
And she couldn't 'a' told, I'll bet my hat,
What on earth she was laughin' at!

But all o' the fun o' the tale hain't done!—
Fer a drizzlin' rain had jest begun,
And a-havin' 'bout four mile' to ride,
I jest concluded I'd better light
Out fer Jeff's and save my hide,—
Fer *it was a-goin' to storm, that night!*
So we went down to the barn, and John
Saddled my beast, and I got on;
And he told me somepin' to not ferget,
And when I left, he was *laughin'* yet.

And, 'proachin' on to my journey's end,
The great big draps o' the rain come down,
And the thunder growled in a way to lend

An awful look to the lowerin' frown
The dull sky wore; and the lightnin' glanced
Tel my old mare jest *more'n* pranced,
And tossed her head, and bugged her eyes
To about four times their natchurl size,
As the big black lips of the clouds 'ud drap
Out some oath of a thunderclap,
And threaten on in an undertone
That chilled a feller clean to the bone!

But I struck shelter soon enough
To save myse'f. And the house was jammed
With the women-folks, and the weddin'-
    stuff :—
A great, long table, fairly *crammed*
With big pound-cakes—and chops and steaks—
And roasts and stews—and stumick-aches
Of every fashion, form, and size,
From twisters up to punkin-pies!
And candies, oranges, and figs,
And reezins,—all the "whilligigs"
And "jim-cracks" that the law allows
On sich occasions!—Bobs and bows
Of gigglin' girls, with corkscrew curls,
And fancy ribbons, reds and blues,
And "beau-ketchers" and "curliques"
To beat the world! And seven o'clock
Brought old Jeff;—and brought—*the groom,*—
With a sideboard-collar on, and stock
That choked him so, he hadn't room
To *swaller* in, er even sneeze,

Er clear his th'oat with any ease
Er comfort—and a good square cough
Would saw his Adam's apple off!

But as fer *Patience*—*My!* Oomh-*oomh!*—
I never saw her look so sweet!—
Her face was cream and roses, too;
And then them eyes o' heavenly blue
Jest made an angel all complete!
And when she split 'em up in smiles
And splintered 'em around the room,
And danced acrost and met the groom,
And *laughed out loud*—It kind o' spiles
My language when I come to that—
Fer, as she laid away his hat,
Thinks I, *"The papers hid inside*
Of that said hat must make a bride
A happy one fer all her life,
Er else a *wrecked* and *wretched wife!"*
And, someway, then, I thought of *John*,—
Then looked towards *Patience*. . . . She was
    gone!—
The door stood open, and the rain
Was dashin' in; and sharp and plain
Above the storm we heerd a cry—
A ringin', laughin', loud "Good-by!"
That died away, as fleet and fast
A hoss's hoofs went splashin' past!
And that was all. 'Twas done that quick! . . .
You've heerd o' fellers "lookin' sick"?
I wisht you'd seen *the groom* jest then—

I wisht you'd seen them two old men,
With starin' eyes that fairly *glared*
At one another, and the scared
And empty faces of the crowd,—
I wisht you could 'a' been allowed
To jest look on and see it all,—
And heerd the girls and women bawl
And wring their hands; and heerd old Jeff
A-cussin' as he swung hisse'f
Upon his hoss, who champed his bit
As though old Nick had holt of it:
And cheek by jowl the two old wrecks
Rode off as though they'd break their necks.

And as we all stood starin' out
Into the night, I felt the brush
Of some one's hand, and turned about,
And heerd a voice that whispered, *"Hush!—
They're waitin' in the kitchen, and
You're wanted. Don't you understand?"*
Well, ef my *memory* serves me now,
I think I winked.—Well, anyhow,
I left the crowd a-gawkin' there,
And jest slipped off around to where
The back door opened, and went in,
And turned and shet the door ag'in,
And maybe *locked* it—couldn't swear,—
A woman's arms around me makes
Me liable to make mistakes.—
I read a marriage license nex',
But as I didn't have my specs

I jest *inferred* it was all right,
And tied the knot so mortal-tight
That Patience and my old friend John
Was safe enough from that time on!

Well, now, I might go on and tell
How all the joke at last leaked out,
And how the youngsters raised the yell
And rode the happy groom about
Upon their shoulders; how the bride
Was kissed a hunderd times beside
The one *I* give her,—tel she cried
And laughed untel she like to died!
I might go on and tell you all
About the supper—and the *ball*.—
You'd ought to see me twist my heel
Through jest one old Furginny reel
Afore you die! er tromp the strings
Of some old fiddle tel she sings
Some old cowtillion, don't you know,
That putts the devil in yer toe!

We kep' the dancin' up tel *four*
O'clock, I reckon—maybe more.—
We hardly heerd the thunders roar,
Er *thought* about the *storm* that blowed—
And them two fellers on the road!
Tel all at onc't we heerd the door
Bu'st open, and a voice that *swore*,—
And old Jeff Thompson tuck the floor.
He shuck hisse'f and looked around

Like some old dog about half-drowned—
His hat, I reckon, *weighed ten pound*
To say the least, and I'll say, *shore,*
His *overcoat weighed fifty* more—
The wettest man you ever saw,
To have so dry a son-in-law!

He sized it all; and Patience laid
Her hand in John's, and looked afraid,
And waited. And a stiller set
O' folks, I *know,* you never met
In any court room, where with dread
They wait to hear a verdick read.

The old man turned his eyes on me:
"And have you married 'em?" says he.
I nodded "Yes." "Well, that'll do,"
He says, "and now we're th'ough with *you,*—
You jest clear out, and I decide
And promise to be satisfied!"
He hadn't nothin' more to say.
I saw, of course, how matters lay,
And left. But as I rode away
I heerd the roosters crow fer day.

A COUNTRY PATHWAY

I COME upon it suddenly, alone—
  A little pathway winding in the weeds
That fringe the roadside; and with dreams my own,
  I wander as it leads.

Full wistfully along the slender way,
  Through summer tan of freckled shade and shine,
I take the path that leads me as it may—
  Its every choice is mine.

A chipmunk, or a sudden-whirring quail,
  Is startled by my step as on I fare—
A garter-snake across the dusty trail
  Glances and—is not there.

Above the arching jimson-weeds flare twos
  And twos of sallow-yellow butterflies,
Like blooms of lorn primroses blowing loose
  When autumn winds arise.

The trail dips—dwindles—broadens then, and lifts
  Itself astride a cross-road dubiously,
And, from the fennel marge beyond it, drifts
  Still onward, beckoning me.

And though it needs must lure me mile on mile
   Out of the public highway, still I go,
My thoughts, far in advance in Indian file,
   Allure me even so.

Why, I am as a long-lost boy that went
   At dusk to bring the cattle to the bars,
And was not found again, though Heaven lent
   His mother all the stars

With which to seek him through that awful night.
   O years of nights as vain!—Stars never rise
But well might miss their glitter in the light
   Of tears in mother-eyes!

So—on, with quickened breaths, I follow still—
   My avant-courier must be obeyed!
Thus am I led, and thus the path, at will,
   Invites me to invade

A meadow's precincts, where my daring guide
   Clambers the steps of an old-fashioned stile,
And stumbles down again, the other side,
   To gambol there a while.

In pranks of hide-and-seek, as on ahead
   I see it running, while the clover-stalks
Shake rosy fists at me, as though they said—
   "You dog our country walks

"And mutilate us with your walking-stick!—
   We will not suffer tamely what you do,
And warn you at your peril,—for we'll sick
   Our bumblebees on you!"

But I smile back, in airy nonchalance,—
   The more determined on my wayward quest,
As some bright memory a moment dawns
   A morning in my breast—

Sending a thrill that hurries me along
   In faulty similes of childish skips,
Enthused with lithe contortions of a song
   Performing on my lips.

In wild meanderings o'er pasture wealth—
   Erratic wanderings through dead'ning lands,
Where sly old brambles, plucking me by stealth,
   Put berries in my hands:

Or the path climbs a boulder—wades a slough—
   Or, rollicking through buttercups and flags,
Goes gaily dancing o'er a deep bayou
   On old tree-trunks and snags:

Or, at the creek, leads o'er a limpid pool
   Upon a bridge the stream itself has made,
With some Spring-freshet for the mighty tool
   That its foundation laid.

I pause a moment here to bend and muse,
　With dreamy eyes, on my reflection, where
A boat-backed bug drifts on a helpless cruise,
　Or wildly oars the air,

As, dimly seen, the pirate of the brook—
　The pike, whose jaunty hulk denotes his speed—
Swings pivoting about, with wary look
　Of low and cunning greed.

Till, filled with other thought, I turn again
　To where the pathway enters in a realm
Of lordly woodland, under sovereign reign
　Of towering oak and elm.

A puritanic quiet here reviles
　The almost whispered warble from the hedge,
And takes a locust's rasping voice and files
　The silence to an edge.

In such a solitude my somber way
　Strays like a misanthrope within a gloom
Of his own shadows—till the perfect day
　Bursts into sudden bloom,

And crowns a long, declining stretch of space,
　Where King Corn's armies lie with flags unfurled,
And where the valley's dint in Nature's face
　Dimples a smiling world.

And lo! through mists that may not be dispelled,
  I see an old farm homestead, as in dreams,
Where, like a gem in costly setting held,
  The old log cabin gleams.

        .   ○   ○   ○   .   .   .

O darling Pathway! lead me bravely on
  Adown your valley-way, and run before
Among the roses crowding up the lawn
  And thronging at the door,—

And carry up the echo there that shall
  Arouse the drowsy dog, that he may bay
The household out to greet the prodigal
  That wanders home to-day.

THE OLD GUITAR

NEGLECTED now is the old guitar
  And moldering into decay;
Fretted with many a rift and scar
  That the dull dust hides away,
While the spider spins a silver star
  In its silent lips to-day.

The keys hold only nerveless strings—
  The sinews of brave old airs
Are pulseless now; and the scarf that clings
  So closely here declares
A sad regret in its ravelings
  And the faded hue it wears.

But the old guitar, with a lenient grace,
  Has cherished a smile for me;
And its features hint of a fairer face
  That comes with a memory
Of a flower-and-perfume-haunted place
  And a moonlit balcony.

Music sweeter than words confess,
  Or the minstrel's powers invent,
Thrilled here once at the light caress
  Of the fairy hands that lent
This excuse for the kiss I press
  On the dear old instrument.

The rose of pearl with the jeweled stem
  Still blooms; and the tiny sets
In the circle all are here; the gem
  In the keys, and the silver frets;
But the dainty fingers that danced o'er them—
  Alas for the heart's regrets!—

Alas for the loosened strings to-day,
  And the wounds of rift and scar
On a worn old heart, with its roundelay
  Enthralled with a stronger bar
That Fate weaves on, through a dull decay
  Like that of the old guitar!

"FRIDAY AFTERNOON"

TO WILLIAM MORRIS PIERSON

[1868–1870]

OF the wealth of facts and fancies
    That our memories may recall,
The old school-day romances
    Are the dearest, after all!—
When some sweet thought revises
    The half-forgotten tune
That opened "Exercises"
    On "Friday Afternoon."

We seem to hear the clicking
    Of the pencil and the pen,
And the solemn, ceaseless ticking
    Of the timepiece ticking then;
And we note the watchful master,
    As he waves the warning rod,
With our own heart beating faster
    Than the boy's who threw the wad.

Some little hand uplifted,
   And the creaking of a shoe:—
A problem left unsifted
   For the teacher's hand to do:
The murmured hum of learning—
   And the flutter of a book;
The smell of something burning,
   And the school's inquiring look.

The opening song, page 20.—
   And the girl, with glancing eyes,
Who hides her smiles, and hushes
   The laugh about to rise,—
Then, with a quick invention,
   Assumes a serious face,
To meet the words, "Attention!
   Every scholar in his place!"

The opening song, page 20.—
   Ah! dear old "Golden Wreath,"
You willed your sweets in plenty;
   And some who look beneath
The leaves of Time will linger,
   And loving tears will start,
As Fancy trails her finger
   O'er the index of the heart.

"Good News from Home"—We hear it
   Welling tremulous, yet clear
And holy as the spirit
   Of the song we used to hear—

"Good news for me"—(A throbbing
    And an aching melody)—
"Has come across the"—(sobbing,
    Yea, and salty) "dark blue sea!"

Or the pæan "Scotland's burning!"
    With its mighty surge and swell
Of chorus, still returning
    To its universal yell—
Till we're almost glad to drop to
    Something sad and full of pain—
And "Skip verse three," and stop, too,
    Ere our hearts are broke again.

Then "the big girls'" compositions,
    With their doubt, and hope, and glow
Of heart and face,—conditions
    Of "the big boys"—even so,—
When themes of "Spring," and "Summer"
    And of "Fall," and "Winter-time"
Droop our heads and hold us dumber
Than the sleigh-bell's fancied chime.

Elocutionary science—
    (Still in changeless infancy!)—
With its "Cataline's Defiance,"
    And "The Banner of the Free":
Or, lured from Grandma's attic,
    A ramshackle "rocker" there,
Adds a skreek of the dramatic
    To the poet's "Old Arm-Chair."

Or the "Speech of Logan" shifts us
   From the pathos, to the fire;
And Tell (with Gessler) lifts us
   Many noble notches higher.—
Till a youngster, far from sunny,
   With sad eyes of watery blue,
Winds up with something "funny,"
   Like "Cock-a-doodle-do!"

Then a dialogue—selected
   For its realistic worth:—
The Cruel Boy detected
   With a turtle turned to earth
Back downward; and, in pleading,
   The Good Boy—strangely gay
At such a sad proceeding—
   Says, "Turn him over, pray!"

So the exercises taper
   Through gradations of delight
To the reading of "The Paper,"
   Which is entertaining—quite!
For it goes ahead and mentions
   "If a certain Mr. O.
Has serious intentions
   That he ought to tell her so."

It also "Asks permission
   To intimate to 'John'
The dubious condition
   Of the ground he's standing on";

And, dropping the suggestion
  To "mind what he's about,"
It stuns him with the question:
  "Does his mother know he's out?"

And among the contributions
  To this "Academic Press"
Are "Versified Effusions"
  By—"Our lady editress"—
Which fact is proudly stated
  By the *Chief* of the concern,—
"Though the verse communicated
  Bears the pen-name 'Fanny Fern.'"

. . . . . .

When all has been recited,
  And the teacher's bell is heard,
And visitors, invited,
  Have dropped a kindly word,
A hush of holy feeling
  Falls down upon us there,
As though the day were kneeling,
  With the twilight for the prayer.

. . . . . .

Midst the wealth of facts and fancies
  That our memories may recall,
Thus the old school-day romances
  Are the dearest, after all!—
When some sweet thought revises
  The half-forgotten tune
That opened "Exercises,"
  On "Friday Afternoon."

"JOHNSON'S BOY"

THE world is turned ag'in' me,
    And people says, "They guess
That nothin' else is in me
    But pure maliciousness!"
I git the blame for doin'
    What other chaps destroy,
And I'm a-goin' to ruin
    Because I'm "Johnson's boy."

That ain't my *name*—I'd ruther
    They'd call me *Ike* or *Pat*—
But they've forgot the other—
    And so have *I,* for that!
I reckon it's as handy,
    When Nibsy breaks his toy,
Or some one steals his candy,
    To say 'twas *"Johnson's boy!"*

You can't git any water
    At the pump, and find the spout
So durn chuck-full o' mortar
    That you have to bore it out;

97

You tackle any scholar
  In Wisdom's wise employ,
And I'll bet you half a dollar
  He'll say it's "Johnson's boy !"

Folks don't know how I suffer
  In my uncomplainin' way—
They think I'm gittin' tougher
  And tougher every day.
Last Sunday night, when Flinder
  Was a-shoutin' out for joy,
And some one shook the winder,
  He prayed for "Johnson's boy."

I'm tired of bein' follered
  By farmers every day,
And then o' bein' collared
  For coaxin' hounds away;
Hounds always plays me double—
  It's a trick they all enjoy—
To git me into trouble,
  Because I'm "Johnson's boy."

But if I git to Heaven,
  I hope the Lord'll see
Some boy has been perfect,
  And lay it on to me;
I'll swell the song sonorous,
  And clap my wings for joy,
And sail off on the chorus—
  "Hurrah for 'Johnson's boy !' "

HER BEAUTIFUL HANDS

O YOUR hands—they are strangely fair!
Fair—for the jewels that sparkle there,—
Fair—for the witchery of the spell
That ivory keys alone can tell;
But when their delicate touches rest
Here in my own do I love them best,
As I clasp with eager, acquisitive spans
My glorious treasure of beautiful hands!

Marvelous—wonderful—beautiful hands!
They can coax roses to bloom in the strands
Of your brown tresses; and ribbons will twine,
Under mysterious touches of thine,
Into such knots as entangle the soul
And fetter the heart under such a control
As only the strength of my love understands—
My passionate love for your beautiful hands.

As I remember the first fair touch
Of those beautiful hands that I love so much,
I seem to thrill as I then was thrilled,
Kissing the glove that I found unfilled—
When I met your gaze, and the queenly bow,

As you said to me, laughingly, "Keep it
    now!" . . .
And dazed and alone in a dream I stand,
Kissing this ghost of your beautiful hand.

When first I loved, in the long ago,
And held your hand as I told you so—
Pressed and caressed it and gave it a kiss
And said "I could die for a hand like this!"
Little I dreamed love's fullness yet
Had to ripen when eyes were wet
And prayers were vain in their wild demands
For one warm touch of your beautiful hands.

  .   .   .   .

Beautiful Hands!—O Beautiful Hands!
Could you reach out of the alien lands
Where you are lingering, and give me, to-night,
Only a touch—were it ever so light—
My heart were soothed, and my weary brain
Would lull itself into rest again;
For there is no solace the world commands
Like the caress of your beautiful hands.

Elizabeth Marine Riley—the poet's mother

NATURAL PERVERSITIES

I AM not prone to moralize
  In scientific doubt
On certain facts that Nature tries
  To puzzle us about,—
For I am no philosopher
  Of wise elucidation,
But speak of things as they occur,
  From simple observation.

I notice *little* things—to wit:—
  I never missed a train
Because I didn't *run* for it;
  I never knew it rain
That my umbrella wasn't lent,—
  Or, when in my possession,
The sun but wore, to all intent,
  A jocular expression.

I never knew a creditor
  To dun me for a debt
But I was "cramped" or "bu'sted"; or
  I never knew one yet,

When I had plenty in my purse,
　To make the least invasion,—
As I, accordingly perverse,
　Have courted no occasion.

Nor do I claim to comprehend
　What Nature has in view
In giving us the very friend
　To trust we oughtn't to.—
But so it is: The trusty gun
　Disastrously exploded
Is always sure to be the one
　We didn't think was loaded.

Our moaning is another's mirth,—
　And what is worse by half,
We say the funniest thing on earth
　And never raise a laugh:
'Mid friends that love us over well,
　And sparkling jests and liquor,
Our hearts somehow are liable
　To melt in tears the quicker.

We reach the wrong when most we seek
　The right; in like effect,
We stay the strong and not the weak—
　Do most when we neglect.—
Neglected genius—truth be said—
　As wild and quick as tinder,
The more you seek to help ahead
　The more you seem to hinder.

I've known the least the greatest, too—
   And, on the selfsame plan,
The biggest fool I ever knew
   Was quite a little man:
We find we ought, and then we won't—
   We prove a thing, then doubt it,—
Know *everything* but when we don't
   Know *anything* about it.

THE SILENT VICTORS

MAY 30, 1878

Dying for victory, cheer on cheer
Thundered on his eager ear.
                    —CHARLES L. HOLSTEIN.

I

DEEP, tender, firm and true, the Nation's heart
    Throbs for her gallant heroes passed away,
Who in grim Battle's drama played their part,
    And slumber here to-day.—

Warm hearts that beat their lives out at the shrine
    Of Freedom, while our country held its breath
As brave battalions wheeled themselves in line
    And marched upon their death:

When Freedom's Flag, its natal wounds scarce
        healed,
    Was torn from peaceful winds and flung again
To shudder in the storm of battle-field—
    The elements of men,—

When every star that glittered was a mark
    For Treason's ball, and every rippling bar
Of red and white was sullied with the dark
    And purple stain of war:

104

When angry guns, like famished beasts of prey,
  Were howling o'er their gory feast of lives,
And sending dismal echoes far away
  To mothers, maids, and wives:—

The mother, kneeling in the empty night,
  With pleading hands uplifted for the son
Who, even as she prayed, had fought the fight—
  The victory had won:

The wife, with trembling hand that wrote to say
  The babe was waiting for the sire's caress—
The letter meeting that upon the way,—
  The babe was fatherless:

The maiden, with her lips, in fancy, pressed
  Against the brow once dewy with her breath,
Now lying numb, unknown, and uncaressed
  Save by the dews of death.

II

What meed of tribute can the poet pay
  The Soldier, but to trail the ivy-vine
Of idle rhyme above his grave to-day
  In epitaph design?—

Or wreathe with laurel-words the icy brows
  That ache no longer with a dream of fame,
But, pillowed lowly in the narrow house,
  Renowned beyond the name.

The dewy tear-drops of the night may fall,
   And tender morning with her shining hand
May brush them from the grasses green and tall
   That undulate the land.—

Yet song of Peace nor din of toil and thrift,
   Nor chanted honors, with the flowers we heap,
Can yield us hope the Hero's head to lift
   Out of its dreamless sleep:

The dear old Flag, whose faintest flutter flies
   A stirring echo through each patriot breast,
Can never coax to life the folded eyes
   That saw its wrongs redressed—

That watched it waver when the fight was hot,
   And blazed with newer courage to its aid,
Regardless of the shower of shell and shot
   Through which the charge was made;—

And when, at last, they saw it plume its wings,
   Like some proud bird in stormy element,
And soar untrammeled on its wanderings,
   They closed in death, content.

III

O Mother, you who miss the smiling face
   Of that dear boy who vanished from your sight,
And left you weeping o'er the vacant place
   He used to fill at night,—

Who left you dazed, bewildered, on a day
    That echoed wild huzzas, and roar of guns
That drowned the farewell words you tried to say
    To incoherent ones;—

Be glad and proud you had the life to give—
    Be comforted through all the years to come,—
Your country has a longer life to live,
    Your son a better home.

O Widow, weeping o'er the orphaned child,
    Who only lifts his questioning eyes to send
A keener pang to grief unreconciled,—
    Teach him to comprehend

He had a father brave enough to stand
    Before the fire of Treason's blazing gun,
That, dying, he might will the rich old land
    Of Freedom to his son.

And, Maiden, living on through lonely years
    In fealty to love's enduring ties,—
With strong faith gleaming through the tender
      tears
    That gather in your eyes,

Look up! and own, in gratefulness of prayer,
    Submission to the will of Heaven's High Host:—
I see your Angel-soldier pacing there,
    Expectant at his post.—

I see the rank and file of armies vast,
  That muster under one supreme control;
I hear the trumpet sound the signal-blast—
  The calling of the roll—

The grand divisions falling into line
  And forming, under voice of One alone
Who gives command, and joins with tongue divine
  The hymn that shakes the Throne.

IV

And thus, in tribute to the forms that rest
  In their last camping-ground, we strew the bloom
And fragrance of the flowers they loved the best,
  In silence o'er the tomb.

With reverent hands we twine the Hero's wreath
  And clasp it tenderly on stake or stone
That stands the sentinel for each beneath
  Whose glory is our own.

While in the violet that greets the sun,
  We see the azure eye of some lost boy;
And in the rose the ruddy cheek of one
  We kissed in childish joy,—

Recalling, haply, when he marched away,
  He laughed his loudest though his eyes were
      wet.—
The kiss he gave his mother's brow that day
  Is there and burning yet:

And through the storm of grief around her tossed,
  One ray of saddest comfort she may see,—
Four hundred thousand sons like hers were lost
  To weeping Liberty.

. . . .

But draw aside the drapery of gloom,
  And let the sunshine chase the clouds away
And gild with brighter glory every tomb
  We decorate to-day:

And in the holy silence reigning round,
  While prayers of perfume bless the atmosphere,
Where loyal souls of love and faith are found,
  Thank God that Peace is here!

And let each angry impulse that may start,
  Be smothered out of every loyal breast;
And, rocked within the cradle of the heart,
  Let every sorrow rest.

SCRAPS

THERE'S a habit I have nurtured,
  From the sentimental time
When my life was like a story,
  And my heart a happy rhyme,—
Of clipping from the paper,
  Or magazine, perhaps,
The idle songs of dreamers,
  Which I treasure as my scraps.

They hide among my letters,
  And they find a cozy nest
In the bosom of my wrapper,
  And the pockets of my vest;
They clamber in my fingers
  Till my dreams of wealth relapse
In fairer dreams than Fortune's
  Though I find them only scraps.

Sometimes I find, in tatters
  Like a beggar, form as fair
As ever gave to Heaven
  The treasure of a prayer;
And words all dim and faded,
  And obliterate in part,
Grow into fadeless meanings
  That are printed on the heart.

Sometimes a childish jingle
 Flings an echo, sweet and clear,
And thrills me as I listen
 To the laughs I used to hear;
And I catch the gleam of faces,
 And the glimmer of glad eyes
That peep at me expectant
 O'er the walls of Paradise.

O syllables of measure!
 Though you wheel yourselves in line,
And await the further order
 Of this eager voice of mine;
You are powerless to follow
 O'er the field my fancy maps,
So I lead you back to silence
 Feeling you are only scraps.

AUGUST

A DAY of torpor in the sullen heat
  Of Summer's passion: In the sluggish
    stream
The panting cattle lave their lazy feet,
  With drowsy eyes, and dream.

Long since the winds have died, and in the sky
  There lives no cloud to hint of Nature's
    grief;
The sun glares ever like an evil eye,
  And withers flower and leaf.

Upon the gleaming harvest-field remote
  The thresher lies deserted, like some old
Dismantled galleon that hangs afloat
  Upon a sea of gold.

The yearning cry of some bewildered bird
  Above an empty nest, and truant boys
Along the river's shady margin heard—
  A harmony of noise—

A melody of wrangling voices blent
   With liquid laughter, and with rippling calls
Of piping lips and thrilling echoes sent
   To mimic waterfalls.

And through the hazy veil the atmosphere
   Has draped about the gleaming face of Day,
The sifted glances of the sun appear
   In splinterings of spray.

The dusty highway, like a cloud of dawn,
   Trails o'er the hillside, and the passer-by,
A tired ghost in misty shroud, toils on
   His journey to the sky.

And down across the valley's drooping sweep,
   Withdrawn to farthest limit of the glade,
The forest stands in silence, drinking deep
   Its purple wine of shade.

The gossamer floats up on phantom wing;
   The sailor-vision voyages the skies
And carries into chaos everything
   That freights the weary eyes:

Till, throbbing on and on, the pulse of heat
   Increases—reaches—passes fever's height,
And Day sinks into slumber, cool and sweet,
   Within the arms of Night.

DEAD IN SIGHT OF FAME

DIED—*Early morning of September 5, 1876, and in the gleaming dawn of "name and fame," Hamilton J. Dunbar.*

DEAD! Dead! Dead!
   We thought him ours alone;
And none so proud to see him tread
The rounds of fame, and lift his head
   Where sunlight ever shone;
But now our aching eyes are dim,
And look through tears in vain for him.

Name! Name! Name!
   It was his diadem;
Nor ever tarnish-taint of shame
Could dim its luster—like a flame
   Reflected in a gem,
He wears it blazing on his brow
Within the courts of Heaven now.

Tears! Tears! Tears!
  Like dews upon the leaf
That bursts at last—from out the years
The blossom of a trust appears
  That blooms above the grief;
And mother, brother, wife and child
Will see it and be reconciled.

IN THE DARK

O IN the depths of midnight
  What fancies haunt the brain!
When even the sigh of the sleeper
  Sounds like a sob of pain.

A sense of awe and of wonder
  I may never well define,—
For the thoughts that come in the shadows
  Never come in the shine.

The old clock down in the parlor
  Like a sleepless mourner grieves,
And the seconds drip in the silence
  As the rain drips from the eaves.

And I think of the hands that signal
  The hours there in the gloom,
And wonder what angel watchers
  Wait in the darkened room.

116

And I think of the smiling faces
    That used to watch and wait,
Till the click of the clock was answered
    By the click of the opening gate.—

They are not there now in the evening—
    Morning or noon—not there;
Yet I know that they keep their vigil,
    And wait for me Somewhere.

THE IRON HORSE

NO song is mine of Arab steed—
   My courser is of nobler blood,
And cleaner limb and fleeter speed,
   And greater strength and hardihood
Than ever cantered wild and free
Across the plains of Araby.

Go search the level desert land
From Sana on to Samarcand—
Wherever Persian prince has been,
Or Dervish, Sheik, or Bedouin,
And I defy you there to point
   Me out a steed the half so fine—
From tip of ear to pastern-joint—
   As this old iron horse of mine.

You do not know what beauty is—
   You do not know what gentleness
   His answer is to my caress!—
Why, look upon this gait of his,—
A touch upon his iron rein—
   He moves with such a stately grace

The sunlight on his burnished mane
    Is barely shaken in its place;
    And at a touch he changes pace,
And, gliding backward, stops again.

And talk of mettle—Ah! my friend,
    Such passion smolders in his breast
That when awakened it will send
    A thrill of rapture wilder than
    E'er palpitated heart of man
    When flaming at its mightiest.
And there's a fierceness in his ire—
    A maddened majesty that leaps
Along his veins in blood of fire,
    Until the path his vision sweeps
Spins out behind him like a thread
    Unraveled from the reel of time,
    As, wheeling on his course sublime,
The earth revolves beneath his tread.

Then stretch away, my gallant steed!
    Thy mission is a noble one:
    Thou bear'st the father to the son,
And sweet relief to bitter need;
Thou bear'st the stranger to his friends;
    Thou bear'st the pilgrim to the shrine,
And back again the prayer he sends
    That God will prosper me and mine,—
The star that on thy forehead gleams
Has blossomed in our brightest dreams.

Then speed thee on thy glorious race!
The mother waits thy ringing pace;
The father leans an anxious ear
The thunder of thy hooves to hear;
The lover listens, far away,
To catch thy keen exultant neigh;
And, where thy breathings roll and rise,
The husband strains his eager eyes,
And laugh of wife and baby-glee
Ring out to greet and welcome thee.
Then stretch away! and when at last
   The master's hand shall gently check
Thy mighty speed, and hold thee fast,
   The world will pat thee on the neck.

DEAD LEAVES

DAWN

AS though a gipsy maiden with dim look,
Sat crooning by the roadside of the year,
So, Autumn, in thy strangeness, thou art here
To read dark fortunes for us from the book
Of fate; thou flingest in the crinkled brook
The trembling maple's gold, and frosty-clear
Thy mocking laughter thrills the atmosphere,
And drifting on its current calls the rook
To other lands. As one who wades, alone,
Deep in the dusk, and hears the minor talk
Of distant melody, and finds the tone,
In some wierd way compelling him to stalk
The paths of childhood o'er,—so I moan,
And like a troubled sleeper, groping, walk.

DUSK

THE frightened herds of clouds across the sky
Trample the sunshine down, and chase the
day
Into the dusky forest-lands of gray
And somber twilight. Far, and faint, and high

The wild goose trails his harrow, with a cry
   Sad as the wail of some poor castaway
   Who sees a vessel drifting far astray
Of his last hope, and lays him down to die.
The children, riotous from school, grow bold
   And quarrel with the wind, whose angry gust
Plucks off the summer hat, and flaps the fold
   Of many a crimson cloak, and twirls the dust
In spiral shapes grotesque, and dims the gold
   Of gleaming tresses with the blur of rust.

NIGHT

FUNERAL Darkness, drear and desolate,
   Muffles the world. The moaning of the wind
   Is piteous with sobs of saddest kind;
And laughter is a phantom at the gate
Of memory. The long-neglected grate
   Within sprouts into flame and lights the mind
   With hopes and wishes long ago refined
To ashes,—long departed friends await
   Our words of welcome: and our lips are dumb
And powerless to greet the ones that press
   Old kisses there. The baby beats its drum,
And fancy marches to the dear caress
   Of mother-arms, and all the gleeful hum
Of home intrudes upon our loneliness.

OVER THE EYES OF GLADNESS

The voice of one hath spoken,
And the bended reed is bruised—
The golden bowl is broken,
And the silver cord is loosed.

OVER the eyes of gladness
The lids of sorrow fall,
And the light of mirth is darkened
Under the funeral pall.

The hearts that throbbed with rapture
In dreams of the future years,
Are wakened from their slumbers,
And their visions drowned in tears.

. . . .

Two buds on the bough in the morning—
Twin buds in the smiling sun,
But the frost of death has fallen
And blighted the bloom of one.

123

One leaf of life still folded,
    Has fallen from the stem,
Leaving the symbol teaching
    There still are two of them,—

For though—through Time's gradations,
    The *living* bud may burst,—
The *withered* one is gathered,
    And blooms in Heaven first.

ONLY A DREAM

ONLY a dream!
           Her head is bent
Over the keys of the instrument,
While her trembling fingers go astray
In the foolish tune she tries to play.
He smiles in his heart, though his deep, sad
    eyes
Never change to a glad surprise
As he finds the answer he seeks confessed
In glowing features, and heaving breast.

Only a dream!
           Though the *fête* is grand,
And a hundred hearts at her command,
She takes no part, for her soul is sick
Of the Coquette's art and the Serpent's
    trick,—
She someway feels she would like to fling
Her sins away as a robe, and spring
Up like a lily pure and white,
And bloom alone for *him* to-night.

Only a dream
                    That the fancy weaves.
The lids unfold like the rose's leaves,
And the upraised eyes are moist and mild
As the prayerful eyes of a drowsy child.
Does she remember the spell they once
Wrought in the past a few short months?
Haply not—yet her lover's eyes
Never change to the glad surprise.

Only a dream!
                    He winds her form
Close in the coil of his curving arm,
And whirls her away in a gust of sound
As wild and sweet as the poets found
In the paradise where the silken tent
Of the Persian blooms in the Orient,—
While ever the chords of the music seem
Whispering sadly,—"Only a dream!"

OUR LITTLE GIRL

HER heart knew naught of sorrow,
Nor the vaguest taint of sin—
'Twas an ever-blooming blossom
Of the purity within:
And her hands knew only touches
Of the mother's gentle care,
And the kisses and caresses
Through the interludes of prayer.

Her baby-feet had journeyed
Such a little distance here,
They could have found no briers
In the path to interfere;
The little cross she carried
Could not weary her, we know,
For it lay as lightly on her
As a shadow on the snow.

And yet the way before us—
O how empty now and drear!—
How ev'n the dews of roses
Seem as dripping tears for her!
And the song-birds all seem crying,
As the winds cry and the rain,
All sobbingly,—"We want—we want
Our little girl again!"

127

THE FUNNY LITTLE FELLOW

'TWAS a Funny Little Fellow
  Of the very purest type,
For he had a heart as mellow
  As an apple over ripe;
And the brightest little twinkle
  When a funny thing occurred,
And the lightest little tinkle
  Of a laugh you ever heard!

His smile was like the glitter
  Of the sun in tropic lands,
And his talk a sweeter twitter
  Than the swallow understands;
Hear him sing—and tell a story—
  Snap a joke—ignite a pun,—
'Twas a capture—rapture—glory,
  An explosion—all in one!

Though he hadn't any money—
　That condiment which tends
To make a fellow "honey"
　For the palate of his friends;—
Sweet simples he compounded—
　Sovereign antidotes for sin
Or taint,—a faith unbounded
　That his friends were genuine.

He wasn't honored, maybe—
　For his songs of praise were slim,—
Yet I never knew a baby
　That wouldn't crow for him;
I never knew a mother
　But urged a kindly claim
Upon him as a brother,
　At the mention of his name.

The sick have ceased their sighing,
　And have even found the grace
Of a smile when they were dying
　As they looked upon his face;
And I've seen his eyes of laughter
　Melt in tears that only ran
As though, swift-dancing after,
　Came the Funny Little Man.

He laughed away the sorrow
　And he laughed away the gloom
We are all so prone to borrow
　From the darkness of the tomb;

And he laughed across the ocean
 Of a happy life, and passed,
With a laugh of glad emotion,
 Into Paradise at last.

And I think the Angels knew him,
 And had gathered to await
His coming, and run to him
 Through the widely opened Gate,
With their faces gleaming sunny
 For his laughter-loving sake,
And thinking, "What a funny
 Little Angel he will make!"

SONG OF THE NEW YEAR

I HEARD the bells at midnight
    Ring in the dawning year;
And above the clanging chorus
    Of the song, I seemed to hear
A choir of mystic voices
    Flinging echoes, ringing clear,
From a band of angels winging
    Through the haunted atmosphere:
            "Ring out the shame and sorrow,
                And the misery and sin,
            That the dawning of the morrow
                May in peace be ushered in."

And I thought of all the trials
    The departed years had cost,
And the blooming hopes and pleasures
    That are withered now and lost;
And with joy I drank the music
    Stealing o'er the feeling there
As the spirit song came pealing
    On the silence everywhere:
            "Ring out the shame and sorrow,
                And the misery and sin,
            That the dawning of the morrow
                May in peace be ushered in."

And I listened as a lover
　To an utterance that flows
In syllables like dewdrops
　From the red lips of a rose,
Till the anthem, fainter growing,
　Climbing higher, chiming on
Up the rounds of happy rhyming,
　Slowly vanished in the dawn:
　　　　　　"Ring out the shame and sorrow,
　　　　　　　And the misery and sin,
　　　　　　That the dawning of the morrow
　　　　　　　May in peace be ushered in."

Then I raised my eyes to Heaven,
　And with trembling lips I pled
For a blessing for the living
　And a pardon for the dead;
And like a ghost of music
　Slowly whispered—lowly sung—
Came the echo pure and holy
　In the happy angel tongue:
　　　　　　"Ring out the shame and sorrow,
　　　　　　　And the misery and sin,
　　　　　　And the dawn of every morrow
　　　　　　　Will in peace be ushered in."

A LETTER TO A FRIEND

THE past is like a story
　　I have listened to in dreams
That vanished in the glory
　　Of the Morning's early gleams;
And—at my shadow glancing—
　　I feel a loss of strength,
As the Day of Life advancing
　　Leaves it shorn of half its length.

But it's all in vain to worry
　　At the rapid race of Time—
And he flies in such a flurry
　　When I trip him with a rhyme,
I'll bother him no longer
　　Than to thank you for the thought
That "my fame is growing stronger
　　As you really think it ought."

And though I fall below it,
　　I might know as much of mirth
To live and die a poet
　　Of unacknowledged worth;
For Fame is but a vagrant—
　　Though a loyal one and brave,
And his laurels ne'er so fragrant
　　As when scattered o'er the grave.

LINES FOR AN ALBUM

I WOULD not trace the hackneyed phrase
   Of shallow words and empty praise,
And prate of "peace" till one might think
My foolish pen was drunk with ink.
Nor will I here the wish express
Of "lasting love and happiness,"
And "cloudless skies"—for after all
"Into each life some rain must fall."
—No. Keep the empty page below,
In my remembrance, white as snow—
Nor sigh to know the secret prayer
My spirit hand has written there.

TO ANNIE

WHEN the lids of dusk are falling
    O'er the dreamy eyes of day,
And the whippoorwills are calling,
    And the lesson laid away,—
May Mem'ry soft and tender
    As the prelude of the night,
Bend over you and render
    As tranquil a delight.

FAME

I

ONCE, in a dream, I saw a man
    With haggard face and tangled hair,
  And eyes that nursed as wild a care
As gaunt Starvation ever can;
And in his hand he held a wand
  Whose magic touch gave life and thought
  Unto a form his fancy wrought
And robed with coloring so grand,
    It seemed the reflex of some child
    Of Heaven, fair and undefiled—
    A face of purity and love—
    To woo him into worlds above:
And as I gazed with dazzled eyes,
    A gleaming smile lit up his lips
    As his bright soul from its eclipse
Went flashing into Paradise.
Then tardy Fame came through the door
And found a picture—nothing more.

II

And once I saw a man, alone,
    In abject poverty, with hand
Uplifted o'er a block of stone
    That took a shape at his command
And smiled upon him, fair and good—
A perfect work of womanhood,

Save that the eyes might never weep,
Nor weary hands be crossed in sleep,
Nor hair that fell from crown to wrist,
Be brushed away, caressed and kissed.
·And as in awe I gazed on her,
  I saw the sculptor's chisel fall—
    I saw him sink, without a moan,
    Sink lifeless at the feet of stone,
And lie there like a worshiper.
  Fame crossed the threshold of the hall,
  And found a statue—that was all.

III

And once I saw a man who drew
  A gloom about him like a cloak,
And wandered aimlessly. The few
  Who spoke of him at all, but spoke
Disparagingly of a mind
The Fates had faultily designed:
Too indolent for modern times—
  Too fanciful, and full of whims—
For, talking to himself in rhymes,
  And scrawling never-heard-of hymns,
The idle life to which he clung
Was worthless as the songs he sung!
I saw him, in my vision, filled
  With rapture o'er a spray of bloom
  The wind threw in his lonely room;
And of the sweet perfume it spilled
He drank to drunkenness, and flung

His long hair back, and laughed and sung
And clapped his hands as children do
At fairy tales they listen to,
While from his flying quill there dripped
Such music on his manuscript
That he who listens to the words
May close his eyes and dream the birds
Are twittering on every hand
A language he can understand.
He journeyed on through life, unknown,
Without one friend to call his own;
He tired.　No kindly hand to press
The cooling touch of tenderness
Upon his burning brow, nor lift
To his parched lips God's freest gift—
No sympathetic sob or sigh
Of trembling lips—no sorrowing eye
Looked out through tears to see him die.
And Fame her greenest laurels brought
To crown a head that heeded not.

And this is Fame! A thing, indeed,
That only comes when least the need:
The wisest minds of every age
The book of life from page to page
Have searched in vain; each lesson conned
Will promise it the page beyond—
Until the last, when dusk of night
Falls over it, and reason's light
Is smothered by that unknown friend
Who signs his *nom de plume,* The End.

Business Department.

THE INDIANAPOLIS JOURNAL.

JNO. C. NEW & SON, Proprietors.

INDIANAPOLIS, IND.. _____ 188_

THE QUEST OF FAME.

I.

Once, in a dream, I saw a man
With haggard face, and tangled hair,
And eyes that nursed as wild a care
As gaunt Starvation ever can,—
And in his hand he held a wand
Whose magic touch gave life and thought
Unto a face his fancy wrought,
And robed with coloring so grand,
It seemed the reflex of some Child
Of Heaven, fair and undefiled—
A star of purity and love
To woo him into worlds above.
And as I gazed, with dazzled eyes,
A gleaming smile lit up his lips
As his bright soul from its eclipse
Went flashing into Paradise.
Then tardy Fame came through the door,
And found—A PICTURE. Nothing more!

Business Department.

THE INDIANAPOLIS JOURNAL.

JNO. C. NEW & SON, PROPRIETORS.

INDIANAPOLIS, IND.,_____ 188_

II

And once I saw a man, alone,
In abject poverty, with hand
Uplifted o'er a block of stone
That took a shape at his command,
And smiled upon him, fair and good —
A perfect work of Womanhood,
Save that the eyes might never weep,
Nor weary hands be crossed in sleep,
Nor hair that fell from brow to wrist
Be brushed away, caressed and kissed.
And as in awe I gazed on her,
I saw the sculptor's chisel fall —
I saw him sink, without a moan,
Sink lifeless at the feet of stone
And lie there like a worshiper.
Fame crossed the threshold of the hall,
And found — A STATUE — that was all!

THE INDIANAPOLIS JOURNAL.

JNO. C. NEW & SON, Proprietors.

INDIANAPOLIS, IND._____ 188_

III

And once I saw a man who drew
A gloom about him like a cloak
And wandered aimlessly. The few
Who spoke of him at all but spoke
Disparagingly of a mind
The Fates had faultily designed, —
Too indolent for modern times —
Too fanciful and full of whims,
For, talking to himself in rhymes,
And scrawling never-heard-of hymns,
The idle life to which he clung
Was worthless as the songs he sung!
I saw him, in my vision, filled
With rapture o'er a spray of bloom
The wind threw in his lonely room;
And of the sweet perfume it spilled
He drank to drunkenness, and flung
His long hair back, and laughed and sung
And clapped his hands as children do
At fairy tales they listen to —

Business Department.

THE INDIANAPOLIS JOURNAL.

JNO. C. NEW & SON, Proprietors.

INDIANAPOLIS, Ind.,_____ 188_

While from his flying quill there dripped
Such music on his manuscript
That he who listens to the words
May close his eyes and dream the birds
Are twittering on every hand
A language he can understand.

      He journeyed on through life unknown—
Without one friend to call his own—
He tired — no kindly hand to press
The cooling touch of tenderness
Upon his burning brow, nor lift
To his parched lips God's first gift—
No sympathetic sob or sigh
Of trembling lips — no sorrowing eye
Looked out through tears to see him die.
And Fame her greatest laurels brought
To crown a head that heeded not.

And this is Fame! A thing, indeed,
That only comes when least the need.

Business Department.

THE INDIANAPOLIS JOURNAL.

JNO. C. NEW & SON, Proprietors.

INDIANAPOLIS, IND., _____ 188__

The wisest minds of every age
The book of life from page to page
Have searched in vain — Each lesson conned
Will promise it the page beyond —
Until the last — when dusk of night
Falls over it, and Reason's light
Is smothered by that unknown friend
Who signs his _non de plume_, The End.

———— James Whitcomb Riley.

AN EMPTY NEST

I FIND an old deserted nest,
  Half-hidden in the underbrush:
A withered leaf, in phantom jest,
  Has nestled in it like a thrush
With weary, palpitating breast.

I muse as one in sad surprise
  Who seeks his childhood's home once more,
And finds it in a strange disguise
  Of vacant rooms and naked floor,
With sudden tear-drops in his eyes.

An empty nest! It used to bear
  A happy burden, when the breeze
Of summer rocked it, and a pair
  Of merry tattlers told the trees
What treasures they had hidden there.

But Fancy, flitting through the gleams
  Of youth's sunshiny atmosphere,
Has fallen in the past, and seems,
  Like this poor leaflet nestled here,—
A phantom guest of empty dreams.

MY FATHER'S HALLS

MY father's halls, so rich and rare,
 Are desolate and bleak and bare;
My father's heart and halls are one,
Since I, their life and light, am gone.

O, valiant knight, with hand of steel
And heart of gold, hear my appeal:
Release me from the spoiler's charms,
And bear me to my father's arms.

THE HARP OF THE MINSTREL

THE harp of the minstrel has never a tone
    As sad as the song in his bosom to-night,
For the magical touch of his fingers alone
    Can not waken the echoes that breathe it aright;
But oh! as the smile of the moon may impart
    A sorrow to one in an alien clime,
Let the light of the melody fall on the heart,
    And cadence his grief into musical rhyme.

The faces have faded, the eyes have grown dim
    That once were his passionate love and his pride;
And alas! all the smiles that once blossomed for him
    Have fallen away as the flowers have died.
The hands that entwined him the laureate's wreath
    And crowned him with fame in the long, long ago,
Like the laurels are withered and folded beneath
    The grass and the stubble—the frost and the
        snow.

Then sigh, if thou wilt, as the whispering strings
    Strive ever in vain for the utterance clear,
And think of the sorrowful spirit that sings,
    And jewel the song with the gem of a tear.

141

For the harp of the minstrel has never a tone
  As sad as the song in his bosom to-night,
And the magical touch of his fingers alone
  Can not waken the echoes that breathe it aright.

HONEY DRIPPING FROM THE COMB

HOW slight a thing may set one's fancy
            drifting
    Upon the dead sea of the Past!—A view—
Sometimes an odor—or a rooster lifting
        A far-off *"Ooh! ooh-ooh!"*

And suddenly we find ourselves astray
    In some wood's-pasture of the Long Ago—
Or idly dream again upon a day
        Of rest we used to know.

I bit an apple but a moment since—
    A wilted apple that the worm had spurned,—
Yet hidden in the taste were happy hints
        Of good old days returned.—

And so my heart, like some enraptured lute,
    Tinkles a tune so tender and complete,
God's blessing must be resting on the fruit—
        So bitter, yet so sweet!

JOHN WALSH

A STRANGE life—strangely passed!
     We may not read the soul
When God has folded up the scroll
          In death at last.
We may not—dare not say of one
Whose task of life as well was done
As he could do it,—"This is lost,
And prayers may never pay the cost."

Who listens to the song
     That sings within the breast,
     Should ever hear the good expressed
          Above the wrong.
And he who leans an eager ear
To catch the discord, he will hear
The echoes of his own weak heart
Beat out the most discordant part.

Whose tender heart could build
     Affection's bower above
     A heart where baby nests of love
          Were ever filled,—

With upward growth may reach and twine
About the children, grown divine,
That once were his a time so brief
His very joy was more than grief.

O Sorrow—"Peace, be still!"
  God reads the riddle right;
   And we who grope in constant night
     But serve His will;
And when sometime the doubt is gone,
And darkness blossoms into dawn,—
"God keeps the good," we then will say:
" 'Tis but the dross He throws away."

ORLIE WILDE

A GODDESS, with a siren's grace,—
A sun-haired girl on a craggy place
Above a bay where fish-boats lay
Drifting about like birds of prey.

Wrought was she of a painter's dream,—
Wise only as are artists wise,
My artist-friend, Rolf Herschkelhiem,
With deep sad eyes of oversize,
And face of melancholy guise.

I pressed him that he tell to me
This masterpiece's history.
He turned—*returned*—and thus beguiled
Me with the tale of Orlie Wilde:—

"We artists live ideally:
We breed our firmest facts of air;
We make our own reality—
We dream a thing and it is so.
The fairest scenes we ever see
Are mirages of memory;

146

The sweetest thoughts we ever know
We plagiarize from Long Ago:
And as the girl on canvas there
Is marvelously rare and fair,
'Tis only inasmuch as she
Is dumb and may not speak to me!"
He tapped me with his mahlstick—then
The picture,—and went on again:

"Orlie Wilde, the fisher's child—
I see her yet, as fair and mild
As ever nursling summer day
Dreamed on the bosom of the bay:
For I was twenty then, and went
Alone and long-haired—all content
With promises of sounding name
And fantasies of future fame,
And thoughts that now my mind discards
As editor a fledgling bard's.

"At evening once I chanced to go,
With pencil and portfolio,
Adown the street of silver sand
That winds beneath this craggy land,
To make a sketch of some old scurf
Of driftage, nosing through the surf
A splintered mast, with knarl and strand
Of rigging-rope and tattered threads
Of flag and streamer and of sail
That fluttered idly in the gale

Or whipped themselves to sadder shreds.
The while I wrought, half listlessly,
On my dismantled subject, came
A sea-bird, settling on the same
With plaintive moan, as though that he
Had lost his mate upon the sea;
And—with my melancholy trend—
It brought dim dreams half understood—
It wrought upon my morbid mood,—
I thought of my own voyagings
That had no end—that have no end.—
And, like the sea-bird, I made moan
That I was loveless and alone.
And when at last with weary wings
It went upon its wanderings,
With upturned face I watched its flight
Until this picture met my sight:
A goddess, with a siren's grace,—
A sun-haired girl on a craggy place
Above a bay where fish-boats lay
Drifting about like birds of prey.

"In airy poise she, gazing, stood
A matchless form of womanhood,
That brought a thought that if for me
Such eyes had sought across the sea,
I could have swum the widest tide
That ever mariner defied,
And, at the shore, could on have gone
To that high crag she stood upon,

To there entreat and say, 'My Sweet,
Behold thy servant at thy feet.'
And to my soul I said: 'Above,
There stands the idol of thy love!'

"In this rapt, awed, ecstatic state
I gazed—till lo! I was aware
A fisherman had joined her there—
A weary man, with halting gait,
Who toiled beneath a basket's weight:
Her father, as I guessed, for she
Had run to meet him gleefully
And ta'en his burden to herself,
That perched upon her shoulder's shelf
So lightly that she, tripping, neared
A jutting crag and disappeared;
But she left the echo of a song
That thrills me yet, and will as long
As I have being! . . .

                    . . . "Evenings came
And went,—but each the same—the same:
She watched above, and even so
I stood there watching from below;
Till, grown so bold at last, I sung,—
(What matter now the theme thereof!)—
It brought an answer from her tongue—
Faint as the murmur of a dove,
Yet all the more the song of love. . . .

"I turned and looked upon the bay,
With palm to forehead—eyes a-blur
In the sea's smile—meant but for her!—
I saw the fish-boats far away
In misty distance, lightly drawn
In chalk-dots on the horizon—
Looked back at her, long, wistfully,—
And, pushing off an empty skiff,
I beckoned her to quit the cliff
And yield me her rare company
Upon a little pleasure-cruise.—
She stood, as loathful to refuse,
To muse for full a moment's time,—
Then answered back in pantomime
'She feared some danger from the sea
Were she discovered thus with me.'
I motioned then to ask her if
I might not join her on the cliff;
And back again, with graceful wave
Of lifted arm, she anwer gave
'She feared some danger from the sea.'

"Impatient, piqued, impetuous, I
Sprang in the boat, and flung 'Good-by'
From pouted mouth with angry hand,
And madly pulled away from land
With lusty stroke, despite that she
Held out her hands entreatingly:
And when far out, with covert eye

I shoreward glanced, I saw her fly
In reckless haste adown the crag,
Her hair a-flutter like a flag
Of gold that danced across the strand
In little mists of silver sand.
All curious I, pausing, tried
To fancy what it all implied,—
When suddenly I found my feet
Were wet; and, underneath the seat
On which I sat, I heard the sound
Of gurgling waters, and I found
The boat aleak alarmingly. . . .
I turned and looked upon the sea,
Whose every wave seemed mocking me;
I saw the fishers' sails once more—
In dimmer distance than before;
I saw the sea-bird wheeling by,
With foolish wish that *I* could fly:
I thought of firm earth, home and friends—
I thought of everything that tends
To drive a man to frenzy and
To wholly lose his own command;
I thought of all my waywardness—
Thought of a mother's deep distress;
Of youthful follies yet unpurged—
Sins, as the seas, about me surged—
Thought of the printer's ready pen
To-morrow drowning me again;—
A million things without a name—
I thought of everything but—Fame. . . .

"A memory yet is in my mind,
So keenly clear and sharp-defined,
I picture every phase and line
Of life and death, and neither mine,—
While some fair seraph, golden-haired,
Bends over me,—with white arms bared,
That strongly plait themselves about
My drowning weight and lift me out—
With joy too great for words to state
Or tongue to dare articulate !

"And this seraphic ocean-child
And heroine was Orlie Wilde:
And thus it was I came to hear
Her voice's music in my ear—
Ay, thus it was Fate paved the way
That I walk desolate to-day !" . . .

The artist paused and bowed his face
Within his palms a little space,
While reverently on his form
I bent my gaze and marked a storm
That shook his frame as wrathfully
As some typhoon of agony,
And fraught with sobs—the more profound
For that peculiar laughing sound
We hear when strong men weep. . . . I leant
With warmest sympathy—I bent
To stroke with soothing hand his brow,
He murmuring—" 'Tis over now !—

And shall I tie the silken thread
Of my frail romance?" "Yes," I said.—
He faintly smiled; and then, with brow
In kneading palm, as one in dread—
His tasseled cap pushed from his head;—
" 'Her voice's music,' I repeat,"
He said,—" 'twas sweet—O passing sweet!—
Though she herself, in uttering
Its melody, proved not the thing
Of loveliness my dreams made meet
For me—there, yearning, at her feet—
Prone at her feet—a worshiper,—
For lo! she spake a tongue," moaned he,
"Unknown to me;—unknown to me
As mine to her—as mine to her."

THAT OTHER MAUD MULLER

MAUD MULLER worked at making hay,
　　And cleared her forty cents a day.

Her clothes were coarse, but her health was fine,
And so she worked in the sweet sunshine

Singing as glad as a bird in May
"Barbara Allen" the livelong day.

She often glanced at the far-off town,
And wondered if eggs were up or down.

And the sweet song died of a strange disease,
Leaving a phantom taste of cheese,

And an appetite and a nameless ache
For soda-water and ginger cake.

The Judge rode slowly into view—
Stopped his horse in the shade and drew

His fine-cut out, while the blushing Maud
Marveled much at the kind he "chawed."

"He was dry as a fish," he said with a wink,
"And kind o' thought that a good square drink

Would brace him up." So the cup was filled
With the crystal wine that old spring spilled;

And she gave it him with a sun-browned hand.
"Thanks," said the Judge in accents bland;

"A thousand thanks! for a sweeter draught,
From a fairer hand"—but there he laughed.

And the sweet girl stood in the sun that day,
And raked the Judge instead of the hay.

A MAN OF MANY PARTS

IT was a man of many parts,
  Who in his coffer mind
Had stored the Classics and the Arts
  And Sciences combined;
The purest gems of poesy
  Came flashing from his pen—
The wholesome truths of History
  He gave his fellow men.

He knew the stars from "Dog" to Mars;
  And he could tell you, too,
Their distances—as though the cars
  Had often checked him through—
And time 'twould take to reach the sun,
  Or by the "Milky Way,"
Drop in upon the moon, or run
  The homeward trip, or stay.

With Logic at his fingers' ends,
  Theology in mind,
He often entertained his friends
  Until they died resigned;
And with inquiring mind intent
  Upon Alchemic arts
A dynamite experiment—

  .   .   .   .

A man of many parts!

THE FROG

WHO am I but the Frog—the Frog!
   My realm is the dark bayou,
And my throne is the muddy and moss-grown log
   That the poison-vine clings to—
And the blacksnakes slide in the slimy tide
   Where the ghost of the moon looks blue.

What am I but a King—a King!—
   For the royal robes I wear—
A scepter, too, and a signet-ring,
   As vassals and serfs declare:
And a voice, god wot, that is equaled not
   In the wide world anywhere!

I can talk to the Night—the Night!—
   Under her big black wing
She tells me the tale of the world outright,
   And the secret of everything;
For she knows you all, from the time you crawl,
   To the doom that death will bring.

The Storm swoops down, and he blows—and
　　blows,—
　　While I drum on his swollen cheek,
And croak in his angered eye that glows
　　With the lurid lightning's streak;
While the rushes drown in the watery frown
　　That his bursting passions leak.

And I can see through the sky—the sky—
　　As clear as a piece of glass;
And I can tell you the how and why
　　Of the things that come to pass—
And whether the dead are there instead,
　　Or under the graveyard grass.

To your Sovereign lord all hail—all hail!—
　　To your Prince on his throne so grim!
Let the moon swing low, and the high stars trail
　　Their heads in the dust to him;
And the wide world sing: Long live the King,
　　And grace to his royal whim!

DEAD SELVES

H OW many of my selves are dead?
  The ghosts of many haunt me: Lo,
The baby in the tiny bed
With rockers on, is blanketed
  And sleeping in the long ago;
And so I ask, with shaking head,
How many of my selves are dead?

A little face with drowsy eyes
  And lisping lips comes mistily
From out the faded past, and tries
The prayers a mother breathed with sighs
  Of anxious care in teaching me;
But face and form and prayers have fled—
How many of my selves are dead?

The little naked feet that slipped
  In truant paths, and led the way
Through dead'ning pasture-lands, and tripped
O'er tangled poison-vines, and dipped
  In streams forbidden—where are they?
In vain I listen for their tread—
How many of my selves are dead?

The awkward boy the teacher caught
   Inditing letters filled with love,
Who was compelled, for all he fought,
To read aloud each tender thought
   Of "Sugar Lump" and "Turtle Dove."
I wonder where he hides his head—
How many of my selves are dead?

The earnest features of a youth
   With manly fringe on lip and chin,
With eager tongue to tell the truth,
To offer love and life, forsooth,
   So brave was he to woo and win;
A prouder man was never wed—
How many of my selves are dead?

The great, strong hands so all-inclined
   To welcome toil, or smooth the care
From mother-brows, or quick to find
A leisure-scrap of any kind,
   To toss the baby in the air,
Or clap at babbling things it said—
How many of my selves are dead?

The pact of brawn and scheming brain—
   Conspiring in the plots of wealth,
Still delving, till the lengthened chain,
Unwindlassed in the mines of gain,
   Recoils with dregs of ruined health
And pain and poverty instead—
How many of my selves are dead?

The faltering step, the faded hair—
　　Head, heart and soul, all echoing
With maundering fancies that declare
That life and love were never there,
　　Nor ever joy in anything,
Nor wounded heart that ever bled—
How many of my selves are dead?

So many of my selves are dead,
　　That, bending here above the brink
Of my last grave, with dizzy head,
I find my spirit comforted,
　　For all the idle things I think:
It can but be a peaceful bed,
Since all my other selves are dead.

A DREAM OF LONG AGO

LYING listless in the mosses
    Underneath a tree that tosses
Flakes of sunshine, and embosses
    Its green shadow with the snow—
Drowsy-eyed, I think in slumber
Born of fancies without number—
Tangled fancies that encumber
    Me with dreams of long ago.

Ripples of the river singing;
And the water-lilies swinging
Bells of Parian, and ringing
    Peals of perfume faint and fine,
While old forms and fairy faces
Leap from out their hiding-places
In the past, with glad embraces
    Fraught with kisses sweet as wine.

Willows dip their slender fingers
O'er the little fisher's stringers,
While he baits his hook and lingers
    Till the shadows gather dim;
And afar off comes a calling

163

Like the sounds of water falling,
With the lazy echoes drawling
  Messages of haste to him.

Little naked feet that tinkle
Through the stubble-fields, and twinkle
Down the winding road, and sprinkle
  Little mists of dusty rain,
While in pasture-lands the cattle
Cease their grazing with a rattle
Of the bells whose clappers tattle
  To their masters down the lane.

Trees that hold their tempting treasures
O'er the orchard's hedge embrasures,
Furnish their forbidden pleasures
  As in Eden lands of old;
And the coming of the master
Indicates a like disaster
To the frightened heart that faster
  Beats pulsations manifold.

Puckered lips whose pipings tingle
In staccato notes that mingle
Musically with the jingle—
  Haunted winds that lightly fan
Mellow twilights, crimson-tinted
By the sun, and picture-printed
Like a book that sweetly hinted
  Of the Nights Arabian.

Porticoes with columns plaited
And entwined with vines and freighted
With a bloom all radiated
   With the light of moon and star;
Where some tender voice is winging
In sad flights of song, and singing
To the dancing fingers flinging
   Dripping from the sweet guitar.

Would my dreams were never taken
From me: that with faith unshaken
I might sleep and never waken
   On a weary world of woe!
Links of love would never sever
As I dreamed them, never, never!
I would glide along forever
   Through the dreams of long ago.

CRAQUEODOOM

THE Crankadox leaned o'er the edge of the
        moon
  And wistfully gazed on the sea
Where the Gryxabodill madly whistled a tune
  To the air of "Ti-fol-de-ding-dee."
The quavering shriek of the Fly-up-the-creek
  Was fitfully wafted afar
To the Queen of the Wunks as she powdered her
        cheek
  With the pulverized rays of a star.

The Gool closed his ear on the voice of the Grig,
  And his heart it grew heavy as lead
As he marked the Baldekin adjusting his wing
  On the opposite side of his head,
And the air it grew chill as the Gryxabodill
  Raised his dank, dripping fins to the skies,
And plead with the Plunk for the use of her bill
  To pick the tears out of his eyes.

The ghost of the Zhack flitted by in a trance,
  And the Squidjum hid under a tub

As he heard the loud hooves of the Hooken ad-
    vance
  With a rub-a-dub—dub-a-dub—dub!
And the Crankadox cried, as he lay down and died,
  "My fate there is none to bewail,"
While the Queen of the Wunks drifted over the
    tide
  With a long piece of crape to her tail.

JUNE

O QUEENLY month of indolent repose!
  I drink thy breath in sips of rare perfume,
As in thy downy lap of clover-bloom
I nestle like a drowsy child and doze
The lazy hours away. The zephyr throws
  The shifting shuttle of the Summer's loom
  And weaves a damask-work of gleam and gloom
Before thy listless feet. The lily blows
A bugle-call of fragrance o'er the glade;
  And, wheeling into ranks, with plume and spear,
Thy harvest-armies gather on parade;
  While, faint and far away, yet pure and clear,
A voice calls out of alien lands of shade:—
  All hail the Peerless Goddess of the Year!

James Whitcomb Riley and his mother

WASH LOWRY'S REMINISCENCE

AND you're the poet of this concern?
 I've seed your name in print
A dozen times, but I'll be dern
 I'd 'a' never 'a' took the hint
O' the size you are—fur I'd pictured you
 A kind of a tallish man—
Dark-complected and sallor too,
 And on the consumpted plan.

'Stid o' that you're little and small,
 With a milk-and-water face—
'Thout no snap in your eyes at all,
 Or nothin' to suit the case!
Kind o' look like a—I don't know—
 One o' these fair-ground chaps
That runs a thingamajig to blow,
 Or a candy-stand perhaps.

'Ll I've allus thought that poetry
   Was a sort of a—some disease—
For I knowed a poet once, and he
   Was techy and hard to please,
And moody-like, and kindo' sad
   And didn't seem to mix
With other folks—like his health was bad,
   Or his liver out o' fix.

Used to teach for a livelihood—
   There's folks in Pipe Crick yit
Remembers him—and he was good
   At cipherin' I'll admit—
And posted up in G'ography
   But when it comes to tact,
And gittin' along with the school, you see,
   He fizzled, and that's a fact!

Boarded with us for fourteen months
   And in all that time I'll say
We never catched him a sleepin' once
   Or idle a single day.
But shucks! It made him worse and worse
   A-writin' rhymes and stuff,
And the school committee used to furse
   'At the school wa'n't good enough.

He wa'n't as strict as he ought to been,
   And never was known to whip,
Or even to keep a scholard in
   At work at his penmanship;

'Stid o' that he'd learn 'em notes,
  And have 'em every day,
Spilin' hymns and a-splittin' th'oats
  With his "Do-sol-fa-me-ra!"

Tell finally it was jest agreed
  We'd have to let him go,
And we all felt bad—we did indeed,
  When we come to tell him so;
For I remember, he turned so white,
  And smiled so sad, somehow,
I someway felt it wasn't right
  And I'm shore it wasn't now!

He hadn't no complaints at all—
  He bid the school adieu,
And all o' the scholards great and small
  Was mighty sorry too!
And when he closed that afternoon
  They sung some lines that he
Had writ a purpose, to some old tune
  That suited the case, you see.

And then he lingered and delayed
  And wouldn't go away—
And shut himself in his room and stayed
  A-writin' from day to day;
And kep' a-gittin' stranger still,
  And thinner all the time,
You know, as any feller will
  On nothin' else but rhyme.

He didn't seem adzactly right,
  Or like he was crossed in love,
He'd work away night after night,
  And walk the floor above;
We'd hear him read and talk, and sing
  So lonesome-like and low,
My woman's cried like everything—
  'Way in the night, you know.

And when at last he tuck to bed
  He'd have his ink and pen;
"So's he could coat the muse" he said,
  "He'd die contented then";
And jest before he past away
  He read with dyin' gaze
The epitaph that stands to-day
  To show you where he lays.

And ever sence then I've allus thought
  That poetry's some disease,
And them like you that's got it ought
  To watch their q's and p's;
And leave the sweets of rhyme, to sup
  On the wholesome draughts of toil,
And git your health recruited up
  By plowin' in rougher soil.

THE ANCIENT PRINTERMAN

"O PRINTERMAN of sallow face,
 And look of absent guile,
Is it the 'copy' on your 'case'
 That causes you to smile?
Or is it some old treasure scrap
 You call from Memory's file?

"I fain would guess its mystery—
 For often I can trace
A fellow dreamer's history
 Whene'er it haunts the face;
Your fancy's running riot
 In a retrospective race!

"Ah, Printerman, you're straying
 Afar from 'stick' and type—
Your heart has 'gone a-maying,'
 And you taste old kisses, ripe
Again on lips that pucker
 At your old asthmatic pipe!

173

"You are dreaming of old pleasures
   That have faded from your view;
And the music-burdened measures
   Of the laughs you listen to
Are now but angel-echoes—
   O, have I spoken true?"

The ancient Printer hinted
   With a motion full of grace
—To where the words were printed
   On a card above his "case,"—
"I am deaf and dumb!"   I left him
   With a smile upon his face.

PRIOR TO MISS BELLE'S APPEARANCE

WHAT makes you come *here* fer, Mister,
  So much to *our* house?—*Say?*
Come to see our big sister!—
An' Charley he says 'at you kissed her
  An' he ketched you, th'uther day!—
Didn' you, Charley?—But we p'omised Belle
An' crossed our heart to never to tell—
'Cause *she* gived us some o' them-er
Chawk'lut-drops 'at you bringed to her!

Charley he's my little b'uther—
  An' we has a-mostest fun,
Don't we, Charley?—Our Muther,
Whenever we whips one anuther,
  Tries to whip *us*—an' we *run*—
Don't we, Charley?—An' nen, bime-by,
Nen she gives us cake—an' pie—
Don't she, Charley?—when we come in
An' p'omise never to do it ag'in!

175

He's named Charley.—I'm *Willie*—
    An' I'm got the purtiest name!
But Uncle Bob *he* calls me "Billy"—
    Don't he, Charley?—'N' our filly
        We named " Billy," the same
    Ist like me! An' our Ma said
'At "Bob puts foolishnuss into our head!"—
    Didn' she, Charley?—An' *she* don't know
Much about *boys!*—'Cause Bob said so!

Baby's a funniest feller!
    Nain't no hair on his head—
Is they, Charley?—It's meller
    Wite up there! An' ef Belle er
        Us ask wuz *we* that way, Ma said,—
    "Yes; an' yer *Pa's* head wuz soft as that,
An' it's that way yet!"—An' Pa grabs his hat
    An' says, "Yes, childern, she's right about Pa—
'Cause that's the reason he married yer Ma!"

An' our Ma says 'at "Belle couldn'
    Ketch nothin' at all but ist *'bows'!*"—
An' *Pa* says 'at "you're soft as puddun!"—
    An' *Uncle Bob* says "you're a good-un—
        'Cause he can tell by yer nose!"—
    Didn' he, Charley?—An' when Belle'll play
In the poller on th' pianer, some day,
    Bob makes up funny songs about you,
Till she gits mad—like he wants her to!

Our sister *Fanny* she's *'leven* ~~sight~~
  Years old! 'At's mucher 'an *I*— ~~hear~~
Ain't it, Charley? . . . I'm seven!— ~~hear~~
But our sister Fanny's in *Heaven!* ~~sight~~
  Nere's where you go ef you die!— ~~hear~~
Don't you Charley?—Nen you has *wings*— ~~hear & sight~~
Ist like Fanny!—an' *purtiest things!*— ~~sight~~
Don't you, Charley?—An' nen you can *fly*— ~~hear, feel~~
Ist fly—an' *ever'*thing! . . . Wisht *I'd* die! ~~feel~~

WHEN MOTHER COMBED MY HAIR

WHEN Memory, with gentle hand,
 Has led me to that foreign land
Of childhood days, I long to be
Again the boy on bended knee,
With head a-bow, and drowsy smile
Hid in a mother's lap the while,
With tender touch and kindly care,
She bends above and combs my hair.

Ere threats of Time, or ghosts of cares
Had paled it to the hue it wears,
Its tangled threads of amber light
Fell o'er a forehead, fair and white,
That only knew the light caress
Of loving hands, or sudden press
Of kisses that were sifted there
The times when mother combed my hair.

But its last gleams of gold have slipped
Away; and Sorrow's manuscript
Is fashioned of the snowy brow—
So lined and underscored now

That you, to see it, scarce would guess
It e'er had felt the fond caress
Of loving lips, or known the care
Of those dear hands that combed my hair.

.   .   .   .

I am so tired! Let me be
A moment at my mother's knee;
One moment—that I may forget
The trials waiting for me yet:
One moment free from every pain—
O! Mother! Comb my hair again!
And I will, oh, so humbly bow,
For I've a wife that combs it now.

A WRANGDILLION

DEXERY-TETHERY! down in the dike,
   Under the ooze and the slime,
Nestles the wraith of a reticent Gryke,
   Blubbering bubbles of rhyme:
Though the reeds touch him and tickle his teeth—
   Though the Graigroll and the Cheest
Pluck at the leaves of his laureate-wreath,
   Nothing affects him the least.

He sinks to the dregs in the dead o' the night,
   And he shuffles the shadows about
As he gathers the stars in a nest of delight
   And sets there and hatches them out:
The Zhederrill peers from his watery mine
   In scorn with the Will-o'-the-wisp,
As he twinkles his eyes in a whisper of shine
   That ends in a luminous lisp.

180

The Morning is born like a baby of gold,
    And it lies in a spasm of pink,
And rallies the Cheest for the horrible cold
    He has dragged to the willowy brink,
The Gryke blots his tears with a scrap of his
        grief,
    And growls at the wary Graigroll
As he twunkers a tune on a Tiljicum leaf
    And hums like a telegraph pole.

GEORGE MULLEN'S CONFESSION

FOR the sake of guilty conscience, and the heart
that ticks the time
Of the clockworks of my nature, I desire to say
that I'm
A weak and sinful creature, as regards my daily
walk
The last five years and better. It ain't worth while
to talk—

I've been too mean to tell it! I've been so hard,
you see,
And full of pride, and—onry—now there's the word
for me—
Just onry—and to show you, I'll give my history
With vital points in question, and I think you'll all
agree.

I was always stiff and stubborn since I could recol-
lect,
And had an awful temper, and never would reflect;
And always into trouble—I remember once at
school
The teacher tried to flog me, and I reversed that
rule.

O I was bad I tell you! And it's a funny move
That a fellow wild as I was could ever fall in love;
And it's a funny notion that an animal like me,
Under a girl's weak fingers was as tame as tame
    could be!

But it's so, and sets me thinking of the easy way
    she had
Of cooling down my temper—though I'd be fight-
    ing mad.
"My Lion Queen" I called her—when a spell of
    mine occurred
She'd come in a den of feelings and quell them
    with a word.

I'll tell you how she loved me—and what her peo-
    ple thought:
When I asked to marry Annie they said "they reck-
    oned not—
That I cut too many didoes and monkey-shines to
    suit
Their idea of a son-in-law, and I could go, to boot!"

I tell you that thing riled me! Why, I felt my face
    turn white,
And my teeth shut like a steel trap, and the fingers
    of my right
Hand pained me with their pressure—all the rest's
    a mystery
Till I heard my Annie saying—"I'm going, too, you
    see."

We were coming through the gateway, and she
    wavered for a spell
When she heard her mother crying and her raving
    father yell
That she wa'n't no child of his'n—like an actor in
    a play
We saw at Independence, coming through the other
    day.

Well! that's the way we started. And for days
    and weeks and months
And even years we journeyed on, regretting never
    once
Of starting out together upon the path of life—
A kind o' sort o' husband, but a mighty loving
    wife,—

And the cutest little baby—little Grace—I see her
    now
A-standin' on the pig-pen as her mother milked the
    cow—
And I can hear her shouting—as I stood unloading
    straw,—
"I'm ain't as big as papa, but I'm biggerest'n ma."

Now folks that never married don't seem to under-
    stand
That a little baby's language is the sweetest ever
    planned—

Why, I tell you it's pure music, and I'll just go on
    to say
That I sometimes have a notion that the angels talk
    that way!

There's a chapter in this story I'd be happy to de-
    stroy;
I could burn it up before you with a mighty sight
    of joy;
But I'll go ahead and give it—not in detail, no, my
    friend,
For it takes five years of reading before you find
    the end.

My Annie's folks relented—at least, in some de-
    gree;
They sent one time for Annie, but they didn't send
    for me.
The old man wrote the message with a heart as hot
    and dry
As a furnace—"Annie Mullen, come and see your
    mother die."

I saw the slur intended—why I fancied I could see
The old man shoot the insult like a poison dart at
    me;
And in that heat of passion I swore an inward oath
That if Annie pleased her father she could never
    please us both.

I watched her—dark and sullen—as she hurried on
    her shawl;
I watched her—calm and cruel, though I saw her
    tear-drops fall;
I watched her—cold and heartless, though I heard
    her moaning, call
For mercy from high Heaven—and I smiled
    throughout it all.

Why even when she kissed me, and her tears were
    on my brow,
As she murmured, "George, forgive me—I must go
    to mother now!"
Such hate there was within me that I answered not
    at all,
But calm, and cold and cruel, I smiled throughout
    it all.

But a shadow in the doorway caught my eye, and
    then the face
Full of innocence and sunshine of little baby Grace.
And I snatched her up and kissed her, and I soft-
    ened through and through
For a minute when she told me "I must kiss her
    muvver too."

I remember, at the starting, how I tried to freeze
    again
As I watched them slowly driving down the little
    crooked lane—

When Annie shouted something that ended in a
    cry,
And how I tried to whistle and it fizzled in a sigh.

I remember running after, with a glimmer in my
    sight—
Pretending I'd discovered that the traces wasn't
    right;
And the last that I remember, as they disappeared
    from view,
Was little Grace a-calling, "I see papa! Howdy-
    do!"

And left alone to ponder, I again took up my hate
For the old man who would chuckle that I was
    desolate;
And I mouthed my wrongs in mutters till my pride
    called up the pain
His last insult had given me—until I smiled again

Till the wild beast in my nature was raging in the
    den—
With no one now to quell it, and I wrote a letter
    then
Full of hissing things, and heated with so hot a heat
    of hate
That my pen flashed out black lightning at a most
    terrific rate.

I wrote that "she had wronged me when she went
    away from me—
Though to see her dying mother 'twas her father's
    victory,
And a woman that could waver when her husband's
    pride was rent
Was no longer worthy of it." And I shut the house
    and went.

To tell of my long exile would be of little good—
Though I couldn't half-way tell it, and I wouldn't
    if I could!
I could tell of California—of a wild and vicious
    life;
Of trackless plains, and mountains, and the In-
    dian's scalping-knife.

I could tell of gloomy forests howling wild with
    threats of death;
I could tell of fiery deserts that have scorched me
    with their breath;
I could tell of wretched outcasts by the hundreds,
    great and small,
And could claim the nasty honor of the greatest of
    them all.

I could tell of toil and hardship; and of sickness
    and disease,
And hollow-eyed starvation, but I tell you, friend,
    that these

Are trifles in comparison with what a fellow feels
With that bloodhound, Remorsefulness, forever at
his heels.

I remember—worn and weary of the long, long
years of care,
When the frost of time was making early harvest of
my hair—
I remember, wrecked and hopeless of a rest be-
neath the sky,
My resolve to quit the country, and to seek the
East, and die.

I remember my long journey, like a dull, oppressive dream,
Across the empty prairies till I caught the distant
gleam
Of a city in the beauty of its broad and shining
stream
On whose bosom, flocked together, float the mighty
swans of steam.

I remember drifting with them till I found myself
again
In the rush and roar and rattle of the engine and
the train;
And when from my surroundings something spoke
of child and wife,
It seemed the train was rumbling through a tunnel
in my life.

Then I remember something—like a sudden burst
    of light—
That don't exactly tell it, but I couldn't tell it
    right—
A something clinging to me with its arms around
    my neck—
A little girl, for instance—or an angel, I expect—

For she kissed me, cried and called me "her dear
    papa," and I felt
My heart was pure virgin gold, and just about to
    melt—
And so it did—it melted in a mist of gleaming rain
When she took my hand and whispered, "My
    mama's on the train."

There's some things I can dwell on, and get off
    pretty well,
But the balance of this story I know I couldn't tell;
So I ain't going to try it, for to tell the reason
    why—
I'm so chicken-hearted lately I'd be certain 'most
    to cry.

"TIRED OUT"

"TIRED out!" Yet face and brow
  Do not look aweary now,
And the eyelids lie like two
Pure, white rose-leaves washed with dew.
Was her life so hard a task?—
Strange that we forget to ask
What the lips now dumb for aye
Could have told us yesterday!

"Tired out!" A faded scrawl
Pinned upon the ragged shawl—
Nothing else to leave a clue
Even of a friend or two,
Who might come to fold the hands,
Or smooth back the dripping strands
Of her tresses, or to wet
Them anew with fond regret.

"Tired out!" We can but guess
Of her little happiness—
Long ago, in some fair land,
When a lover held her hand
In the dream that frees us all,
Soon or later, from its thrall—
Be it either false or true,
We, at last, must tire, too.

HARLIE

"FOLD the little waxen hands
Lightly. Let your warmest tears
Speak regrets, but never fears,—
    Heaven understands!
Let the sad heart, o'er the tomb,
Lift again and burst in bloom
Fragrant with a prayer as sweet
As the lily at your feet.

Bend and kiss the folded eyes—
They are only feigning sleep
While their truant glances peep
    Into Paradise.
See, the face, though cold and white,
Holds a hint of some delight
E'en with Death, whose finger-tips
Rest upon the frozen lips.

When, within the years to come,
Vanished echoes live once more—
Pattering footsteps on the floor,
    And the sounds of home,—
Let your arms in fancy fold
Little Harlie as of old—
As of old and as he waits
At the City's golden gates.

SAY SOMETHING TO ME

SAY something to me! I've waited so
　　long—
　Waited and wondered in vain;
Only a sentence would fall like a song
　Over this listening pain—
Over a silence that glowers and frowns,—
　Even my pencil to-night
Slips in the dews of my sorrow and wounds
　Each tender word that I write.

Say something to me—if only to tell
　Me you remember the past;
Let the sweet words, like the notes of a bell,
　Ring out my vigil at last.
O it were better, far better than this
　Doubt and distrust in the breast,—
For in the wine of a fanciful kiss
　I could taste Heaven, and—rest.

Say something to me! I kneel and I plead,
　In my wild need, for a word;
If my poor heart from this silence were
　　freed,
　I could soar up like a bird
In the glad morning, and twitter and sing,
　Carol and warble and cry
Blithe as the lark as he cruises awing
　Over the deeps of the sky.

LEONAINIE

LEONAINIE—Angels named her;
　　And they took the light
Of the laughing stars and framed her
　　In a smile of white;
　　　　And they made her hair of gloomy
　　　　Midnight, and her eyes of bloomy
　　　　Moonshine, and they brought her to
　　　　　me
　　In the solemn night.—

In a solemn night of summer,
　　When my heart of gloom
Blossomed up to greet the comer
　　Like a rose in bloom;
　　　　All forebodings that distressed me
　　　　I forgot as Joy caressed me—
　　　　(*Lying* Joy! that caught and pressed
　　　　　me
　　In the arms of doom!)

Only spake the little lisper
　　In the Angel-tongue;
Yet I, listening, heard her whisper,—
　　"Songs are only sung

Here below that they may grieve
   you—
Tales but told you to deceive you,—
So must Leonainie leave you
While her love is young."

Then God smiled and it was morning.
   Matchless and supreme
Heaven's glory seemed adorning
   Earth with its esteem:
      Every heart but mine seemed gifted
      With the voice of prayer, and lifted
      Where my Leonainie drifted
   From me like a dream.

A TEST OF LOVE

"Now who shall say he loves me not."

HE wooed her first in an atmosphere
    Of tender and low-breathed sighs;
But the pang of her laugh went cutting clear
    To the soul of the enterprise;
"You beg so pert for the kiss you seek
    It reminds me, John," she said,
"Of a poodle pet that jumps to 'speak'
    For a crumb or a crust of bread."

And flashing up, with the blush that flushed
    His face like a tableau-light,
Came a bitter threat that his white lips
      hushed
    To a chill, hoarse-voiced "Good night!"
And again her laugh, like a knell that tolled,
    And a wide-eyed mock surprise,—
"Why, John," she said, "you have taken
    cold
    In the chill air of your sighs!"

And then he turned, and with teeth tight
    clenched,
  He told her he hated her,—
That his love for her from his heart he
    wrenched
  Like a corpse from a sepulcher.
And then she called him "a ghoul all red
  With the quintessence of crimes"—
"But I know you love me now," she said,
  And kissed him a hundred times.

FATHER WILLIAM

A NEW VERSION BY LEE O. HARRIS AND JAMES
WHITCOMB RILEY

"YOU are old, Father William, and though one
would think
All the veins in your body were dry,
Yet the end of your nose is red as a pink;
I beg your indulgence, but why?"

"You see," Father William replied, "in my youth—
'Tis a thing I must ever regret—
It worried me so to keep up with the truth
That my nose has a flush on it yet."

"You are old," said the youth, "and I grieve to de-
tect
A feverish gleam in your eye;
Yet I'm willing to give you full time to reflect.
Now, pray, can you answer me why?"

"Alas," said the sage, "I was tempted to choose
Me a wife in my earlier years,
And the grief, when I think that she didn't refuse,
Has reddened my eyelids with tears."

198

Birthplace James Whitcomb Riley, Greenfield, Indiana

"You are old, Father William," the young man said,
  "And you never touch wine, you declare,
Yet you sleep with your feet at the head of the bed;
  Now answer me that if you dare."

"In my youth," said the sage, "I was told it was
      true,
  That the world turned around in the night;
I cherished the lesson, my boy, and I knew
  That at morning my feet would be right."

"You are old," said the youth, "and it grieved me to
      note,
  As you recently fell through the door,
That 'full as a goose' had been chalked on your
      coat;
  Now answer me that I implore."

"My boy," said the sage, "I have answered you fair,
  While you stuck to the point in dispute,
But this is a personal matter, and there
  Is my answer—the toe of my boot."

WHAT THE WIND SAID

I MUSE to-day, in a listless way,
  In the gleam of a summer land;
I close my eyes as a lover may
  At the touch of his sweetheart's hand,
And I hear these things in the whisperings
  Of the zephyrs round me fanned:—

I am the Wind, and I rule mankind,
  And I hold a sovereign reign
Over the lands, as God designed,
  And the waters they contain:
Lo! the bound of the wide world round
  Falleth in my domain!

I was born on a stormy morn
  In a kingdom walled with snow,
Whose crystal cities laugh to scorn
  The proudest the world can show;
And the daylight's glare is frozen there
  In the breath of the blasts that blow.

Life to me was a jubilee
  From the first of my youthful days:
Clinking my icy toys with glee—
  Playing my childish plays;
Filling my hands with the silver sands
  To scatter a thousand ways:

Chasing the flakes that the Polar shakes
  From his shaggy coat of white,
Or hunting the trace of the track he makes
  And sweeping it from sight,
As he turned to glare from the slippery stair
  Of the iceberg's farthest height.

Till I grew so strong that I strayed ere long
  From my home of ice and chill;
With an eager heart and a merry song
  I traveled the snows until
I heard the thaws in the ice-crag's jaws
  Crunched with a hungry will;

And the angry crash of the waves that dash
  Themselves on the jaggèd shore
Where the splintered masts of the ice-wrecks
      flash,
  And the frightened breakers roar
In wild unrest on the ocean's breast
  For a thousand leagues or more.

And the grand old sea invited me
  With a million beckoning hands,
And I spread my wings for a flight as free
  As ever a sailor plans
When his thoughts are wild and his heart be-
    guiled
  With the dreams of foreign lands.

I passed a ship on its homeward trip,
  With a weary and toil-worn crew;
And I kissed their flag with a welcome lip,
  And so glad a gale I blew
That the sailors quaffed their grog and
    laughed
  At the work I made them do.

I drifted by where sea-groves lie
  Like brides in the fond caress
Of the warm sunshine and the tender sky—
  Where the ocean, passionless
And tranquil, lies like a child whose eyes
  Are blurred with drowsiness.

I drank the air and the perfume there,
  And bathed in a fountain's spray;
And I smoothed the wings and the plumage
    rare
  Of a bird for his roundelay,
And fluttered a rag from a signal-crag
  For a wretched castaway.

With a sea-gull resting on my breast,
   I launched on a madder flight:
And I lashed the waves to a wild unrest,
   And howled with a fierce delight
Till the daylight slept; and I wailed and
      wept
   Like a fretful babe all night.

For I heard the boom of a gun strike doom;
   And the gleam of a blood-red star
Glared at me through the mirk and gloom
   From the lighthouse tower afar;
And I held my breath at the shriek of death
   That came from the harbor bar.

For I am the Wind, and I rule mankind,
   And I hold a sovereign reign
Over the lands, as God designed,
   And the waters they contain:
Lo! the bound of the wide world round
   Falleth in my domain!

I journeyed on, when the night was gone,
   O'er a coast of oak and pine;
And I followed a path that a stream had
      drawn
   Through a land of vale and vine,
And here and there was a village fair
   In a nest of shade and shine.

I passed o'er lakes where the sunshine shakes
    And shivers his golden lance
On the glittering shield of the wave that
       breaks
    Where the fish-boats dip and dance,
And the trader sails where the mist unveils
    The glory of old romance.

I joyed to stand where the jeweled hand
    Of the maiden-morning lies
On the tawny brow of the mountain-land.
    Where the eagle shrieks and cries,
And holds his throne to himself alone
    From the light of human eyes.

Adown deep glades where the forest shades
    Are dim as the dusk of day—
Where only the foot of the wild beast wades,
    Or the Indian dares to stray,
As the blacksnakes glide through the reeds
       and hide
    In the swamp-depths grim and gray.

And I turned and fled from the place of
       dread
    To the far-off haunts of men.
"In the city's heart is rest," I said,—
    But I found it not, and when
I saw but care and vice reign there
    I was filled with wrath again:

And I blew a spark in the midnight dark
  Till it flashed to an angry flame
And scarred the sky with a lurid mark
  As red as the blush of shame:
And a hint of hell was the dying yell
  That up from the ruins came.

The bells went wild, and the black smoke
      piled
  Its pillars against the night,
Till I gathered them, like flocks defiled,
  And scattered them left and right,
While the holocaust's red tresses tossed
  As a maddened Fury's might.

"Ye overthrown!" did I jeer and groan—
  "Ho! who is your master?—say!—
Ye shapes that writhe in the slag and moan
  Your slow-charred souls away—
Ye worse than worst of things accurst—
  Ye dead leaves of a day!"

I am the Wind, and I rule mankind,
  And I hold a sovereign reign
Over the lands, as God designed,
  And the waters they contain:
Lo! the bound of the wide world round
  Falleth in my domain!

        • • • • • • •

I wake, as one from a dream half done,
  And gaze with a dazzled eye
On an autumn leaf like a scrap of sun
  That the wind goes whirling by,
While afar I hear, with a chill of fear,
  The winter storm-king sigh.

MORTON

THE warm pulse of the nation has grown
    chill;
  The muffled heart of Freedom, like a knell,
Throbs solemnly for one whose earthly will
  Wrought every mission well.

Whose glowing reason towered above the sea
  Of dark disaster like a beacon light,
And led the Ship of State, unscathed and free,
  Out of the gulfs of night.

When Treason, rabid-mouthed, and fanged with
    steel,
  Lay growling o'er the bones of fallen braves.
And when beneath the tyrant's iron heel
  Were ground the hearts of slaves,

And War, with all his train of horrors, leapt
  Across the fortress-walls of Liberty
With havoc, e'en the marble goddess wept
  With tears of blood to see.

Throughout it all his brave and kingly mind
　Kept loyal vigil o'er the patriot's vow,
And yet the flag he lifted to the wind
　Is drooping o'er him now.

And Peace—all pallid from the battle-field
　When first again it hovered o'er the land,
And found his voice above it like a shield,
　Had nestled in his hand.

　　　.　　.　　.　　.　　.　　.　　,　　.

O throne of State and gilded Senate halls—
　Though thousands throng your aisles and gal-
　　　leries—
How empty are ye! and what silence falls
　On your hilarities!

And yet, though great the loss to us appears,
　The consolation sweetens all our pain—
Though hushed the voice, through all the coming
　　　years
　Its echoes will remain.

AN AUTUMNAL EXTRAVAGANZA

WITH a sweeter voice than birds
    Dare to twitter in their sleep,
Pipe for me a tune of words,
    Till my dancing fancies leap
Into freedom vaster far
Than the realms of Reason are!
Sing for me with wilder fire
    Than the lover ever sung,
From the time he twanged the lyre,
    When the world was baby-young.

O, my maiden Autumn, you—
You have filled me through and through,
With a passion so intense,
All of earthly eloquence
    Fails, and falls, and swoons away
In your presence. Like as one
Who essays to look the sun
    Fairly in the face, I say,
Though my eyes you dazzle blind
Greater dazzled is my mind.
So, my Autumn, let me kneel
    At your feet and worship you!
Be my sweetheart; let me feel

Your caress; and tell me too
Why your smiles bewilder me—
Glancing into laughter, then
Trancing into calm again,
Till your meaning drowning lies
In the dim depths of your eyes.
Let me see the things you see
Down the depths of mystery!
Blow aside the hazy veil
    From the daylight of your face
With the fragrance-ladened gale
    Of your saucy breath and chase
    Every dimple to its place.
Lift your gipsy finger-tips
To the roses of your lips,
And fling down to me a bud;
    But an unblown kiss—but one—
It shall blossom in my blood,
    Even after life is done—
When I dare to touch the brow
Your rare hair is veiling now—
When the rich, red-golden strands
Of the treasure in my hands
Shall be all of worldly worth
Heaven lifted from the earth,
Like a banner to have set
On its highest minaret.

THE ROSE

IT tossed its head at the wooing breeze;
  And the sun, like a bashful swain,
Beamed on it through the waving trees
  With a passion all in vain,—
For my rose laughed in a crimson glee,
And hid in the leaves in wait for me.

The honey-bee came there to sing
  His love through the languid hours,
And vaunt of his hives, as a proud old king
  Might boast of his palace-towers:
But my rose bowed in a mockery,
And hid in the leaves in wait for me.

The humming-bird, like a courtier gay,
  Dipped down with a dalliant song,
And twanged his wings through the roundelay
  Of love the whole day long:
Yet my rose turned from his minstrelsy
And hid in the leaves in wait for me.

The firefly came in the twilight dim
  My red, red rose to woo—
Till quenched was the flame of love in him,
  And the light of his lantern too,
As my rose wept with dewdrops three
And hid in the leaves in wait for me.

And I said: I will cull my own sweet rose—
  Some day I will claim as mine
The priceless worth of the flower that knows
  No change, but a bloom divine—
The bloom of a fadeless constancy
That hides in the leaves in wait for me!

But time passed by in a strange disguise,
  And I marked it not, but lay
In a lazy dream, with drowsy eyes,
  Till the summer slipped away,
And a chill wind sang in a minor key:
"Where is the rose that waits for thee?"

.   .   .   .

I dream to-day, o'er a purple stain
  Of bloom on a withered stalk,
Pelted down by the autumn rain
  In the dust of the garden-walk,
That an Angel-rose in the world to be
Will hide in the leaves in wait for me.

THE MERMAN

I

WHO would be
A merman gay,
Singing alone,
Sitting alone,
With a mermaid's knee,
For instance—hey—
For a throne?

II

I would be a merman gay;
I would sit and sing the whole day long;
I would fill my lungs with the strongest brine,
And squirt it up in a spray of song,
And soak my head in my liquid voice;
I'd curl my tail in curves divine,
And let each curve in a kink rejoice.
I'd tackle the mermaids under the sea,
And yank 'em around till they yanked me,
Sportively, sportively;
And then we would wiggle away, away,
To the pea-green groves on the coast of day,
Chasing each other sportively.

III

There would be neither moon nor star;
But the waves would twang like a wet guitar—
Low thunder and thrum in the darkness grum—
    Neither moon nor star;
We would shriek aloud in the dismal dales—
Shriek at each other and squawk and squeal:
    "All night!" rakishly, rakishly;
They would pelt me with oysters and
    wiggletails,
Laughing and clapping their hands at me,
    "All night!" prankishly, prankishly;
But I would toss them back in mine,
Lobsters and turtles of quaint design;
Then leaping out in an abrupt way,
I'd snatch them bald in my devilish glee,
And skip away when they snatched at me,
    Fiendishly, fiendishly.
O, what a jolly life I'd lead,
Ah, what a "bang-up" life indeed!
Soft are the mermaids under the sea—
We would live merrily, merrily.

THE RAINY MORNING

THE dawn of the day was dreary,
    And the lowering clouds o'erhead
Wept in a silent sorrow
    Where the sweet sunshine lay dead;
And a wind came out of the eastward
    Like an endless sigh of pain,
And the leaves fell down in the pathway
    And writhed in the falling rain.

I had tried in a brave endeavor
    To chord my harp with the sun,
But the strings would slacken ever,
    And the task was a weary one:
And so, like a child impatient
    And sick of a discontent,
I bowed in a shower of tear-drops
    And mourned with the instrument.

And lo! as I bowed, the splendor
    Of the sun bent over me,
With a touch as warm and tender
    As a father's hand might be:
And, even as I felt its presence,
    My clouded soul grew bright,
And the tears, like the rain of morning,
    Melted in mists of light.

WE ARE NOT ALWAYS GLAD WHEN
WE SMILE

WE are not always glad when we smile:
    Though we wear a fair face and are gay,
  And the world we deceive
  May not ever believe
We could laugh in a happier way.—
Yet, down in the deeps of the soul,
  Ofttimes, with our faces aglow,
    There's an ache and a moan
    That we know of alone,
And as only the hopeless may know.

We are not always glad when we smile,—
  For the heart, in a tempest of pain,
    May live in the guise
    Of a smile in the eyes
  As a rainbow may live in the rain;
And the stormiest night of our woe
  May hang out a radiant star
    Whose light in the sky
    Of despair is a lie
As black as the thunder-clouds are.

We are not always glad when we smile!—
   But the conscience is quick to record,
      All the sorrow and sin
      We are hiding within
   Is plain in the sight of the Lord:
And ever, O ever, till pride
   And evasion shall cease to defile
      The sacred recess
      Of the soul, we confess
We are not always glad when we smile.

A SUMMER SUNRISE

AFTER LEE O. HARRIS

THE master-hand whose pencils trace
 This wondrous landscape of the morn,
Is but the sun, whose glowing face
Reflects the rapture and the grace
 Of inspiration Heaven-born.

And yet with vision-dazzled eyes,
 I see the lotus-lands of old,
Where odorous breezes fall and rise,
And mountains, peering in the skies,
 Stand ankle-deep in lakes of gold.

And, spangled with the shine and shade,
 I see the rivers raveled out
In strands of silver, slowly fade
In threads of light along the glade
 Where truant roses hide and pout.

218

The tamarind on gleaming sands
  Droops drowsily beneath the heat;
And bowed as though aweary, stands
The stately palm, with lazy hands
  That fold their shadows round his feet.

And mistily, as through a veil,
  I catch the glances of a sea
Of sapphire, dimpled with a gale
Toward Colch's blowing, where the sail
  Of Jason's Argo beckons me.

And gazing on and farther yet,
  I see the isles enchanted, bright
With fretted spire and parapet,
And gilded mosque and minaret,
  That glitter in the crimson light.

But as I gaze, the city's walls
  Are keenly smitten with a gleam
Of pallid splendor, that appalls
The fancy as the ruin falls
  In ashen embers of a dream.

Yet over all the waking earth
  The tears of night are brushed away,
And eyes are lit with love and mirth,
And benisons of richest worth
  Go up to bless the new-born day.

DAS KRIST KINDEL

I HAD fed the fire and stirred it, till the sparkles
      in delight
Snapped their saucy little fingers at the chill De-
      cember night;
And in dressing-gown and slippers, I had tilted back
      "my throne"—
The old split-bottomed rocker—and was musing all
      alone.

I could hear the hungry Winter prowling round the
      outer door,
And the tread of muffled footsteps on the white
      piazza floor;
But the sounds came to me only as the murmur of
      a stream
That mingled with the current of a lazy-flowing
      dream.

Like a fragrant incense rising, curled the smoke of
      my cigar,
With the lamplight gleaming through it like a mist-
      enfolded star;—

And as I gazed, the vapor like a curtain rolled away,
With a sound of bells that tinkled, and the clatter
of a sleigh.

And in a vision, painted like a picture in the air,
I saw the elfish figure of a man with frosty hair—
A quaint old man that chuckled with a laugh as he
appeared,
And with ruddy cheeks like embers in the ashes of
his beard.

He poised himself grotesquely, in an attitude of
mirth,
On a damask-covered hassock that was sitting on
the hearth;
And at a magic signal of his stubby little thumb,
I saw the fireplace changing to a bright proscenium.

And looking there, I marveled as I saw a mimic
stage
Alive with little actors of a very tender age;
And some so very tiny that they tottered as they
walked,
And lisped and purled and gurgled like the brook-
lets, when they talked.

And their faces were like lilies, and their eyes like
purest dew,
And their tresses like the shadows that the shine is
woven through;

And they each had little burdens, and a little tale
      to tell
Of fairy lore, and giants, and delights delectable.

And they mixed and intermingled, weaving melody
      with joy,
Till the magic circle clustered round a blooming
      baby-boy;
And they threw aside their treasures in an ecstacy
      of glee,
And bent, with dazzled faces and with parted lips,
      to see.

'Twas a wondrous little fellow, with a dainty dou-
      ble-chin,
And chubby cheeks, and dimples for the smiles to
      blossom in;
And he looked as ripe and rosy, on his bed of straw
      and reeds,
As a mellow little pippin that had tumbled in the
      weeds.

And I saw the happy mother, and a group sur-
      rounding her
That knelt with costly presents of frankincense and
      myrrh;
And I thrilled with awe and wonder, as a murmur
      on the air
Came drifting o'er the hearing in a melody of
      prayer:—

By the splendor in the heavens, and the hush upon
the sea,
And the majesty of silence reigning over Galilee,—
We feel Thy kingly presence, and we humbly bow
the knee
And lift our hearts and voices in gratefulness to
Thee.

Thy messenger has spoken, and our doubts have
fled and gone
As the dark and spectral shadows of the night be-
fore the dawn;
And, in the kindly shelter of the light around us
drawn,
We would nestle down forever in the breast we
lean upon.

You have given us a shepherd—You have given
us a guide,
And the light of Heaven grew dimmer when You
sent him from Your side,—
But he comes to lead Thy children where the gates
will open wide
To welcome his returning when his works are
glorified.

By the splendor in the heavens, and the hush upon
the sea,
And the majesty of silence reigning over Galilee,—

*We feel Thy kingly presence, and we humbly bow
    the knee
And lift our hearts and voices in gratefulness to
    Thee.*

Then the vision, slowly failing, with the words of
    the refrain,
Fell swooning in the moonlight through the frosty
    window-pane;
And I heard the clock proclaiming, like an eager
    sentinel
Who brings the world good tidings,—"It is Christ-
    mas—all is well!"

AN OLD YEAR'S ADDRESS

"I HAVE twankled the strings of the twinkling
      rain;
  I have burnished the meteor's mail;
    I have bridled the wind
    When he whinnied and whined
  With a bunch of stars tied to his tail;
But my sky-rocket hopes, hanging over the past,
Must fuzzle and fazzle and fizzle at last!"

I had waded far out in a drizzling dream,
  And my fancies had spattered my eyes
    With a vision of dread,
    With a number ten head,
  And a form of diminutive size—
That wavered and wagged in a singular way
As he wound himself up and proceeded to say,—

"I have trimmed all my corns with the blade of the
      moon;
  I have picked every tooth with a star:
    And I thrill to recall
    That I went through it all
  Like a tune through a tickled guitar.

I have ripped up the rainbow and raveled the ends
When the sun and myself were particular friends."

And pausing again, and producing a sponge
    And wiping the tears from his eyes,
        He sank in a chair
        With a technical air
    That he struggled in vain to disguise,—
For a sigh that he breathed, as I over him leant,
Was haunted and hot with a peppermint scent.

"Alas!" he continued in quavering tones
    As a pang rippled over his face,
        "The life was too fast
        For the pleasure to last
    In my very unfortunate case;
And I'm going"—he said as he turned to adjust
A fuse in his bosom,—"I'm going to—BUST!"

I shrieked and awoke with the sullen che-boom
    Of a five-pounder filling my ears;
        And a roseate bloom
        Of a light in the room
    I saw through the mist of my tears,—
But my guest of the night never saw the display,
He had fuzzled and fazzled and fizzled away!

A NEW YEAR'S PLAINT

In words like weeds, I'll wrap me o'er,
Like coarsest clothes against the cold;
But that large grief which these enfold
Is given in outline and no more.
                                        —TENNYSON.

THE bells that lift their yawning throats
    And lolling tongues with wrangling cries
Flung up in harsh, discordant notes,
    As though in anger, at the skies,—
Are filled with echoings replete,
    With purest tinkles of delight—
So I would have a something sweet
    Ring in the song I sing to-night.

As when a blotch of ugly guise
    On some poor artist's naked floor
Becomes a picture in his eyes,
    And he forgets that he is poor,—
So I look out upon the night,
    That ushers in the dawning year,
And in a vacant blur of light
    I see these fantasies appear.

I see a home whose windows gleam
  Like facets of a mighty gem
That some poor king's distorted dream
  Has fastened in his diadem.
And I behold a throng that reels
  In revelry of dance and mirth,
With hearts of love beneath their heels,
  And in their bosoms hearts of earth.

O Luxury, as false and grand
  As in the mystic tales of old,
When genii answered man's command,
  And built of nothing halls of gold!
O Banquet, bright with pallid jets,
  And tropic blooms, and vases caught
In palms of naked statuettes,
  Ye can not color as ye ought!

For, crouching in the storm without,
  I see the figure of a child,
In little ragged roundabout,
  Who stares with eyes that never smiled—
And he, in fancy can but taste
  The dainties of the kingly fare,
And pick the crumbs that go to waste
  Where none have learned to kneel in prayer.

Go, Pride, and throw your goblet down—
  The "merry greeting" best appears
On loving lips that never drown
  Its worth but in the wine of tears;

Go, close your coffers like your hearts,
  And shut your hearts against the poor,
Go, strut through all your pretty parts
  But take the "Welcome" from your door.

LUTHER BENSON

AFTER READING HIS AUTOBIOGRAPHY

POOR victim of that vulture curse
  That hovers o'er the universe,
With ready talons quick to strike
In every human heart alike,
And cruel beak to stab and tear
In virtue's vitals everywhere,—
You need no sympathy of mine
To aid you, for a strength divine
Encircles you, and lifts you clear
Above this earthly atmosphere.

And yet I can but call you poor,
As, looking through the open door
Of your sad life, I only see
A broad landscape of misery,
And catch through mists of pitying tears
The ruins of your younger years,
I see a father's shielding arm
Thrown round you in a wild alarm—
Struck down, and powerless to free
Or aid you in your agony.

230

I see a happy home grow dark
And desolate—the latest spark
Of hope is passing in eclipse—
The prayer upon a mother's lips
Has fallen with her latest breath
In ashes on the lips of death—
I see a penitent who reels,
And writhes, and clasps his hands, and
  kneels,
And moans for mercy for the sake
Of that fond heart he dared to break.

And lo! as when in Galilee
A voice above the troubled sea
Commanded "Peace; be still!" the flood
That rolled in tempest-waves of blood
Within you, fell in calm so sweet
It ripples round the Saviour's feet;
And all your noble nature thrilled
With brightest hope and faith, and filled
Your thirsty soul with joy and peace
And praise to Him who gave release.

"DREAM"

BECAUSE her eyes were far too deep
    And holy for a laugh to leap
Across the brink where sorrow tried
To drown within the amber tide;
Because the looks, whose ripples kissed
The trembling lids through tender mist,
Were dazzled with a radiant gleam—
Because of this I called her "Dream."

Because the roses growing wild
About her features when she smiled
Were ever dewed with tears that fell
With tenderness ineffable;
Because her lips might spill a kiss
That, dripping in a world like this,
Would tincture death's myrrh-bitter stream
To sweetness—so I called her "Dream."

Because I could not understand
The magic touches of a hand
That seemed, beneath her strange control,
To smooth the plumage of the soul

And calm it, till, with folded wings,
It half forgot its flutterings,
And, nestled in her palm, did seem
To trill a song that called her "Dream."

Because I saw her, in a sleep
As dark and desolate and deep
And fleeting as the taunting night
That flings a vision of delight
To some lorn martyr as he lies
In slumber ere the day he dies—
Because she vanished like a gleam
Of glory, do I call her "Dream."

WHEN EVENING SHADOWS FALL

WHEN evening shadows fall,
   She hangs her cares away
Like empty garments on the wall
   That hides her from the day;
And while old memories throng,
   And vanished voices call,
She lifts her grateful heart in song
   When evening shadows fall.

Her weary hands forget
   The burdens of the day.
The weight of sorrow and regret
   In music rolls away;
And from the day's dull tomb,
   That holds her in its thrall,
Her soul springs up in lily bloom
   When evening shadows fall.

O weary heart and hand,
   Go bravely to the strife—
No victory is half so grand
   As that which conquers life!

WHEN EVENING SHADOWS FALL.

When evening shadows fall,
  She hangs her cares away,
Like empty garments on the wall,
  That hides her from the day;
And while old memories throng,
  And vanished voices call,
She lifts her grateful heart in song
  When evening shadows fall.

Her weary hands forget
  The burdens of the day,
The weight of sorrow and regret
  In music rolls away,
And from the day's dull tomb,
  That holds her in its thrall,
Her soul springs up in lily bloom
  When Evening shadows fall.

O weary heart and hand,
  Go bravely to the strife—
No victory is half so grand
  As that which conquers life!
One Day shall yet be their—
  The day that waits for all
Whose prayerful eyes are things divine
  When evening shadows fall.

J. W. Riley
Nov 25 '78

One day shall yet be thine—
  The day that waits for all
Whose prayerful eyes are things divine
  When evening shadows fall.

YLLADMAR

HER hair was, oh, so dense a blur
    Of darkness, midnight envied her;
And stars grew dimmer in the skies
To see the glory of her eyes;
And all the summer rain of light
That showered from the moon at night
Fell o'er her features as the gloom
Of twilight o'er a lily-bloom.

The crimson fruitage of her lips
Was ripe and lush with sweeter wine
Than burgundy or muscadine
Or vintage that the burgher sips
In some old garden on the Rhine:
And I to taste of it could well
Believe my heart a crucible
Of molten love—and I could feel
The drunken soul within me reel
And rock and stagger till it fell.

And do you wonder that I bowed
Before her splendor as a cloud
Of storm the golden-sandaled sun
Had set his conquering foot upon?
And did she will it, I could lie
In writhing rapture down and die
A death so full of precious pain
I'd waken up to die again.

A FANTASY

A FANTASY that came to me
  As wild and wantonly designed
As ever any dream might be
  Unraveled from a madman's mind,—
A tangle-work of tissue, wrought
  By cunning of the spider-brain,
  And woven, in an hour of pain,
To trap the giddy flies of thought—

I stood beneath a summer moon
  All swollen to uncanny girth,
And hanging, like the sun at noon,
  Above the center of the earth;
  But with a sad and sallow light,
  As it had sickened of the night
And fallen in a pallid swoon.
Around me I could hear the rush
  Of sullen winds, and feel the whir
Of unseen wings apast me brush
  Like phantoms round a sepulcher;
And, like a carpeting of plush,

A lawn unrolled beneath my feet,
Bespangled o'er with flowers as sweet
To look upon as those that nod
Within the garden-fields of God,
But odorless as those that blow
In ashes in the shades below.

And on my hearing fell a storm
  Of gusty music, sadder yet
  Than every whimper of regret
That sobbing utterance could form,
  And patched with scraps of sound that seemed
  Torn out of tunes that demons dreamed,
  And pitched to such a piercing key,
  It stabbed the ear with agony;
  And when at last it lulled and died,
  I stood aghast and terrified.
I shuddered and I shut my eyes,
  And still could see, and feel aware
  Some mystic presence waited there;
And staring, with a dazed surprise,
  I saw a creature so divine
  That never subtle thought of mine
  May reproduce to inner sight
  So fair a vision of delight.

A syllable of dew that drips
From out a lily's laughing lips
Could not be sweeter than the word
I listened to, yet never heard.—

For, oh, the woman hiding there
Within the shadows of her hair,
Spake to me in an undertone
So delicate, my soul alone
But understood it as a moan
Of some weak melody of wind
A heavenward breeze had left behind.

A tracery of trees, grotesque
  Against the sky, behind her seen,
Like shapeless shapes of arabesque
  Wrought in an Oriental screen;
And tall, austere and statuesque
  She loomed before it—e'en as though
  The spirit-hand of Angelo
  Had chiseled her to life complete,
  With chips of moonshine round her feet.
And I grew jealous of the dusk,
  To see it softly touch her face,
  As lover-like, with fond embrace,
It folded round her like a husk:
But when the glitter of her hand,
  Like wasted glory, beckoned me,
  My eyes grew blurred and dull and dim—
  My vision failed—I could not see—
I could not stir—I could but stand,
  Till, quivering in every limb,
  I flung me prone, as though to swim

The tide of grass whose waves of green
Went rolling ocean-wide between
My helpless shipwrecked heart and her
Who claimed me for a worshiper.

And writhing thus in my despair,
　I heard a weird, unearthly sound,
　That seemed to lift me from the ground
And hold me floating in the air.
I looked, and lo! I saw her bow
　Above a harp within her hands;
A crown of blossoms bound her brow,
　And on her harp were twisted strands
Of silken starlight, rippling o'er
With music never heard before
By mortal ears; and, at the strain,
I felt my Spirit snap its chain
And break away,—and I could see
It as it turned and fled from me
To greet its mistress, where she smiled
To see the phantom dancing wild
And wizard-like before the spell
Her mystic fingers knew so well.

A DREAM

I DREAMED I was a spider;
  A big, fat, hungry spider;
A lusty, rusty spider
  With a dozen palsied limbs;
With a dozen limbs that dangled
Where three wretched flies were tangled
And their buzzing wings were strangled
  In the middle of their hymns.

And I mocked them like a demon;
A demoniacal demon
Who delights to be a demon
  For the sake of sin alone.
And with fondly false embraces
Did I weave my mystic laces
Round their horror-stricken faces
  Till I muffled every groan.

And I smiled to see them weeping,
For to see an insect weeping,
Sadly, sorrowfully weeping,
  Fattens every spider's mirth;

And to note a fly's heart quaking,
And with anguish ever aching
Till you see it slowly breaking
  Is the sweetest thing on earth.

I experienced a pleasure,
Such a highly-flavored pleasure,
Such intoxicating pleasure,
  That I drank of it like wine;
And my mortal soul engages
That no spider on the pages
Of the history of ages
  Felt a rapture more divine.

I careened around and capered—
Madly, mystically capered—
For three days and nights I capered
  Round my web in wild delight;
Till with fierce ambition burning,
And an inward thirst and yearning
I hastened my returning
  With a fiendish appetite.

And I found my victims dying,
"Ha!" they whispered, "we are dying!"
Faintly whispered, "we are dying,
  And our earthly course is run."
And the scene was so impressing
That I breathed a special blessing,
As I killed them with caressing
  And devoured them one by one.

DREAMER, SAY

DREAMER, say, will you dream for me
    A wild sweet dream of a foreign land,
Whose border sips of a foaming sea
    With lips of coral and silver sand;
Where warm winds loll on the shady deeps,
    Or lave themselves in the tearful mist
The great wild wave of the breaker weeps
    O'er crags of opal and amethyst?

Dreamer, say, will you dream a dream
    Of tropic shades in the lands of shine,
Where the lily leans o'er an amber stream
    That flows like a rill of wasted wine,—
Where the palm-trees, lifting their shields of
      green,
    Parry the shafts of the Indian sun
Whose splintering vengeance falls between
    The reeds below where the waters run?

Dreamer, say, will you dream of love
    That lives in a land of sweet perfume,
Where the stars drip down from the skies above
    In molten spatters of bud and bloom?
Where never the weary eyes are wet,
    And never a sob in the balmy air,
And only the laugh of the paroquet
    Breaks the sleep of the silence there?

BRYANT

THE harp has fallen from the master's hand;
　Mute is the music, voiceless are the strings,
　　Save such faint discord as the wild wind flings
In sad Æolian murmurs through the land.
The tide of melody, whose billows grand
　Flowed o'er the world in clearest utterings,
　　Now, in receding current, sobs and sings
That song we never wholly understand.
* * O, eyes where glorious prophecies belong,
　And gracious reverence to humbly bow,
And kingly spirit, proud, and pure, and strong;
　O, pallid minstrel with the laureled brow,
And lips so long attuned to sacred song,
　How sweet must be the heavenly anthem now!

BABYHOOD

HEIGH-HO! Babyhood! Tell me where you
        linger!
  Let's toddle home again, for we have gone astray;
Take this eager hand of mine and lead me by the
    finger
  Back to the lotus-lands of the far-away!

Turn back the leaves of life.—Don't read the
        story.—
  Let's find the pictures, and fancy all the rest;
We can fill the written pages with a brighter glory
  Than old Time, the story-teller, at his very best.

Turn to the brook where the honeysuckle tipping
  O'er its vase of perfume spills it on the breeze,
And the bee and humming-bird in ecstacy are sip-
        ping
  From the fairy flagons of the blooming locust-
        trees.

Turn to the lane where we used to "teeter-totter,"
　　Printing little foot-palms in the mellow mold—
Laughing at the lazy cattle wading in the water
　　Where the ripples dimple round the buttercups of
　　　　gold;

Where the dusky turtle lies basking on the gravel
　　Of the sunny sand-bar in the middle tide,
And the ghostly dragon-fly pauses in his travel
　　To rest like a blossom where the water-lily died.

Heigh-ho! Babyhood! Tell me where you linger!
　　Let's toddle home again, for we have gone astray;
Take this eager hand of mine and lead me by the
　　　　finger
　　Back to the lotus-lands of the far-away!

LIBERTY

NEW CASTLE, JULY 4, 1878.

I

FOR a hundred years the pulse of time
  Has throbbed for Liberty;
For a hundred years the grand old clime,
  Columbia has been free;
    For a hundred years our country's love,
    The Stars and Stripes has waved above.

Away far out on the gulf of years—
  Misty and faint and white
Through the fogs of wrong—a sail appears,
  And the Mayflower heaves in sight,
    And drifts again, with its little flock
    Of a hundred souls, on Plymouth Rock.

Do you see them there—as long, long since—
  Through the lens of History;

249

Do you see them there as their chieftain prints
  In the snow his bended knee,
    And lifts his voice through the wintry blast
    In thanks for a peaceful home at last?

Though the skies are dark and the coast is bleak,
  And the storm is wild and fierce,
Its frozen flake on the upturned cheek
  Of the Pilgrim melts in tears,
    And the dawn that springs from the darkness
      there
    Is the morning light of an answered prayer.

The morning light of the day of Peace
  That gladdens the aching eyes,
And gives to the soul that sweet release
  That the present verifies,—
    Nor a snow so deep, nor a wind so chill
    To quench the flame of a freeman's will!

II

Days of toil when the bleeding hand
  Of the pioneer grew numb,
When the untilled tracts of the barren land
  Where the weary ones had come
    Could offer nought from a fruitful soil
    To stay the strength of the stranger's toil.

Days of pain, when the heart beat low,
  And the empty hours went by
Pitiless, with the wail of woe
  And the moan of Hunger's cry.
    When the trembling hands upraised in prayer
    Had only the strength to hold them there.

Days when the voice of hope had fled—
  Days when the eyes grown weak
Were folded to, and the tears they shed
  Were frost on a frozen cheek—
    When the storm bent down from the skies
        and gave
    A shroud of snow for the Pilgrim's grave.

Days at last when the smiling sun
  Glanced down from a summer sky,
And a music rang where the rivers run,
  And the waves went laughing by;
    And the rose peeped over the mossy bank
    While the wild deer stood in the stream and
        drank.

And the birds sang out so loud and good,
  In a symphony so clear
And pure and sweet that the woodman stood
  With his ax upraised to hear,
    And to shape the words of the tongue unknown
    Into a language all his own:—

I

Sing! every bird, to-day!
  Sing for the sky so clear,
    And the gracious breath of the atmosphere
Shall waft our cares away.
Sing! sing! for the sunshine free;
Sing through the land from sea to sea;
Lift each voice in the highest key
      And sing for Liberty!

2

Sing for the arms that fling
  Their fetters in the dust
    And lift their hands in higher trust
Unto the one Great King;
Sing for the patriot heart and hand;
Sing for the country they have planned;
Sing that the world may understand
      This is Freedom's land!

3

Sing in the tones of prayer,
  Sing till the soaring soul
    Shall float above the world's control
In Freedom everywhere!

Sing for the good that is to be,
Sing for the eyes that are to see
The land where man at last is free,
    O sing for Liberty!

III

A holy quiet reigned, save where the hand
Of labor sent a murmur through the land,
And happy voices in a harmony
Taught every lisping breeze a melody.
A nest of cabins, where the smoke upcurled
A breathing incense to the other world.
A land of languor from the sun of noon,
That fainted slowly to the pallid moon,
Till stars, thick-scattered in the garden-land
Of Heaven by the great Jehovah's hand,
Had blossomed into light to look upon
The dusky warrior with his arrow drawn,
As skulking from the covert of the night
With serpent cunning and a fiend's delight,
With murderous spirit, and a yell of hate
The voice of Hell might tremble to translate:
When the fond mother's tender lullaby
Went quavering in shrieks all suddenly,
And baby-lips were dabbled with the stain
Of crimson at the bosom of the slain,
And peaceful homes and fortunes ruined—lost
In smoldering embers of the holocaust.

Yet on and on, through years of gloom and strife,
Our country struggled into stronger life;
Till colonies, like footprints in the sand
Marked Freedom's pathway winding through the
      land—
And not the footprints to be swept away
Before the storm we hatched in Boston Bay,—
But footprints where the path of war begun
That led to Bunker Hill and Lexington,—
For he who "dared to lead where others dared
To follow" found the promise there declared
Of Liberty, in blood of Freedom's host
Baptized to Father, Son and Holy Ghost!

Oh, there were times when every patriot breast
Was riotous with sentiments expressed
In tones that swelled in volume till the sound
Of lusty war itself was well-nigh drowned.
Oh, those were times when happy eyes with tears
Brimmed o'er as all the misty doubts and fears
Were washed away, and Hope with gracious mien,
Reigned from her throne again a sovereign queen
Until at last, upon a day like this
When flowers were blushing at the summer's kiss,
And when the sky was cloudless as the face
Of some sweet infant in its angel grace,—
There came a sound of music, thrown afloat
Upon the balmy air—a clanging note
Reiterated from the brazen throat

Of Independence Bell: A sound so sweet,
The clamoring throngs of people on the streets
Were stilled as at the solemn voice of prayer,
And heads were bowed, and lips were moving there
That made no sound—until the spell had passed,
And then, as when all sudden comes the blast
Of some tornado, came the cheer on cheer
Of every eager voice, while far and near
The echoing bells upon the atmosphere
Set glorious rumors floating, till the ear
Of every listening patriot tingled clear,
And thrilled with joy and jubilee to hear.

I

Stir all your echoes up,
  O Independence Bell,
And pour from your inverted cup
  The song we love so well.

Lift high your happy voice,
  And swing your iron tongue
Till syllables of praise rejoice
  That never yet were sung.

Ring in the gleaming dawn
  Of Freedom—Toll the knell
Of Tyranny, and then ring on,
  O Independence Bell.—

Ring on, and drown the moan
  Above the patriot slain
Till sorrow's voice shall catch the tone
  And join the glad refrain.

Ring out the wounds of wrong
  And rankle in the breast;
Your music like a slumber-song
  Will lull revenge to rest.

Ring out from Occident
  To Orient, and peal
From continent to continent
  The mighty joy you feel.

Ring! Independence Bell!
  Ring on till worlds to be
Shall listen to the tale you tell
  Of love and Liberty!

IV

O Liberty—the dearest word
A bleeding country ever heard,—
We lay our hopes upon thy shrine
And offer up our lives for thine.
You gave us many happy years
Of peace and plenty ere the tears
A mourning country wept were dried
Above the graves of those who died

Upon thy threshold.   And again
When newer wars were bred, and men
Went marching in the cannon's breath
And died for thee and loved the death,
While, high above them, gleaming bright,
The dear old flag remained in sight,
And lighted up their dying eyes
With smiles that brightened paradise.
O Liberty, it is thy power
To gladden us in every hour
Of gloom, and lead us by thy hand
 As little children through a land
Of bud and blossom; while the days
Are filled with sunshine, and thy praise
Is warbled in the roundelays
Of joyous birds, and in the song
Of waters, murmuring along
The paths of peace, whose flowery fringe
Has roses finding deeper tinge
Of crimson, looking on themselves
Reflected—leaning from the shelves
Of cliff and crag and mossy mound
Of emerald splendor shadow-drowned.—
We hail thy presence, as you come
With bugle blast and rolling drum,
And booming guns and shouts of glee
Commingled in a symphony
That thrills the worlds that throng to see
The glory of thy pageantry.

And with thy praise, we breathe a prayer
That God who leaves you in our care
May favor us from this day on
With thy dear presence—till the dawn
Of Heaven, breaking on thy face,
Lights up thy first abiding place.

Old Seminary at Greenfield where Riley attended school and later
lived for a time

TOM VAN ARDEN

TOM VAN ARDEN, my old friend,
  Our warm fellowship is one
Far too old to comprehend
  Where its bond was first begun:
    Mirage-like before my gaze
    Gleams a land of other days,
    Where two truant boys, astray,
    Dream their lazy lives away.

There's a vision, in the guise
  Of Midsummer, where the Past
Like a weary beggar lies
  In the shadow Time has cast;
    And as blends the bloom of trees
    With the drowsy hum of bees,
    Fragrant thoughts and murmurs blend,
    Tom Van Arden, my old friend.

Tom Van Arden, my old friend,
  All the pleasures we have known
Thrill me now as I extend
  This old hand and grasp your own—

Feeling, in the rude caress,
All affection's tenderness;
Feeling, though the touch be rough,
Our old souls are soft enough.

So we'll make a mellow hour:
    Fill your pipe, and taste the wine—
Warp your face, if it be sour,
    I can spare a smile from mine;
        If it sharpen up your wit,
        Let me feel the edge of it—
        I have eager ears to lend,
        Tom Van Arden, my old friend.

Tom Van Arden, my old friend,
    Are we "lucky dogs," indeed?
Are we all that we pretend
    In the jolly life we lead?—
        Bachelors, we must confess,
        Boast of "single blessedness"
        To the world, but not alone—
        Man's best sorrow is his own!

And the saddest truth is this,—
    Life to us has never proved
What we tasted in the kiss
    Of the women we have loved:
        Vainly we congratulate
        Our escape from such a fate
        As their lying lips could send,
        Tom Van Arden, my old friend!

Tom Van Arden, my old friend,
  Hearts, like fruit upon the stem,
Ripen sweetest, I contend,
    As the frost falls over them:
      Your regard for me to-day
      Makes November taste of May,
      And through every vein of rhyme
      Pours the blood of summer-time.

When our souls are cramped with youth
  Happiness seems far away
In the future, while, in truth,
  We look back on it to-day
      Through our tears, nor dare to boast,—
      "Better to have loved and lost!"
      Broken hearts are hard to mend,
      Tom Van Arden, my old friend.

Tom Van Arden, my old friend,
  I grow prosy, and you tire;
Fill the glasses while I bend
    To prod up the failing fire. . . .
      You are restless:—I presume
      There's a dampness in the room.—
      Much of warmth our nature begs,
      With rheumatics in our legs! . . .

Humph! the legs we used to fling
  Limber-jointed in the dance,
When we heard the fiddle ring
  Up the curtain of Romance,

And in crowded public halls
Played with hearts like jugglers' balls.—
Feats of mountebanks, depend!—
Tom Van Arden, my old friend.

Tom Van Arden, my old friend,
  Pardon, then, this theme of mine:
While the firelight leaps to lend
  Higher color to the wine,—
    I propose a health to those
    Who have *homes,* and home's repose,
    Wife- and child-love without end!
    . . . Tom Van Arden, my old friend.

T. C. PHILIPS

O NOBLE heart, and brave impetuous hand!
     So all engrossed in work of public weal
  Thou couldst not pause thy own distress to feel
While maladies of Wrong oppressed the land.
The hopes that marshaled at thy pen's command
     To cheer the Right, had not the power to heal
     The ever-aching wounds thou didst conceal
Beneath a front so stoically bland
That no one guessed thy inward agony,—
     Until the Master, leaning from his throne,
     Heard some soul wailing in an undertone,
And bending lower down, discovered thee,
     And clasped thy weary hand within His own
And lifted thee to rest eternally.

A DREAM UNFINISHED

ONLY a dream unfinished; only a form at rest
    With weary hands clasped lightly over a peace-
    ful breast.

And the lonesome light of summer through the
    open doorway falls,
But it wakes no laugh in the parlor—no voice in
    the vacant halls.

It throws no spell of music over the slumbrous air;
It meets no step on the carpet—no form in the
    easy chair.

It finds no queenly presence blessing the solitude
With the gracious benediction of royal womanhood.

It finds no willowy figure tilting the cage that
    swings
With the little pale canary that forgets the song
    he sings.

No face at the open window to welcome the fra-
    grant breeze;
No touch at the old piano to waken the sleeping
    keys.

The idle book lies open, and the folded leaf is
    pressed
Over the half-told story while death relates the
    rest.

Only a dream unfinished; only a form at rest,
With weary hands clasped lightly over a peaceful
    breast.

The light steals into the corner where the darkest
    shadows are,
And sweeps with its golden fingers the strings of
    the mute guitar.

And over the drooping mosses it clambers the rus-
    tic stand,
And over the ivy's tresses it trails a trembling
    hand.

But it brings no smile from the darkness—it calls
    no face from the gloom—
No song flows out of the silence that aches in the
    empty room.

And we look in vain for the dawning in the depths
    of our despair,
Where the weary voice goes wailing through the
    empty aisles of prayer.

And the hands reach out through the darkness for
    the touches we have known
When the icy palms lay warmly in the pressure of
    our own.

When the folded eyes were gleaming with a glory
    God designed
To light a way to Heaven by the smiles they left
    behind.

Only a dream unfinished; only a form at rest,
With weary hands clasped lightly over a peaceful
    breast.

A CHILD'S HOME—LONG AGO

READ AT AN OLD SETTLERS' MEETING AT OAKLAND,
INDIANA, AUGUST 3, 1878.

THE terse old maxim of the poet's pen,
   "What constitutes a state? High-minded men,"
Holds such a wealth of truth, when one reflects,
It seems more like a sermon than a text.
Yet looking dimly backward o'er the years
Where first the face of progress, through our tears,
Smiles on us, where within the forest gloom
The bud of Indiana bursts in bloom;
We can but see, from Lake of Michigan,
To where Ohio rolls, the work of man—
From where our eastern boundary-line is pressed,
To where the Wabash revels on the west;
A broad expanse of fair and fertile land,
Like some rich landscape, from a master's hand,
That in its rustic frame, we well might call
The fairest picture on Columbia's wall—
A picture now—a masterpiece divine,
That, ere the artist's hand in its design

Had traced this loveliness, was but a blot
Of ugly pigment on a barren spot—
A blur of color on a hueless ground
Where scarce a hint of beauty could be found.
But patiently the hand of labor wrought,
And from each touch new inspiration caught;
Toiled on through disadvantages untold,
And at each onward step found firmer hold,
And obstacles that threatened long delay
He climbed above and went upon his way,
Until at last, exulting, he could see
The sweet reward of patient industry;
And beauties he had hardly dared to dream,
In hill and vale, and cliff and winding stream,
Spread out before his vision, till the soul
Within him seemed to leap beyond control,
And hover over lands the genii made
Of sifted sunshine and of dew-washed shade.

And who, indeed, that loves his native state,
Has not a heart to throb and palpitate
With ecstacy, as o'er her wintry past,
He sees the sun of summer dawn at last,
And catches, through the misty shower of light,
Dim glimpses of the orchards' bloom of white,
And fields beyond where, waving empty sleeves,
The "scarecrow" beckons to the feathered thieves
That perch, and perk their nimble heads away,
And flit away with harsh, discordant cry,
Or shading with his hand, his dazzled eyes,
Looks out across the deadened paradise,

Where wild flowers blossom, and the ivy clings,
And from the ruined oak the grapevine swings,
While high above upon the leafless tree
The red-head drummer beats his reveille,
And, like an army thronging at the sound,
The soldier corn-stalks on their battle-ground
March on to harvest victories, and flaunt
Their banners o'er the battlements of want!

And musing thus to-day, the pioneer
Whose brawny arm has grubbed a pathway here,
Stands, haply; with his vision backward turned
To where the log-heap of the past was burned,
And sees again, as in some shadowy dream,
The wild deer bending o'er the hidden stream,
Or sniffing, with his antlers lifted high,
The gawky crane, as he comes trailing by,
And drops in shallow tides below to wade
On tilting legs through dusky depths of shade,
While just across the glossy otter slips
Like some wet shadow 'neath the ripple's lips
As, drifting from the thicket-hid bayou,
The wild duck paddles past his rendezvous,
And overhead the beech and sycamore,
That lean their giant forms from either shore,
Clasp hands and bow their heads, as though to bless
In whispered prayer the sleeping wilderness.
A scene of such magnificent expanse
Of nameless grandeur that the utterance
Of even feathered orators is faint.
For here the dove's most melancholy plaint

Invokes no echo, and the killdeer's call
Swoons in the murmur of the waterfall
That, faint and far away and undefined,
Falls like a ghost of sound upon the mind.
The voice of nature's very self drops low,
As though she whispered of the long ago,
When down the wandering stream the rude canoe
Of some lone trapper glided into view,
And loitered down the watery path that led
Through forest depths that only knew the tread
Of savage beasts; and wild barbarians
That skulked about with blood upon their hands
And murder in their hearts. The light of day
Might barely pierce the gloominess that lay
Like some dark pall across the water's face,
And folded all the land in its embrace;
The panther's whimper, and the bear's low growl—
The snake's sharp rattle, and the wolf's wild howl;
The owl's grim chuckle, as it rose and fell
In alternation with the Indian's yell,
Made fitting prelude for the gory plays
That were enacted in the early days.

But fancy, soaring o'er the storm of grief
Like that lone bird that brought the olive leaf,
Brings only peace—an amulet whose spell
Works stranger marvels than the tongue can tell—
For o'er the vision, like a mirage, falls
The old log cabin with its dingy walls,
And crippled chimney with its crutch-like prop
Beneath a sagging shoulder at the top:

The coonskin battened fast on either side—
The wisps of leaf-tobacco—"cut-and-dried";
The yellow strands of quartered apples, hung
In rich festoons that tangle in among
The morning-glory vines that clamber o'er
The little clapboard roof above the door:
The old well-sweep that drops a courtesy
To every thirsting soul so graciously,
The stranger, as he drains the dripping gourd,
Intuitively murmurs, "Thank the Lord!"
Again through mists of memory arise
The simple scenes of home before the eyes:—
The happy mother, humming, with her wheel,
The dear old melodies that used to steal
So drowsily upon the summer air,
The house-dog hid his bone, forgot his care,
And nestled at her feet, to dream, perchance,
Some cooling dream of winter-time romance:
The square of sunshine through the open door
That notched its edge across the puncheon floor,
And made a golden coverlet whereon
The god of slumber had a picture drawn
Of Babyhood, in all the loveliness
Of dimpled cheek and limb and linsey dress:
The bough-filled fireplace, and the mantel wide,
Its fire-scorched ankles stretched on either side,
Where, perched upon its shoulders 'neath the joist,
The old clock hiccoughed, harsh and husky-voiced,
And snarled the premonition, dire and dread,
When it should hammer Time upon the head:

Tomatoes, red and yellow, in a row,
Preserved not then for diet, but for show,—
Like rare and precious jewels in the rough
Whose worth was not appraised at half enough:
The jars of jelly, with their dusty tops;
The bunch of pennyroyal; the cordial drops;
The flask of camphor, and the vial of squills,
The box of buttons, garden-seeds, and pills;
And, ending all the mantel's bric-à-brac,
The old, time-honored "Family Almanack."
And Memory, with a mother's touch of love,
Climbs with us to the dusky loft above,
Where drowsily we trail our fingers in
The mealy treasures of the harvest bin;
And, feeling with our hands the open track,
We pat the bag of barley on the back;
And, groping onward through the mellow gloom,
We catch the hidden apple's faint perfume,
And, mingling with it, fragrant hints of pear
And musky melon ripening somewhere.
Again we stretch our limbs upon the bed
Where first our simple childish prayers were said;
And while, without, the gallant cricket trills
A challenge to the solemn whippoorwills,
And, filing on the chorus with his glee,
The katydid whets all the harmony
To feather-edge of incoherent song,
We drop asleep, and peacefully along
The current of our dreams we glide away
To the dim harbor of another day,

Where brown toil waits for us, and where labor
    stands
To welcome us with rough and horny hands.

And who will mock the rude, unpolished ways
That swayed us in the good old-fashioned days
When labor wore the badge of manhood, set
Upon his tawny brow in pearls of sweat?
Who dares to-day to turn a scornful eye
On labor in his swarthy majesty?
Or wreathe about his lips the sneer of pride
Where brawny toil stands towering at his side?
By industry alone we gauge the worth
Of all the richer nations of the earth;
And side by side with honesty and toil
Prosperity walks round the furrowed soil
That belts the world, and o'er the ocean ledge
Tilts up the horn of plenty on its edge.
'Tis not the subject fawning to the king,
'Tis not the citizen, low cowering
Before the throne of state.—'Twas God's intent
Each man should be a king—a president;
And while through human veins the blood of pride
Shall ebb and flow in Labor's rolling tide,
The brow of toil shall wear the diadem,
And justice gleaming there, the central gem,
Shall radiate the time when we shall see
Each man rewarded as his works shall be.
Thank God for this bright promise! Lift the voice
Till all the waiting multitudes rejoice;

Reach out across the sea and clap your hands
Till voices waken out of foreign lands
To join the song, while listening Heaven waits
To roll an answering anthem through the gates.

THE FLYING ISLANDS OF THE NIGHT

"A thynge of wytchencreft—an idle dreme."

FOR the Song's sake; even so:
Humor it, and let it go
All untamed and wild of wing—
Leave it ever truanting.

Be its flight elusive!—Lo,
For the Song's sake—even so.—
Yield it but an ear as kind
As thou perkest to the wind.

Who will name us what the seas
Have sung on for centuries?
For the Song's sake! Even so—
Sing, O Seas! and Breezes, blow!

Sing! or Wave or Wind or Bird—
Sing! nor ever afterward
Clear thy meaning to us—No!—
For the Song's sake. Even so.

DRAMATIS PERSONÆ

KRUNG	King—*of the* Spirks
CRESTILLOMEEM	*The* Queen—*Second Consort to* Krung
SPRAIVOLL	*The* Tune-Fool
AMPHINE	Prince—*Son of* Krung
DWAINIE	*A* Princess—*of the* Wunks
JUCKLET	*A* Dwarf—*of the* Spirks
CREECH *and*	
GRITCHFANG	Nightmares

Counselors, Courtiers, Heralds, etc.

THE FLYING ISLANDS OF THE NIGHT

ACT I

SCENE I. Spirkland. *Time, Moondawn. Interior Court of* KRUNG. *A vast, pendant star burns dimly in dome above throne.* CRESTILLOMEEM *discovered languidly reclining at foot of empty throne, an overturned goblet lying near, as though just drained. The* Queen, *in seeming dazed, ecstatic state, raptly gazing upward, listening. Swarming forms and features in air above, seen eeriely coming and going, blending and intermingling in domed ceiling-spaces of court. Weird music. Mystic, luminous, beautiful faces detached from swarm, float singly forward,—tremulously, and in succession, poising in mid-air and chanting.*

FIRST FACE

And who hath known her—like as *I*
Have known her?—since the envying sky

Filched from her cheeks its morning hue,
And from her eyes its glory, too,
Of dazzling shine and diamond-dew.

Second Face

I knew her—long and long before
High Æo loosed her palm and thought:
"What awful splendor have I wrought
To dazzle earth and Heaven, too!"

Third Face

I knew her—long ere Night was o'er—
Ere Æo yet conjectured what
To fashion Day of—ay, before
He sprinkled stars across the floor
Of dark, and swept that form of mine,
E'en as a fleck of blinded shine,
Back to the black where light was not.

Fourth Face

Ere day was dreamt, I saw her face
Lift from some starry hiding-place
Where our old moon was kneeling while
She lit its features with her smile.

Fifth Face

I knew her while these islands yet
Were nestlings—ere they feathered wing,

Or e'en could gape with them or get
Apoise the laziest-ambling breeze,
Or cheep, chirp out, or anything!
When Time crooned rhymes of nurseries
Above them—nodded, dozed and slept,
And knew it not, till, wakening,
The morning stars agreed to sing
And Heaven's first tender dews were wept.

SIXTH FACE

I knew her when the jealous hands
Of Angels set her sculptured form
Upon a pedestal of storm
And let her to this land with strands
Of twisted lightnings.

SEVENTH FACE

And I heard
Her voice ere she could tone a word
Of any but the Seraph-tongue.—
And O sad-sweeter than all sung-
Or word-said things!—to hear her say,
Between the tears she dashed away:—
"Lo, launched from the offended sight
Of Æo!—anguish infinite
Is ours, O Sisterhood of Sin!
Yet is thy service mine by right,
And, sweet as I may rule it, thus

Shall Sin's myrrh-savor taste to us—
Sin's Empress—let my reign begin!"

Chorus of Swarming Faces

We follow thee forever on!
Through darkest night and dimmest dawn;
Through storm and calm—through shower and
    shine,
Hear thou our voices answering thine:
> We follow—*craving* but to be
> Thy followers.—We follow thee—
> We follow, follow, follow thee!

We follow ever on and on—
O'er hill and hollow, brake and lawn;
Through gruesome vale and dread ravine
Where light of day is never seen.—
> We waver not in loyalty,—
> Unfaltering we follow thee—
> We follow, follow, follow thee!

We follow ever on and on!
The shroud of night around us drawn,
Though wet with mists, is wild-ashine
With stars to light that path of thine;—
> The glowworms, too, befriend us—we
> Shall fail not as we follow thee.
> We follow, follow, follow thee!

We follow ever on and on.—
The notchèd reeds we pipe upon
Are pithed with music, keener blown
And blither where thou leadest lone—
        Glad pangs of its ecstatic glee
        Shall reach thee as we follow thee.
        We follow, follow, follow thee!

We follow ever on and on:
We know the ways thy feet have gone,—
The grass is greener, and the bloom
Of roses richer in perfume—
        And the birds of every blooming tree
        Sing sweeter as we follow thee.
        We follow, follow, follow thee!

We follow ever on and on;
For wheresoever thou hast gone
We hasten joyous, knowing there
Is sweeter sin than otherwhere—
        Leave still its latest cup, that we
        May drain it as we follow thee.
        We follow, follow, follow thee!

[*Throughout final stanzas, faces in foreground and
    forms in background slowly vanish, and voices
    gradually fail to sheer silence.*—Crestillo-
    meem *rises and wistfully gazes and listens;
    then, evidently regaining wonted self, looks to
    be assured of being wholly alone—then speaks.*]

CRESTILLOMEEM

The Throne is throwing wide its gilded arms
To welcome me.   The Throne of Krung! Ha! ha!
Leap up, ye lazy echoes, and laugh loud!
For I, Crestillomeem, the Queen—ha! ha!
Do fling my richest mirth into your mouths
That ye may fatten ripe with mockery!
I marvel what the kingdom would become
Were I not here to nurse it like a babe
And dandle it above the reach and clutch
Of intermeddlers in the royal line
And their attendant serfs.   *Ho!* Jucklet, ho!
'Tis time my knarled warp of nice anatomy
Were here, to weave us on upon our mesh
Of silken villanies.   *Ho!* Jucklet, ho!

[*Lifts secret door in pave and drops a star-bud
    through opening. Enter* JUCKLET *from below.*]

JUCKLET

Spang sprit! my gracious Queen! but thou hast
        scorched
My left ear to a cinder! and my head
Rings like a ding-dong on the coast of death!
For, patient hate! thy hasty signal burst
Full in my face as hitherward I came!
But though my lug be fried to crisp, and my
Singed wig stinks like a little sun-stewed Wunk,
I stretch my fragrant presence at thy feet
And kiss thy sandal with a blistered lip.

CRESTILLOMEEM

Hold! rare-done fool, lest I may bid the cook
To bake thee brown! How fares the King by this?

JUCKLET

Safe couched midmost his lordly hoard of books,
I left him sleeping like a quinsied babe
Next the guest-chamber of a poor man's house:
But ere I came away, to rest mine ears,
I salved his welded lids, uncorked his nose,
And o'er the odorous blossom of his lips
Re-squeezed the tinctured sponge, and felt his pulse
Come staggering back to regularity.
And four hours hence his Highness will awake
And *Peace* will take a nap!

CRESTILLOMEEM

Ha! What mean you?

JUCKLET [*Ominously*]

I mean that he suspects our knaveries.—
Some covert spy is burrowed in the court—
Nay, and I pray thee startle not *aloud*,
But mute thy very heart in its out-throb,
And let the blanching of thy cheeks but be
A whispering sort of pallor!

CRESTILLOMEEM

A spy?—Here?

JUCKLET

Ay, *here*—and haply even *now*. And one
Whose unseen eye seems ever focused keen
Upon our action, and whose hungering ear
Eats every crumb of counsel that we drop
In these our secret interviews!—For he—
The King—through all his talking-sleep to-day
Hath jabbered of intrigue, conspiracy—
Of treachery and hate in fellowship,
With dire designs upon his royal bulk,
To oust it from the Throne.

CRESTILLOMEEM

He spake my name?

JUCKLET

O Queen, he speaks not ever but thy name
Makes melody of every sentence.—Yea,
He thinks thee even true to him as thou
Art fickle, false and subtle! O how blind
And lame, and deaf and dumb, and worn and weak,
And faint, and sick, and all-commodious
His dear love is! In sooth, O wifely one,
Thy malleable spouse doth mind me of

That pliant hero of the bald old catch
"The Lovely Husband."—Shall I wreak the thing?

[*Sings—with much affected gravity and grimace*]

O a lovely husband he was known,
He loved his wife and her a-lone;
She reaped the harvest he had sown;
She ate the meat; he picked the bone.
    With mixed admirers every size,
    She smiled on each without disguise;
    This lovely husband closed his eyes
    Lest he might take her by surprise.

[*Aside, exclamatory*]

Chorious uproarious!

[*Then pantomime as though pulling at bell-rope—
    singing in pent, explosive utterance*]
Trot!
    Run!
        Wasn't he a handy hubby?

What
    Fun
        She could plot and plan!
Not
    One
        Other such a dandy hubby
        As this lovely man!

CRESTILLOMEEM

Or talk or tune, wilt thou wind up thy tongue
Nor let it tangle in a knot of words!
What said the King?

JUCKLET [*With recovered reverence*]

He said: "Crestillomeem—
O that *she* knew this thick distress of mine!—
Her counsel would *anoint* me and her voice
Would flow in limpid wisdom o'er my woes
And, like a love-balm, lave my secret grief
And lull my sleepless heart!" [*Aside*] And so
      went on,
Struggling all maudlin in the wrangled web
That well-nigh hath cocooned him!

CRESTILLOMEEM

Did he yield
No hint of this mysterious distress
He needs must hold sequestered from his Queen?
What said he in his talking-sleep by which
Some clue were gained of how and when and
      whence
His trouble came?

JUCKLET

In one strange phase he spake
As though some sprited lady talked with him.—

Full courteously he said: "In woman's guise
Thou comest, yet I think thou art, in sooth,
But woman in thy form.—Thy words are strange
And leave me mystified. I feel the truth
Of all thou hast declared, and yet so vague
And shadow-like thy meaning is to me,
I know not how to act to ward the blow
Thou sayest is hanging o'er me even now."
And then, with open hands held pleadingly,
He asked, "Who *is* my foe?"—And o'er his face
A sudden pallor flashed, like death itself,
As though, if answer had been given, it
Had fallen like a curse.

CRESTILLOMEEM

I'll stake my soul
Thrice over in the grinning teeth of doom,
'Tis Dwainie of the Wunks who peeks and peers
With those fine eyes of hers in our affairs
And carries Krung, in some disguise, these hints
Of our intent! See thou that silence falls
Forever on her lips, and that the sight
She wastes upon our secret action blurs
With gray and grisly scum that shall for aye
Conceal us from her gaze while she writhes blind
And fangless as the fat worms of the grave!
Here! take this tuft of downy druze, and when
Thou comest on her, fronting full and fair,
Say *"Sherzham!"* thrice, and fluff it in her face.

JUCKLET

Thou knowest scanty magic, O my Queen,
But all thou dost is fairly excellent—
An *this* charm work, thou shalt have fuller faith
Than still I must withhold.

[*Takes charm, with extravagant salutation*]

CRESTILLOMEEM

Thou gibing knave!
Thou thing! Dost dare to name my sorcery
As any trifling gift? Behold what might
Be thine an thy deserving wavered not
In stable and abiding service to
Thy Queen!

[*She presses suddenly her palm upon his eyes, then
lifts her softly opening hand upward, his gaze
following, where, slowly shaping in the air
above them, appears semblance—or counter-
self—of* CRESTILLOMEEM, *clothed in most radiant youth, her maiden-face bent downward
to a moonlit sward, where kneels a lover-knight
—flawless in manly symmetry and princely
beauty,—yet none other than the counter-self
of* JUCKLET, *eeriely and with strange sweetness
singing, to some curiously tinkling instrument,
the praises of its queenly mistress:* JUCKLET
and CRESTILLOMEEM *transfixed below—trancedly gazing on their mystic selves above.*]

SEMBLANCE OF JUCKLET [*Sings*]

Crestillomeem!
> *Crestillomeem!*
Soul of my slumber!—Dream of my dream!
Moonlight may fall not as goldenly fair
As falls the gold of thine opulent hair—
Nay, nor the starlight as dazzlingly gleam
As gleam thine eyes, 'Meema—Crestillomeem!—
> *Star of the skies, 'Meema—*
>> *Crestillomeem!*

SEMBLANCE OF CRESTILLOMEEM [*Sings*]

O Prince divine!
> *O Prince divine!*
Tempt thou me not with that sweet voice of thine!
Though my proud brow bear the blaze of a crown,
Lo, at thy feet must its glory bow down,
That from the dust thou mayest lift me to shine
Heaven'd in thy heart's rapture, O Prince divine!—
> *Queen of thy love ever,*
>> *O Prince divine!*

SEMBLANCE OF JUCKLET [*Sings*]

Crestillomeem!
> *Crestillomeem!*
Our life shall flow as a musical stream—
Windingly—placidly on it shall wend,

Marged with mazhoora-bloom banks without end—
Word-birds shall call thee and dreamily scream,
"Where dost thou cruise, 'Meema—Crestillomeem?
Whither away, 'Meema?—
Crestillomeem!"

DUO

[*Vision and voices gradually failing away*]

Crestillomeem!
Crestillomeem!
Soul of my slumber!—Dream of my dream!
Star of Love's light, 'Meema—Crestillomeem!
Crescent of Night, 'Meema!—
Crestillomeem!

[*With song, vision likewise fails utterly*]

CRESTILLOMEEM

[*To* JUCKLET, *still trancedly staring upward*]

How now, thou clabber-brainèd spudge!—
Thou squelk!—thou—

JUCKLET

Nay, O Queen! contort me not
To more condensèd littleness than now
My shamèd frame incurreth on itself,

Seeing what might fare with it, didst *thou* will
Kindly to nip it with thy magic *here*
And leave it living in that form i' the air,
Forever pranking o'er the daisied sward
In wake of sandal-prints that dint the dews
As lightly as, in thy late maidenhood,
Thine own must needs have done in flighting from
The dread encroachments of the King.

CRESTILLOMEEM

Nay—peace!

JUCKLET

So be it, O sweet Mystic.—But I crave
One service of thy magic yet.—*Amphine!*—
Breed me some special, damnèd philter for
Amphine—the *fair* Amphine!—to chuck it him,
Some serenade-tide, in a sodden slug
O' pastry, 'twixt the door-crack and a screech
O' rusty hinges.—Hey! Amphine, the *fair!*—
And let me, too, elect his doom, O Queen!—
Listed against thee, he, too, doubtless hath
Been favored with an outline of our scheme.—
And I would kick my soul all over hell
If I might juggle his fine figure up
In such a shape as mine!

CRESTILLOMEEM

Then this:—When thou
Canst come upon him bent above a flower,

Or any blooming thing, and thou, arear,
Shalt reach it first and, thwartwise, touch it fair,
And with thy knuckle flick him on the knee,—
Then—his fine form will shrink and shrivel up
As warty as a toad's—so hideous,
Thine own shall seem a marvel of rare grace!
Though idly speak'st thou of my mystic skill,
'Twas that which won the King for me;—'twas that
Bereft him of his daughter ere we had
Been wedded yet a haed:—She strangely went
Astray one moonset from the palace-steps—
She went—nor yet returned.—Was it not strange?—
She would be wedded to an alien prince
The morrow midnight—to a prince whose sire
I once knew, in lost hours of lute and song,
When *he* was but a prince—*I* but a mouth
For him to lift up sippingly and drain
To lees most ultimate of stammering sobs
And maudlin wanderings of blinded breath.

JUCKLET [*Aside*]

Twigg-brebblets! but her Majesty hath speech
That doth bejuice all metaphor to drip
And spray and mist of sweetness!

CRESTILLOMEEM [*Confusedly*]

                        Where was I?
O, ay!—The princess went—she strangely went!—
E'en as I deemed her lover-princeling would

As strangely go, were she not soon restored.—
As so he did:—That airy penalty
The jocund Fates provide our love-lorn wights
In this glad island: So for thrice three nights
They spun the prince his line and marked him pay
It out (despite all warnings of his doom)
In fast and sleepless search for her—and *then*
They tripped his fumbling feet and he fell—UP!—
Up!—as 'tis writ—sheer past Heaven's flinching
      walls
And topmost cornices.—Up—up and on!—
And, it is grimly guessed of those who thus
For such a term bemoan an absent love,
And so fall *up*wise, they must needs fall on—
And on and on—and on—and on—and on!
Ha! ha!

JUCKLET

    Quahh! but the prince's holden breath
Must ache his throat by this! But, O my Queen,
What of the princess?—and—

CRESTILLOMEEM

                The princess?—Ay—
The princess! Ay, she went—she strangely went!
And when the dainty vagrant came not back—
Both sire and son in apprehensive throes
Of royal grief—the very Throne befogged
In sighs and tears!—when all hope waned at last,

And all the spies of Spirkland, in her quest,
Came straggling empty-handed home again,—
Why, then the wise King sleeved his rainy eyes
And sagely thought the pretty princess had
Strayed to the island's edge and tumbled off.
I could have set his mind at ease on that—
I could have told him,—*yea,* she tumbled off—
I tumbled her!—and tumbled her so plump,
She tumbled in an under-island, then
Just slow-unmooring from our own and poised
For unknown voyagings of flight afar
And all remote of latitudes of ours.—
Ay, into that land I tumbled her from which
But one charm known to art can tumble her
Back into this,—and *that* charm (guilt be praised!)
Is lodged not in the wit nor the desire
Of my rare lore.

JUCKLET

Thereinasmuch find joy!
But dost thou know that rumors flutter now
Among thy subjects of thy sorceries?—
The art being *banned,* thou knowest; or, unhoused,
Is unleashed pitilessly by the grim,
Facetious body of the dridular
Upon the one who fain had loosed the curse
On others.—An my counsel be worth aught,
Then have a care thy spells do not revert
Upon thyself, nor yet mine own poor hulk
O' fearsomeness!

CRESTILLOMEEM

                    Ha! ha! No vaguest need
Of apprehension there!—While Krung remains—

[*She abruptly pauses—startled first, then listening
    curiously and with awed interest. Voice of ex-
    quisite melodiousness and fervor heard sing-
    ing.*]

VOICE

When kings are kings, and kings are men—
        And the lonesome rain is raining!—
O who shall rule from the red throne then,
And who shall covet the scepter when—
        When the winds are all complaining?

When men are men, and men are kings—
        And the lonesome rain is raining!—
O who shall list as the minstrel sings
Of the crown's fiat, or the signet-ring's,
        When the winds are all complaining?

CRESTILLOMEEM

Whence flows such sweetness, and what voice is
        that?

JUCKLET

The voice of Spraivoll, an mine ears be whet
And honéd o' late honeyéd memories

Behaunting the deserted purlieus of
The court.

CRESTILLOMEEM

And who is Spraivoll, and what song
Is that besung so blinding exquisite
Of cadenced mystery?

JUCKLET

Spraivoll—O Queen,—
Spraivoll The Tune-Fool is she fitly named
By those who meet her ere the day long wanes
And naught but janiteering sparsely frets
The cushioned silences and stagnant dusts
Indifferently resuscitated by
The drowsy varlets in mock servitude
Of so refurbishing the royal halls:
She cometh, alien, from Wunkland—so
Hath she deposed to divers questioners
Who have been smitten of her voice—as rich
In melody as she is poor in mind.
She hath been roosting, pitied of the hinds
And scullions, round about the palace here
For half a node.

CRESTILLOMEEM

And pray, where is she perched—
This wild-bird woman with her wondrous throat?

JUCKLET

Under some dingy cornice, like enough—
Though *wild-bird* she is not, being plumèd in,
Not feathers, but one fustianed stole—the like
Of which so shameth her fair face one needs
Must swear some lusty oaths, but that they shape
Themselves full gentlewise in mildest prayer:—
Not *wild-bird;*—nay, nor *woman*—though, in truth,
She ith a licensed idiot, and drifts
About, as restless and as useless, too,
As any lazy breeze in summer-time.
I'll call her forth to greet your Majesty.
Ho! Spraivoll! Ho! my twittering birdster, flit
Thou hither.

[*Enter* SPRAIVOLL—*from behind group of statuary
—singing*]

SPRAIVOLL

Ting-aling! Ling-ting! Tingle-tee!
The moon spins round and round for me!
Wind it up with a golden key.
Ting-aling! Ling-ting! Tingle-tee!

CRESTILLOMEEM

Who art thou, and what the strange
Elusive beauty and intent of thy

Sweet song? What singest thou, vague, mystic-
     bird—
What doth The Tune-Fool sing? Ay, sing me what.

SPRAIVOLL [*Singing*]

What sings the breene on the wertling-vine,
    And the tweck on the bamner-stem?
Their song, to me, is the same as mine,
    As mine is the same to them—to them—
      As mine is the same to them.

In star-starved glooms where the plustre looms
    With its slender boughs above,
Their song sprays down with the fragrant
     blooms,—
    And the song they sing is love—is love—
      And the song they sing is love.

JUCKLET

Your Majesty may be surprised somewhat,
But Spraivoll can not talk,—her only mode
Of speech is melody; and thou might'st put
The dowered fool a thousand queries, and,
In like return, receive a thousand songs,
All set to differing tunes—as full of naught
As space is full of emptiness.

CRESTILLOMEEM

               A fool?—
And with a gift so all-divine!—A fool?

The old Riley homestead, Greenfield

JUCKLET

Ay, warranted!—The Flying Islands all
Might flock in mighty counsel—molt, and shake
Their loosened feathers, and sort every tuft,
Nor ever most minutely quarry there
One other Spraivoll, itching with her voice
Such favored spot of cuticle as she
Alone selects here in our blissful realm.

CRESTILLOMEEM

Out, jester, on thy cumbrous wordiness!
Come hither, Tune-Fool, and be not afraid,
For I like fools so well I married one:
And since thou art a *Queen* of fools, and he
A *King,* why, I've a mind to bring ye two
Together in some wise.   Canst use thy song
All times in such entrancing spirit one
Who lists must so needs list, e'en though the song
Go on unceasingly indefinite?

SPRAIVOLL [*Singing*]

If one should ask me for a song,
    Then I should answer, and my tongue
Would twitter, trill and troll along
    Until the song were done.

Or should one ask me for my tongue,
    And I should answer with a song,
I'd trill it till the song were sung,
    And troll it all along.

CRESTILLOMEEM

Thou art indeed a fool, and one, I think,
To serve my present purposes.   Give ear.—
And Jucklet, thou, go to the King and bide
His waking : then repeat these words :—*"The Queen
Impatiently awaits his Majesty,
And craves his presence in the Tower of Stars,
That she may there express full tenderly
Her great solicitude."*   And *then*, end thus,—
*"So much she bade, and drooped her glowing face
Deep in the showerings of her golden hair,
And with a flashing gesture of her arm
Turned all the moonlight pallid, saying 'Haste!' "*

JUCKLET

And would it not be well to hang a pearl
Or twain upon thy silken lashes?

CRESTILLOMEEM
                                        Go!

JUCKLET [*Exit, singing*]

This lovely husband's loyal breast
Heaved only as she might suggest,—
To every whimsy she expressed
He proudly bowed and acquiesced.
    He plotted with her, blithe and gay—
    In no flirtation said her nay,—

He even took her to the play,
Excused himself and came away.

CRESTILLOMEEM [*To Spraivoll*]

Now, Tune-Fool, *junior*, let me theme *thee* for
A song:—An Empress once, with angel in
Her face and devil in her heart, had wish
To breed confusion to her sovereign lord,
And work the downfall of his haughty son—
The issue of a former marriage—who
Bellowsed her hatred to the whitest heat,
For that her own son, by a former lord,
Was born a hideous dwarf, and reared aside
From the sire's knowing or his princely own—
That *none,* in sooth, might ever chance to guess
The hapless mother of the hapless child.
The Fiends that scar her thus, protect her still
With outward beauty of both face and form.—
It so is written, and so must remain
Till magic greater than their own is found
To hurl against her. So is she secure
And proof above all fear. Now, listen well!—
Her present lord is haunted with a dream,
That he is soon to pass, and so prepares
(*All havoc hath been wrangled with the drugs!*)
The Throne for the ascension of the son,
His cursèd heir, who still doth baffle all
Her arts against him, e'en as though he were
Protected by a skill beyond her own.

Soh! she, the Queen, doth rule the King in all
Save this affectionate perversity
Of favor for the son whom he would raise
To his own place.—And but for this the King
Long since had tasted death and kissed his fate
As one might kiss a bride! But so his Queen
Must needs withhold, not deal, the final blow,
She yet doth bind him, spelled, still trusting her;
And, by her craft and wanton flatteries,
Doth sway his love to every purpose but
The one most coveted.—And for this end
She would make use of thee;—and if thou dost
Her will, as her good pleasure shall direct,
Why, thou shalt sing at court, in silken tire,
Thy brow bound with wild diamonds, and thy hair
Sown with such gems as laugh hysteric lights
From glittering quespar, guenk and plennocynth,—
Ay, even panoplied as might the fair
Form of a very princess be, thy voice
Shall woo the echoes of the listening Throne.

SPRAIVOLL [*Crooning abstractedly*]

And O shall one—high brother of the air,
In deeps of space—shall he have dream as fair?—
And shall that dream be this?—In some strange
        place
Of long-lost lands he finds her waiting face—
Comes marveling upon it, unaware,
Set moonwise in the midnight of her hair,

And is behaunted with old nights of May,
So his glad lips do purl a roundelay
Purloinèd from the echo-triller's beak,
Seen keenly notching at some star's blanch cheek
With its ecstatic twitterings, through dusk
And sheen of dewy boughs of bloom and musk.
For him, Love, light again the eyes of her
That show nor tears nor laughter nor surprise—
For him undim their glamour and the blur
Of dreams drawn from the depths of deepest skies.
He doth not know if any lily blows
As fair of feature, nor of any rose.

CRESTILLOMEEM [*Aside*]

O this weird woman! she doth drug mine ears
With her uncanny sumptuousness of song!
[*To Spraivoll*] Nay, nay! Give o'er thy tuneful
    maunderings
And mark me further, Tune-Fool—ay, and well:—
At present doth the King lie in a sleep
Drug-wrought and deep as death—the after-phase
Of an unconscious state, in which each act
Of his throughout his waking hours is so
Rehearsed, in manner, motion, deed and word,
Her spies (the Queen's) that watch him, serving
    there
As guardians o'er his royal slumbers, may
Inform her of her lord's most secret thought.
And lo, her plans have ripened even now
Till, *should he come upon this Throne to-night,*

Where eagerly his counselors will bide
His coming,—she, the Queen, hath reason to
Suspect her long-designèd purposes
May fall in jeopardy;—but if he *fail,*
Through *any* means, to lend his presence there,—
Then, by a wheedled mandate, *is his Queen*
Empowered with all Sovereignty to reign
And work the royal purposes instead.
Therefore, the Queen hath set an interview—
A conference to be holden with the King,
Which is ordained to fall on noon to-night,
Twelve star-twirls ere the nick the Throne con-
      venes.—
And with her thou shalt go, and bide in wait
Until she signal thee to sing; and then
Shalt thou so work upon his mellow mood
With that un-Spirkly magic of thy voice—
So all bedaze his waking thought with dreams,—
The Queen may, all unnoticed, slip away,
And leave thee singing to a throneless King.

SPRAIVOLL [*Singing*]

And who shall sing for the haughty son
    While the good King droops his head?—
And will he dream, when the song is done,
    That a princess fair lies dead?

CRESTILLOMEEM

The haughty son hath found *his* "Song"—*sweet*
    curse!—

And may she sing his everlasting dirge!
She comes from that near-floating land of thine,
Naming herself a princess of that realm
So strangely peopled we would fain evade
All mergence, and remain as strange to them
As they to us. No less this Dwainie hath
Most sinuously writhed and lithed her way
Into court favor here—hath glidden past
The King's encharmèd sight and sleeked herself
Within the very altars of his house—
His line—his blood—his very life:—*AMPHINE!*
Not any Spirkland gentlemaiden might
Aspire so high as *she* hath dared to dare!—
For she, with her fair skin and finer ways,
And beauty second only to the Queen's,
Hath caught the Prince betwixt her mellow palms
And stroked him flutterless. Didst ever thou
In thy land hear of *Dwainie of the Wunks?*

SPRAIVOLL [*Singing*]

Ay, Dwainie!—My Dwainie!
        The lurloo ever sings,
A tremor in his flossy crest
        And in his glossy wings.
And Dwainie!—My Dwainie!
        The winno-welvers call;—
But Dwainie hides in Spirkland
        And answers not at all.

The teeper twitters Dwainie!—
        The tcheucker on his spray

Teeters up and down the wind
          And will not fly away:
And Dwainie!—My Dwainie!
          The drowsy oovers drawl;—
But Dwainie hides in Spirkland
          And answers not at all.

O Dwainie!—My Dwainie!
          The breezes hold their breath—
The stars are pale as blossoms,
          And the night as still as death:
And Dwainie!—My Dwainie!
          The fainting echoes fall;—
But Dwainie hides in Spirkland
          And answers not at all.

CRESTILLOMEEM

A melody ecstatic! and—thy words,
Although so meaningless, seem something more—
A vague and shadowy something, eerie-like,
That maketh one to shiver over-chilled
With curious, creeping sweetnesses of pain
And catching breaths that flutter tremulous
With sighs that dry the throat out icily.—
But save thy music! Come! that I may make
Thee ready for thy royal auditor.   [*Exeunt*]

END ACT I

ACT II

SCENE I. *A garden of* KRUNG'S *Palace, screened from the moon with netted glenk-vines and blooming zhoomer-boughs, all glimmeringly lighted with star-flakes. An arbor, near which is a table spread with a repast—two seats, drawn either side. A playing fountain, at marge of which* AMPHINE *sits thrumming a trentoraine.*

AMPHINE [*Improvising*]

Ah, help me! but her face and brow
Are lovelier than lilies are
Beneath the light of moon and star
That smile as they are smiling now—
White lilies in a pallid swoon
Of sweetest white beneath the moon—
White lilies in a flood of bright
Pure lucidness of liquid light
Cascading down some plenilune
When all the azure overhead

309

Blooms like a dazzling daisy-bed.—
So luminous her face and brow,
The luster of their glory, shed
In memory, even, blinds me now.

[*Plaintively addressing instrument*]

O warbling strand of silver, where, O where
Hast thou unraveled that sweet voice of thine
And left its silken murmurs quavering
In limp thrills of delight?   O golden wire,
Where hast thou spilled thy precious twinker-
      ings?—
What thirsty ear hath drained thy melody,
And left me but a wild, delirious drop
To tincture all my soul with vain desire?

[*Improvising*]

Her face—her brow—her hair unfurled!—
And O the oval chin below,
Carved, like a cunning cameo,
With one exquisite dimple, swirled
With swimming shine and shade, and whirled
The daintiest vortex poets know—
The sweetest whirlpool ever twirled
By Cupid's finger-tip,—and so,
The deadliest maelstrom in the world.

[*Pauses—Enter unperceived,* DWAINIE, *behind, in
      upper bower*]

AMPHINE [*Again addressing instrument*]

O Trentoraine! how like an emptièd vase
Thou art—whose clustering blooms of song have
        drooped
And faded, one by one, and fallen away
And left to me but dry and tuneless stems
And crisp and withered tendrils of a voice
Whose thrilling tone, now like a throttled sound,
Lies stifled, faint, and gasping all in vain
For utterance.

[*Again improvising*]

        And O mad wars of blinding blurs
        And flashings of lance-blades of light,
        Whet glitteringly athwart the sight
        That dares confront those eyes of hers!
        Let any dewdrop soak the hue
        Of any violet through and through,
        And then be colorless and dull,
        Compared with eyes so beautiful!
        I swear ye that her eyes be bright
        As noonday, yet as dark as night—
        As bright as be the burnished bars
        Of rainbows set in sunny skies,
        And yet as deep and dark, her eyes,
        And lustrous black as blown-out stars.

[*Pauses* — DWAINIE *still unperceived, radiantly
    smiling and wafting kisses down from trellis-
    window above*]

AMPHINE   [*Again to instrument*]

O empty husk of song!
If deep within my heart the music thou
Hast stored away might find an issuance,
A fount of limpid laughter would leap up
And gurgle from my lips, and all the winds
Would revel with it, riotous with joy;
And Dwainie, in her beauty, would lean o'er
The battlements of night, and, like the moon,
The glory of her face would light the world—
For I would sing of love.

DWAINIE

And she would hear,—
And, reaching overhead among the stars,
Would scatter them like daisies at thy feet.

AMPHINE

O voice, where art thou floating on the air?—
O Seraph-soul, where art thou hovering?

DWAINIE

I hover in the zephyr of thy sighs,
And tremble lest thy love for me shall fail
To buoy me thus forever on the breath
Of such a dream as Heaven envies.

AMPHINE

Ah!

[*Turning, discovers* DWAINIE—*she still feigning invisibility, while he, with lifted eyes and wistful gaze, preludes with instrument — then sings.*]

Linger, my Dwainie! Dwainie, lily-fair,
Stay yet thy step upon the casement-stair—
Poised be thy slipper-tip as is the tine
Of some still star.—Ah, Dwainie—Dwainie mine,
    Yet linger—linger there!

Thy face, O Dwainie, lily-pure and fair,
Gleams i' the dusk, as in thy dusky hair
The moony zhoomer glimmers, or the shine
Of thy swift smile.—Ah, Dwainie—Dwainie mine,
    Yet linger—linger there!

With lifted wrist, whereround the laughing air
Hath blown a mist of lawn and clasped it there,
Waft finger-thipt adieus that spray the wine
Of thy waste kisses toward me, Dwainie mine—
    Yet linger—linger there!

What unloosed splendor is there may compare
With thy hand's unfurled glory, anywhere?
What glint of dazzling dew or jewel fine

May mate thine eyes?—Ah, Dwainie—Dwainie
    mine!
        Yet linger—linger there!

My soul confronts thee: On thy brow and hair
It lays its tenderness like palms of prayer—
It touches sacredly those lips of thine
And swoons across thy spirit, Dwainie mine,
      The while thou lingerest there.

[*Drops trentoraine, and, with open arms, gazes
      yearningly on* DWAINIE]

DWAINIE [*Raptly*]

Thy words do wing my being dovewise!

AMPHINE

                        Then,
Thou lovest!—O my homing dove, veer down
And nestle in the warm home of my breast!
So empty are mine arms, so full my heart,
The one must hold thee, or the other burst.

DWAINIE [*Throwing herself in his embrace*]

Æo's own hand methinks hath flung me here:
O hold me that He may not pluck me back!

AMPHINE

So closely will I hold thee that not e'en
The hand of death shall separate us.

DWAINIE

So

May sweet death find us, then, that, woven thus
In the corolla of a ripe caress,
We may drop lightly, like twin plustre-buds,
On Heaven's star-strewn lawn.

AMPHINE

So do I pray.

But tell me, tender heart, an thou dost love,
Where hast thou loitered for so long?—for thou
Didst promise tryst here with me earlier by
Some several layodemes which I have told
Full chafingly against my finger-tips
Till the full complement, save three, are ranged
Thy pitiless accusers, claiming, each,
So many as their joinèd number be
Shalt thou so many times lift up thy lips
For mine's most lingering forgiveness.
So, save thee, O my Sweet! and rest thee, I
Have ordered merl and viands to be brought
For our refreshment here, where, thus alone,
I may sip words with thee as well as wine.
Why hast thou kept me so athirst?—Why, I
Am jealous of the flattered solitudes
In which thou walkest.   [*They sit at table*]

DWAINIE

Nay, I will not tell,

Since, an I yielded, countless questions, like

In idlest worth, would waste our interview
In speculations vain.—Let this suffice:—
I stayed to talk with one whom, long ago,
I met and knew, and grew to love, forsooth,
In dreamy Wunkland.—Talked of mellow nights,
And long, long hours of golden olden times
When girlish happiness locked hands with me
And we went spinning round, with naked feet
In swaths of bruisèd roses ankle-deep;
When laughter rang unsilenced, unrebuked,
And prayers went unremembered, oozing clean
From the drowsed memory, as from the eyes
The pure, sweet mother-face that bent above
Glimmered and wavered, blurred, bent closer still
A timeless instant, like a shadowy flame,
Then flickered tremulously o'er the brow
And went out in a kiss.

AMPHINE [*Kissing her*]

Not like to *this!*
O blessèd lips whose kiss alone may be
Sweeter than their sweet speech! Speak on, and say
Of what else talked thou and thy friend?

DWAINIE
We talked
Of all the past, ah me! and all the friends
That now await my coming. And we talked
Of O so many things—so many things—
That I but blend them all with dreams of when,

With thy warm hand clasped close in this of mine,
We cross the floating bridge that soon again
Will span the all-unfathomable gulfs
Of nether air betwixt this isle of strife
And my most glorious realm of changeless peace,
Where summer night reigns ever and the moon
Hangs ever ripe and lush with radiance
Above a land where roses float on wings
And fan their fragrance out so lavishly
That Heaven hath hint of it, and oft therefrom
Sends down to us across the odorous seas
Strange argosies of interchanging bud
And blossom, spice and balm.—Sweet—sweet
Beyond all art and wit of uttering.

AMPHINE

O Empress of my listening Soul, speak on,
And tell me all of that rare land of thine!—
For even though I reigned a peerless king
Within mine own, methinks I could fling down
My scepter, signet, crown and royal might,
And so fare down the thornèd path of life
If at its dwindling end my feet might touch
Upon the shores of such a land as thou
Dost paint for me—*thy* realm! Tell on of it—
And tell me if thy sister-woman there
Is like to thee—Yet nay! for an thou didst,
These eyes would lose all speech of sight
And call not back to thine their utter love.
But tell me of thy brothers.—Are they great,

And can they grapple Æo's arguments
Beyond our skill? or wrest a purpose from
The pink side of the moon at Darsten-tide?
Or cipher out the problem of blind stars,
That ever still do safely grope their way
Among the thronging constellations?

DWAINIE

                                        Ay!
Ay, they have leaped all earthland barriers
In mine own isle of wisdom-working Wunks:—
'Twas Wunkland's son that voyaged round the
    moon
And moored his bark within the molten bays
Of bubbling silver: And 'twas Wunkland's son
That talked with Mars—unbuckled Saturn's belt
And tightened it in squeezure of such facts
Therefrom as even *he* dare not disclose
In full till all his followers, as himself,
Have grown them wings, and gat them beaks and
    claws,
With plumage all bescienced to withstand
All tensest flames—glaze-throated, too, and lung'd
To swallow fiercest-spurted jets and cores
Of embered and unquenchable white heat:
'Twas Wunkland's son that alchemized the dews
And bred all colored grasses that he wist—
Divorced the airs and mists and caught the trick
Of azure-tinting earth as well as sky:

'Twas Wunkland's son that bent the rainbow
    straight
And walked it like a street, and so returned
To tell us it was made of hammered shine,
Inlaid with strips of selvage from the sun
And burnished with the rust of rotten stars:
'Twas Wunkland's son that comprehended first
All grosser things, and took our worlds apart
And oiled their works with theories that clicked
In glib articulation with the pulse
And palpitation of the systemed facts.—
And, circling ever round the farthest reach
Of the remotest welkin of all truths,
We stint not our investigations to
Our worlds only, but query still beyond.—
For now our goolores say, below these isles
A million million miles, are *other* worlds—
Not like to ours, but *round,* as bubbles are,
And, like them, ever reeling on through space,
And anchorless through all eternity;—
Not like to ours, for our isles, as they note,
Are living things that fly about at night,
And soar above and cling, throughout the day,
Like bats, beneath the bent sills of the skies:
And I myself have heard, at dawn of moon,
A liquid music filtered through my dreams,
As though 'twere myriads of sweet voices, pent
In some o'erhanging realm, had spilled themselves
In streams of melody that trickled through
The chinks and crannies of a crystal pave.

Until the wasted juice of harmony,
Slow-leaking o'er my senses, laved my soul
In ecstacy divine: And afferhaiks,
Who scour our coasts on missions for the King,
Declare our island's shape is like the zhibb's
When lolling in a trance upon the air
With open wings upslant and motionless.
O such a land it is—so all complete
In all wise inhabitants, and knowledge, lore,
Arts, sciences, perfected government
And kingly wisdom, worth and majesty—
And *Art*—ineffably above all else:—
The art of the *Romancer,*—fabulous
Beyond the miracles of strangest fact;
The art of *Poesy,*—the sanest soul
Is made mad with its uttering; the art
Of *Music,*—words may not e'en whimper what
The jewel-sounds of song yield to the sense;
And, last,—the art of *Knowing what to Know,*
And how to zoon straight toward it like a bee,
Draining or song or poem as it brims
And overruns with raciest spirit-dew.—
And, *after,*—chaos all to sense like thine,
Till there, translated, thou shalt know as I. . . .
So furnished forth in all things lovable
Is my Land-Wondrous—ay, and thine to be,—
O Amphine, love of mine, it lacks but thy
Sweet presence to make it a paradise!

[*Takes up trentoraine*]

And shall I tell thee of the home that waits
For thy glad coming, Amphine?—Listen, then!

Chant-Recitative

A palace veiled in a glimmering dusk;
  Warm breaths of a tropic air,
Drugged with the odorous marzhoo's musk
  And the sumptuous cyncotwaire—
Where the trembling hands of the lilwing's leaves
  The winds caress and fawn,
While the dreamy starlight idly weaves
  Designs for the damask lawn.

Densed in the depths of a dim eclipse
  Of palms, in a flowery space,
A fountain leaps from the marble lips
  Of a girl, with a golden vase
Held atip on a curving wrist,
  Drinking the drops that glance
Laughingly in the glittering mist
  Of her crystal utterance.

Archways looped o'er blooming walks
  That lead through gleaming halls;
And balconies where the word-bird talks
  To the tittering waterfalls:
And casements, gauzed with the filmy sheen
  Of a lace that sifts the sight
Through a ghost of bloom on the haunted screen
  That drips with the dews of light.

Weird, pale shapes of sculptured stone,—
  With marble nymphs agaze
Ever in fonts of amber, sown
  With seeds of gold and sprays
Of emerald mosses, ever drowned,
  Where glimpses of shell and gem
Peer from the depths, as round and round
  The nautilus nods at them.

Faces blurred in a mazy dance,
  With a music, wild and sweet,
Spinning the threads of the mad romance
  That tangles the waltzers' feet:
Twining arms, and warm, swift thrills
  That pulse to the melody,
Till the soul of the dancer dips and fills
  In the wells of ecstacy.

Eyes that melt in a quivering ore
  Of love, and the molten kiss
Jetted forth of the hearts that pour
  Their blood in the molds of bliss.—
Till, worn to a languor slumber-deep,
  The soul of the dreamer lifts
A silken sail on the gulfs of sleep,
  And into the darkness drifts.

[*The instrument falls from her hand*—AMPHINE, *in
  stress of passionate delight, embraces her.*]

Amphine

Thou art not all of earth, O angel one!
Nor do I far miswonder me an thou
Hast peered above the very walls of Heaven!
What hast thou seen there?—Didst on Æo bask
Thine eyes and clothe Him with new splendorings?
And strove He to fling back as bright a smile
As thine, the while He beckoned thee within?
And, tell me, didst thou meet an angel there
A-linger at the gates, nor entering
Till I, her brother, joined her?

Dwainie

                Why, hast thou
A sister dead?—Truth, I have heard of one
Long lost to thee—not dead?

Amphine

               Of her I speak,—
And dead, although we know not certainly,
We moan us ever it must needs be death
Only could hold her from us such long term
Of changeless yearning for her glad return.
She strayed away from us long, long ago.—
O and our memories!—Her wondering eyes
That seemed as though they ever looked on things
We might not see—as haply so they did,—

For she went from us, all so suddenly—
So strangely vanished, leaving never trace
Of her outgoing, that I ofttimes think
Her rapt eyes fell along some certain path
Of special glory paven for her feet,
And fashioned of Æo's supreme desire
That she might bend her steps therein and so
Reach Him again, unseen of our mere eyes.
My sweet, sweet sister!—lost to brother—sire—
And, to *her* heart, one dearer than all else,—
Her *lover*—lost indeed!

DWAINIE

Nay, do not grieve
Thee thus, O loving heart! Thy sister yet
May come to thee in some glad way the Fates
Are fashioning the while thy tear-drops fall!
So calm thee, while I speak of thine own self.—
For I have listened to a whistling bird
That pipes of waiting danger. Didst thou note
No strange behavior of thy sire of late?

AMPHINE

Ay, he is silent, and he walks as one
In some fixed melancholy, or as one
Half waking.—Even his worshiped books seem now
But things on shelves.

DWAINIE

    And doth he counsel not
With thee in any wise pertaining to
His ailings, or of matters looking toward
His future purposes or his intents
Regarding thine own future fortunings
And his desires and interests therein?
What bearing hath he shown of late toward thee
By which thou might'st beframe some estimate
Of his mind's placid flow or turbulent?
And hath he not so spoken thee at times
Thou hast been 'wildered of his words, or grieved
Of his strange manner?

AMPHINE

    Once he stayed me on
The palace-stair and whispered, "Lo, my son,
Thy young reign draweth nigh—prepare!"—So
  passed
And vanished as a wraith, so wan he was!

DWAINIE

And didst thou ever reason on this thing,
Nor ask thyself what dims thy father's eye
And makes a brooding shadow of his form?

AMPHINE

Why, there's a household rumor that he dreams
Death fareth ever at his side, and soon

Shall signal him away.—But *Jucklet* saith
Crestillomeem hath said *the leeches* say
There is no cause for serious concern;
And thus am I assured 'tis nothing more
Than childish fancy of mine aging sire,—
And so, as now, I laugh, full reverently,
And marvel, as I mark his shuffling gait,
And his bestrangered air and murmurous lips,
As by he glideth to and fro, ha! ha!
Ho! ho!—I laugh me many, many times—
Mind, thou, 'tis *reverently* I laugh—ha! ha!—
And wonder, as he glideth ghostly-wise,
If ever *I* shall waver as I walk,
And stumble o'er my beard, and knit my brows,
And o'er the dull mosaics of the pave
Play chequers with mine eyes!   Ha! ha!

DWAINIE [*Aside*]

How dare—
How dare I tell him?   Yet I must—I must!

AMPHINE

Why, art *thou*, too, grown childish, that thou canst
Find thee waste pleasure talking to thyself
And staring frowningly with eyes whose smiles
I need so much?

DWAINIE

Nay, rather say, their tears,
Poor thoughtless Prince!   [*Aside*]   (My magic
    even now

Forecasts his kingly sire's near happening
Of nameless hurt and ache and awful stress
Of agony supreme, when he shall stare
The stark truth in the face!)

AMPHINE

What meanest thou?

DWAINIE

What mean I but thy welfare? Why, I mean,
One hour agone, the Queen, thy mother—

AMPHINE

Nay,

Say only "Queen"!

DWAINIE

—The Queen, one hour agone—
As so I learned from source I need not say—
Sent message craving audience with the King
At noon to-night, within the Tower of Stars.—
Thou knowest, only brief space following
The time of her pent session thereso set
In secret with the King alone, *the Throne*
Is set, too, to convene; and that *the King*
Hath lent his seal unto a mandate that,
Should he withhold his presence there, the Queen
Shall be empowered to preside—to reign—

Solely endowed to work the royal will
In lieu of the good King. Now, therefore, I
Have been advised that she, the Queen, by craft
Connives to hold him absent purposely,
That she may claim the vacancy—for what
Covert design I know not, but I know
It augurs peril to you both, as to
The Throne's own perpetuity. [*Aside*]   (Again
My magic gives me vision terrible:—
The Sorceress' legions balk mine own.—The King
Still hers, yet wavering. O save the King,
Thou Æo!—Render him to us!)

AMPHINE

                    I feel
Thou speakest truth: and yet how know'st thou
    this?

DWAINIE

Ask me not that; my lips are welded close.—
And, *more,*—since I have dared to speak, and thou
To listen,—Jucklet is accessory,
And even now is plotting for thy fall.
But, Passion of my Soul! think not of me,—
For nothing but sheer magic may avail
To work me harm;—but look thou to thyself!
For thou art blameless cause of all the hate
That rankleth in the bosom of the Queen.
So have thine eyes unslumbered ever, that
No step may steal behind thee—for in this

Unlooked-of way thine enemy will come:
This much I know, but for what fell intent
Dare not surmise.—*So look thou, night and day,*
That none may skulk upon thee in this wise
Of dastardly attack. [*Aside*] (Ha! Sorceress!
Thou palest, tossing wild and wantonly
The smothering golden tempest of thy hair.—
What! lying eyes! *ye* dare to utter *tears?*
Help! help! Yield us the King!)

AMPHINE

And thou, O sweet!
How art thou guarded and what shield is thine
Of safety?

DWAINIE

Fear not thou for me at all.—
Possessed am I of wondrous sorcery—
The gift of Holy Magi at my birth:—
Mine enemy must *front* me in assault
And must with mummery of speech assail,
And I will know him in first utterance—
And so may thus disarm him, though he be
A giant thrice in vasty form and force.
[*Singing heard*]
But, list! what wandering minstrel cometh here
In the young night?

VOICE [*In distance—singing*]

The drowsy eyes of the stars grow dim;
The wamboo roosts on the rainbow's rim,
And the moon is a ghost of shine:
The soothing song of the crule is done,
But the song of love is a soother one,
And the song of love is mine.
Then, wake! O wake!
For the sweet song's sake,
Nor let my heart
With the morning break!

AMPHINE

Some serenader! Hist!
What meaneth he so early, and what thus
Within the palace garden-close? Quick; here!
He neareth! Soh! Let us conceal ourselves
And mark his action, wholly unobserved.

[AMPHINE *and* DWAINIE *enter bower*]

VOICE [*Drawing nearer*]

The mist of the morning, chill and gray,
Wraps the night in a shroud of spray;
The sun is a crimson blot:
The moon fades fast, and the stars take wing;
The comet's tail is a fleeting thing—
But the tale of love is not.

Then, wake! O wake!
For the sweet song's sake,
   Nor let my heart
With the morning break!

[*Enter* JUCKLET]

JUCKLET

Eex! what a sumptuous darkness is the Night—
How rich and deep and suave and velvety
Its lovely blackness to a soul like mine!
Ah, Night! thou densest of all mysteries—
Thou eeriest of unfathomable delights,
Whose soundless sheer inscrutability
Is fascination's own ethereal self,
Unseen, and yet embodied—palpable,—
An essence, yet a form of stableness
That stays me—weighs me, as a giant palm
Were laid on either shoulder.—Peace! I cease
Even to strive to grope one further pace,
But stand uncovered and with lifted face.
O but a glamour of inward light
Hath smitten the eyes of my soul to-night!
Groping here in the garden-land,
I feel my fancy's outheld hand
Touch the rim of a realm that seems
Like an isle of bloom in a sea of dreams:
I stand mazed, dazed and alone—alone!—
My heart beats on in an undertone,
And I lean and listen long, and long,

And I hold my breath as I hear again
The chords of a long-dead trentoraine
And the wraith of an old love-song.
Low to myself am I whispering:—
 Glad am I, and the Night knows why—
 Glad am I that the dream came by
 And found me here as of old when I
  Was a ruler and a king.

DWAINIE   [*To Amphine*]

What gentle little monster is this dwarf—
Surely not Jucklet of the court?

AMPHINE   [*Ironically*]

       Ay, ay!
But he'll *ungentle* an thy woman's-heart
Yield him but space. Listen: he mouths again.

JUCKLET

It was an age ago—an age
Turned down in life like a folded page.—
See where the volume falls apart,
And the faded book-mark—'tis my heart,—
Nor mine alone, but another knit
So cunningly in the love of it
That you must look, with a shaking head,
Nor know the quick one from the dead.
Ah! what a broad and sea-like lawn

Is the field of love they bloom upon!—
Waves of its violet-velvet grass
Billowing, with the winds that pass,
And breaking in a snow-white foam
Of lily-crests on the shores of home.
Low to myself am I whispering:—
   Glad am I, and the Night knows why—
   Glad am I that the dream came by
   And found me here as of old when I
      Was a ruler and a king.

[*Abruptly breaking into impassioned vocal burst*]

SONG

   Fold me away in your arms, O Night—
      Night, my Night, with your rich black
         hair!—
   Tumble it down till my yearning sight
   And my unkissed lips are hidden quite
      And my heart is havened there,—
         Under that mystical dark despair—
         Under your rich black hair.

   Oft have I looked in your eyes, O Night—
      Night, my Night, with your rich black
         hair!—
   Looked in your eyes till my face waned white
   And my heart laid hold of a mad delight
      That moaned as I held it there
         Under the deeps of that dark despair—
         Under your rich black hair.

Just for a kiss of your mouth, O Night—
   Night, my Night, with your rich black
      hair!—
Lo! will I wait as a dead man might
Wait for the Judgment's dawning light,
   With my lips in a frozen prayer—
      Under this lovable dark despair—
      Under your rich black hair.

   [With swift change to mood of utter gaiety]

Ho! ho! what will my dainty mistress say
When I shall stand knee-deep in the wet grass
Beneath her lattice, and with upturned eyes
And tongue out-lolling like the clapper of
A bell, outpour her *that?*   I wonder now
If she will not put up her finger thus,
And say, "Hist! heart of mine! the angels call
To thee!" Ho! ho! Or will her blushing face
Light up her dim boudoir and, from her glass,
Flare back to her a flame upsprouting from
The hot-cored socket of a soul whose light
She thought long since had guttered out?—Ho! ho!
Or, haply, will she chastely bend above—
A Parian phantomette, with head atip
And twinkling fingers dusting down the dews
That glitter on the tarapyzma-vines
That riot round her casement—gathering
Lush blooms to pelt me with while I below
All winkingly await the fragrant shower?
Ho! ho! how jolly is this thing of love!

But how much richer, rarer, jollier
Than all the loves is this rare love of mine!
Why, my sweet Princess doth not even dream
I *am* her lover,—for, to here confess,
I have a way of wooing all mine own,
And waste scant speech in creamy compliment
And courtesies all gaumed with winy words.—
In sooth, I do not woo at all—I *win!*
How is it now the old duet doth glide
Itself full ripplingly adown the grooves
Of its quaint melody?—And whoso, by
The *bye,* or by the *way,* or *for the nonce,*
Or, eke ye, *peradventure,* ever durst
Render a duet singly but myself?

[*Singing—with grotesque mimicry of two voices*]

JUCKLET'S OSTENSIBLE DUET

How is it you woo?—and now answer me true,—
  How is it you woo and you win?
*Why, to answer you true,—the first thing that you
    do*
  Is to simply, my dearest—begin.

But how can I begin to woo or to win
  When I don't know a Win from a Woo?
Why, cover your chin with your fan or your fin,
  And I'll introduce them to you.

But what if it drew from my parents a view
   With, my own in no manner akin?
No matter!—your view shall be first of the two,—
   So I hasten to usher them in.

Nay, stay! Shall I grin at the Woo or the Win?
   And what will he do if I *do?*
Why, the Woo will begin with "How pleasant it's
   been!"
   And the Win with "Delighted with you!"

Then supposing he grew very dear to my view—
   I'm speaking, you know, of the Win?
Why, then, you should do what he wanted you to,—
   And now is the time to begin.

The time to begin? O then usher him in—
   Let him say what he wants me to do.
He is here.—He's a twin of yourself,—I am "Win,"
   And you are, my darling, my "Woo"!

   [*Capering and courtesying to feigned audience*]

That song I call most sensible nonsense;
And if the fair and peerless Dwainie were
But here, with that sweet voice of hers, to take
The part of "Woo," I'd be the happiest "Win"
On this side of futurity! Ho! ho!

DWAINIE [*Aside to* AMPHINE]

What means he?

Amphine

        Why, he means that throatless head
Of his needs further chucking down betwixt
His cloven shoulders!

[*Starting forward—Dwainie detaining him*]

Dwainie

         Nay, thou shalt not stir!
See! now the monster hath discovered our
Repast. Hold! Let us mark him further.

Jucklet [*Archly eying viands*]

                     What!
A roasted wheffle and a toc-spiced whum,
Tricked with a larvey and a gherghgling's tail!—
And, sprit me! wine enough to swim them in!
Now I should like to put a question to
The *guests;* but as there *are* none, I direct
Mine interrogatory to the host. [*Bowing to vacancy*]
Am I behind time?—Then I can but trust
My tardy coming may be overlooked
In my most active effort to regain
A gracious tolerance by service now:—
Directing rapt attention to the fact
That I have brought mine appetite along,

I can but feel, ho! ho! that further words
Would be a waste of speech.

[*Sits at table—pours out wine, drinks and eats
voraciously*]

              —There was a time
When I was rather backward in my ways
In courtly company (as though, forsooth,
I felt not, from my very birth, the swish
Of royal blood along my veins, though bred
Amongst the treacled scullions and the thralls
I shot from, like a cork, in youthful years,
Into court favor by my wit's sheer stress
Of fomentation.—*Pah! the stench o' toil!*)
Ay, somehow, as I think, I've all outgrown
That coarse, nice age, wherein one makes a meal
Of two estardles and a fork of soup.
Hey! sanaloo! Lest my starved stomach stand
Awe-stricken and aghast, with mouth agape
Before the rich profusion of this feast,
I lubricate it with a glass of merl
And coax it on to more familiar terms
Of fellowship with those delectables.
[*Pours wine and holds up goblet with mock courtli-
ness*]
Mine host!—Thou of the viewless presence and
Hush-haunted lip:—Thy most imperial,
Ethereal, and immaterial health!
Live till the sun dries up, and comb thy cares

With star-prongs till the comets fizzle out
And fade away and fail and are no more!
       [*Drains and refills goblet*]
And, if thou wilt permit me to observe,—
The gleaming shaft of spirit in this wine
Goes whistling to its mark, and full and **fair**
Zipps to the target-center of my soul!
Why, now am I the veriest gentleman
That ever buttered woman with a smile,
And let her melt and run and drip and ooze
All over and around a wanton heart!
And if my mistress bent above me now,
In all my hideous deformity,
I think she would look over, as it were,
The hump upon my back, and so forget
The kinks and knuckles of my crooked legs,
In this enchanting smile, she needs must leap,
Love-dazzled, and fall faint and fluttering
Within these yawning, all-devouring arms
Of mine! Ho! ho! And yet Crestillomeem
Would have me blight my dainty Dwainie with
This feather from the Devil's wing!—But I
Am far too full of craft to spoil the eyes
That yet shall pour their love like nectar out
Into mine own,—and I am far too deep
For royal wit to wade my purposes.

DWAINIE [*To* AMPHINE]

What can he mean?

AMPHINE [*Chafing in suppressed frenzy*]

Ha! to rush forward and
Tear out his tongue and slap it in his face!

DWAINIE [*To* AMPHINE]

Nay, nay! Hist what he saith!

JUCKLET

How big a fool—
How all magnificent an idiot
Would I be to blight *her*—(my peerless one!—
My very soul's soul!) as Crestillomeem
Doth instigate me to, for *her* hate's sake—
And inward *jealousy,* as well, belike!—
Wouldst have my Dwainie blinded to my charms—
For charms, good sooth, were every several flaw
Of my malformèd outer-self, compared
With that his Handsomeness the Prince Amphine
Shalt change to at a breath of my puff'd cheek,
E'en were it weedy-bearded at the time
With such a stubble as a huntsman well
Might lose his spaniel in! Ho! ho! Ho! ho!
I fear me, O my coy Crestillomeem,
Thine ancient coquetry doth challenge still
Thine own vain admiration overmuch!
I to crush *her?*—when thou, as certainly,
Hast armed me to smite down the only bar
That lies betwixt her love and mine? Ho! ho!

Hey! but the revel I shall riot in
Above the beauteous Prince, instantuously
Made all abhorrent as a reptiled bulk!
Ho! ho! my princely wooer of the fair
Rare lady of mine own superior choice!
Pah! but my very 'maginings of him
Refinèd to that shamèd, sickening shape,
Do so beloathe me of him there be qualms
Expostulating in my forum now!
Ho! what unprincifying properties
Of medication hath her Majesty
Put in my tender charge! Ho! ho! Ho! ho!
Ah, Dwainie! sweetest sweet! what shock to
      thee?—
I wonder when she sees the human toad
Squat at her feet and cock his filmy eyes
Upon her and croak love, if she will not
Call me to tweezer him with two long sticks
And toss him from her path.—O ho! Ho! ho!
Hell bend him o'er some blossom quick, that I
May have one brother in the flesh!

[*Nods drowsily*]

DWAINIE [*To* AMPHINE]

                              Ha! See!
He groweth drunken.—Soh! Bide yet a spell
And I will vex him with my sorcery:
Then shall we hence,—for lo, the node when all
Our sublest arts and strategies must needs

Be quickened into acts and swift results.
Now bide thou here, and in mute silence mark
The righteous penalty that hath accrued
Upon that dwarfèd monster.

[*She stands, still in concealment from the dwarf,
her tense gaze fixed upon him as though in
mute and painful act of incantation.*—JUCKLET
*affected drowsily—yawns and mumbles inco-
herently—stretches, and gradually sinks at full
length on the sward.*—DWAINIE *moves forward*—AMPHINE, *following, is about to set
foot contemptuously on sleeper's breast, but is
caught and held away by* DWAINIE, *who imperiously waves him back, and still, in pantomime,
commanding, bids him turn and hide his face*
—AMPHINE *obeying as though unable to do
otherwise. Dwainie then unbinds her hair, and
throwing it all forward covering her face and
bending till it trails the ground, she lifts to the
knee her dress, and so walks backward in a circle round the sleeping* JUCKLET, *crooning to herself an incoherent song. Then pausing, letting
fall her gown, and rising to full stature, waves
her hands above the sleeper's face, and runs to*
AMPHINE, *who turns about and gazes on her
with new wonderment.*]

DWAINIE [*To* AMPHINE]

Now shalt thou
Look on such scaith as thou hath never dreamed.

[*As she speaks, half averting her face as with mel-
    ancholy apprehension, chorus of lugubrious
    voices heard chanting discordantly*]

VOICES

When the fat moon smiles,
    And the comets kiss,
        And the elves of Spirkland flit
The Whanghoo twunkers
    A tune like this,
        And the Nightmares champ the bit.

[*As chorus dies away, a comet, freighted with
    weird shapes, dips from the night and trails
    near* JUCKLET'S *sleeping figure, while with at-
    tendant goblin-forms, two* Nightmares, CREECH
    and GRITCHFANG, *alight.—The comet kisses,
    switches its tail and disappears, while the two
    goblins hover buzzingly over* JUCKLET, *who
    starts wide-eyed and stares fixedly at them,
    with horribly contorted features.*]

CREECH [*To* GRITCHFANG]

Buzz!
    Buzz!
        Buzz!
            Buzz!
Flutter your wings like your grandmother does!
Tuck in your chin and wheel over and *whir-r-r*

Like a dickerbug fast in the web of the wuhrr!
Reel out your tongue, and untangle your toes
And rattle your claws o'er the bridge of his nose;
Tickle his ears with your feathers and fuzz,
And keep up a hum like your grandmother does!

[JUCKLET *moans and clutches at air convulsively*]

AMPHINE [*Shuddering*]

Most gruesome sight!   See how the poor worm
    writhes!
How must he suffer!

DWAINIE

           Ay, but good is meant—
A far voice sings it so.

GRITCHFANG [*To* CREECH]

Let me dive deep in his nostriline caves
And keep an eye out as to how he behaves:
Fasten him down while I put him to rack—
And don't let him flop from the flat of his back!
[*Shrinks to minute size, while goblin attendants
    pluck from shrubbery a great lily-shaped flower
    which they invert funnel-wise, with small end
    at sleeper's nostrils, hoisting* GRITCHFANG *in
    at top and jostling shape downward gradually*

from sight, and—removing flower,—voice of
GRITCHFANG *continues gleefully from within
sleeper's head*]

Ho! I have bored through the floor of his brains,
And set them all writhing with torturous pains;
And I shriek out the prayer, as I whistle and whiz,
I may be the nightmare that my grandmother is!
[*Reappears, through reversal of flower method, as-
suming former shape, crosses to* CREECH, *and,
joining, the twain dance on sleeper's stomach
in broken time to duo*]

DUO

Whing!
     Whang!
          So our ancestors sang!
And they guzzled hot blood and blew up with a
    bang!—
But they ever tenaciously clung to the rule
To only blow up in the hull of a fool—
To fizz and explode like a cast-iron toad
In the cavernous depths where his victuals were
    stowed—
When chances were ripest and thickest and best
To burst every buttonhole out of his vest!

[*They pause, float high above, and fusing together
into a great square iron weight drop
heavily on chest of sleeper, who moans piteously.*]

AMPHINE   [*Hiding his face*]

Ah! take me hence!

[DWAINIE *leads him off, looking backward as she
   goes and waving her hands imploringly to*
   CREECH *and* GRITCHFANG, *reassuming former
   shapes, in ecstasies of insane delight*]

CREECH   [*To* GRITCHFANG]

Zipp!

      Zipp!

           Zipp!

                  Zipp!

Sting his tongue raw and unravel his lip!
Grope, on the right, down his windpipe, and squeeze
His liver as dry as a petrified wheeze!
[GRITCHFANG—*as before—shrinks and disappears
   at sleeper's mouth*]
Throttle his heart till he's black in the face,
And bury it down in some desolate place
Where only remorse in pent agony lives
To dread the advice that your grandmother gives!

[*The sleeper struggles contortedly, while voice of*
   GRITCHFANG *calls from within*]

GRITCHFANG

Ho-ho! I have clambered the rungs of his ribs
And beriddled his lungs into tatters and dribs;

And I turn up the tube of his heart like a hose
And squirt all the blood to the end of his nose!
I stamp on his stomach and caper and prance,
With my tail tossing round like a boomerang-lance!
And thus may success ever crown my intent
To wander the ways that my grandmother went!

[*Reappears, falls hysterically in* CREECH'S *out-stretched arms.—Then dance and duo.*]

DUO

Whing!

      Whung!

            So our ancestors sung!
And they snorted and pawed, and they hissed and
    they stung,—
Taking special terrific delight in their work
On the fools that they found in the lands of the
    Spirk.—
And each little grain of their powders of pain
They scraped up and pestled again and again—
Mixed in quadruple doses for gluttons and sots,
Till they strangled their dreams with gung-jibbrous
    knots!

[*The comet again trails past, upon which the* Night-mares *leap and disappear.* JUCKLET *staggers to his feet and glares frenziedly around—then starts for opposite exit of comet—is there sud-denly confronted with fiend-faces in the air, bewhiskered with ragged purplish flames that*

*flare audibly and huskily in abrupt alternating
chill gasps and hot welterings of wind.   He
starts back from them, reels and falls prostrate,
groveling terrifiedly in the dust, and chattering,
with eerie music accompanying his broken utterance.*]

JUCKLET

Æo! Æo! Æo!
Thou dost all things know—
  Waving all claims of mine to *dare* to pray,
Save that I needs *must:*—Lo,
  What *may* I pray for?   Yea,
  I have not *any* way,
An *Thou* gainsayest me a tolerance so.—
  I dare not pray
    Forgiveness—too great
    My vast o'ertoppling weight
  Of sinning; nor can I
  Pray my
Poor soul unscourged to go.—
Frame *Thou* my prayer, Æo!

What may I pray for?   Dare
I shape a prayer,
   In sooth,
  For any canceled joy
    Of my mad youth,
  Or any bliss my sin's stress did destroy?
What may I pray for—What?—

That the wild clusters of forget-me-not
      And mignonette
      And violet
Be out of childhood brought,
      And in mine hard heart set
   'A-blooming now as then?—
      With all their petals yet
Bediamonded with dews—
Their sweet, sweet scent let loose
      Full sumptuously again!

What *may* I pray, Æo!
    For the poor hutchèd cot
    Where death sate squat
Midst my first memories?—Lo!
My mother's face—(they, whispering, told me
    so)—
    That face!—so pinchedly
    It blanched up, as they lifted me—
      Its frozen eyelids would
      Not part, nor could
Be ever wetted open with warm tears.
   . . . Who hears
The prayers for all dead-mother-sakes, Æo!

Leastwise *one* mercy:—May
I not have leave to pray
All *self* to pass away—
    Forgetful of all needs mine own—
    Neglectful of all creeds;—alone,

Stand fronting Thy high throne and say:
    To Thee,
O Infinite, I pray
    Shield *Thou* mine enemy!

[*Music throughout supplication gradually softens
    and sweetens into utter gentleness, with scene
    slow-fading into densest night.*]

END ACT II

From a photograph taken when twenty-
two years old

ACT III

SCENE I. *Court of* KRUNG—*Royal* Ministers,
Counselors, *etc., in session.* CRESTILLOMEEM,
*in full blazonry of regal attire, presiding. She
signals a* Herald *at her left, who steps forward.—Blare of trumpets, greeted with ominous murmurings within, blent with tumult
from without.*

HERALD

Hist, ho! Ay, ay! Ay, ay!—Her Majesty,
The All-Glorious and Ever-Gracious Queen,
Crestillomeem, to her most loyal, leal
And right devoted subjects, greeting sends—
Proclaiming, in the absence of the King,
Her royal presence—

[*Voice of* Herald *fails abruptly—utterly.—A
breathless hush falls sudden on the court.—A
sense oppressive—ominous—affects the throng.
Weird music heard of unseen instruments.*]

HERALD [*Huskily striving to be heard*]

Hist, ho! Ay, ay! Ay, ay!—Her Majesty,

351

The All-Glorious and Ever-Gracious Queen,
Crestillomeem—

[*The* Queen *gasps, and clutches at* Herald, *mutely
signing him to silence, her staring eyes fixed on
a shadowy figure, mistily developing before her
into wraith-like form and likeness of The
Tune-Fool,* SPRAIVOLL. *The shape—evidently
invisible and voiceless to all senses but the
Queen's—wavers vaporishly to and fro before
her, moaning and crooning in infinitely sweet-
sad minor cadences a mystic song.*]

WRAITH-SONG OF SPRAIVOLL

I will not hear the dying word
  Of any friend, nor stroke the wing
Of any little wounded bird.
  . . . Love is the deadest thing!

I wist not if I see the smile
  Of prince or wight, in court or lane.—
I only know that afterwhile
  He will not smile again.

The summer blossom, at my feet,
  Swims backward, drowning in the grass.—
I will not stay to name it sweet—
  Sink out! and let me pass!

I have no mind to feel the touch
Of gentle hands on brow and hair.—
The lack of this once pained me much,
And so I have a care.

Dead weeds, and husky-rustling leaves
That beat the dead boughs where ye cling,
And old dead nests beneath the eaves—
Love is the deadest thing!

Ah! once I fared not all alone;
And once—no matter, rain or snow!—
The stars of summer ever shone—
Because I loved him so!

With always tremblings in his hands,
And always blushes unaware,
And always ripples down the strands
Of his long yellow hair.

I needs must weep a little space,
Remembering his laughing eyes
And curving lip, and lifted face
Of rapture and surprise.

O joy is dead in every part,
And life and hope; and so I sing:
In all the graveyard of my heart
Love is the deadest thing!

[*With dying away of song, apparition of* SPRAIVOLL *slowly vanishes.* CRESTILLOMEEM *turns dazedly to throng, and with labored effort strives to reassume imperious mien.—Signs for merl and tremulously drains goblet—sinks back in throne with feigned complacency, mutely waving* Herald *to proceed.*]

HERALD [*Mechanically*]

Hist, ho! Ay, ay! Ay, ay!—Her Majesty,
The All-Glorious and Ever-Gracious Queen,
Crestillomeem, to her most loyal, leal
And right devoted subjects, greeting sends—
Proclaiming, in the absence of the King,
Her royal presence, as by him empowered
To sit and occupy, maintain and hold,
And therefrom rule the Throne, in sovereign
    state,
And work the royal will—[*Confusion*]   Hist,
    ho! Ay, ay!
Ay, ay!—And be it known, the King, in view
Of his approaching dissolution—

[*Sensation among* Counselors, *etc., within, and wild tumult without and cries of "Long live the King!" and "Treason!" "Intrigue!" "Sorcery!"* CRESTILLOMEEM, *in suppressed ire, waving silence, and* Herald *striving to be heard.*]

HERALD

Hist, ho! Ay, ay! Ay, ay!—The King, in view
Of his approaching dissolution, hath
Decreed this instrument—this royal scroll

[*Unrolling and displaying scroll*]

With royal seal thereunto set by Krung's
Most sacred act and sign—

[*General sensation within, and growing tumult
    without, with wrangling cries of "Plot!"
    "Treason!" "Conspiracy!" and "Down with the
    Queen!" "Down with the usurper!" "Down
    with the Sorceress!"*]

CRESTILLOMEEM [*Wildly*]

Who dares to cry
"Conspiracy!" Bring me the traitor-knave!

[*Growing confusion without—sound of rioting.—
    Voice, "Let me be taken! Let me be taken!"
    Enter Guards, dragging JUCKLET forward,
    wild-eyed and hysterical—the Queen's gaze
    fastened on him wonderingly.*]

CRESTILLOMEEM [*To Guards*]

Why bring ye Jucklet hither in this wise?

GUARD

O Queen, 'tis he who cries "Conspiracy!"
And who incites the mob without with cries
Of "Plot!" and "Treason!"

CRESTILLOMEEM [*Starting*]

Ha! Can this be true?
I'll not believe it!—Jucklet is my fool,
But not so vast a fool that he would tempt
His gracious Sovereign's ire. [*To* Guards] Let
him be freed!

[*Then to* JUCKLET, *with mock service*]

Stand hither, O my Fool!

JUCKLET [*To* Queen]

What! I, thy fool?
Ho! ho! *Thy* fool?—ho! ho!—Why, *thou* art
mine!

[*Confusion—cries of "Strike down the traitor!"*
JUCKLET *wrenching himself from grasp of
officers*]

Back, all of ye! I have not waded hell
That I should fear your puny enmity!
Here will I give ye proof of all I say!

[*Presses toward throne, wedging his opposers left
    and right*—CRESTILLOMEEM *sits as though
    stricken speechless—pallid, waving him back*—
    JUCKLET, *fairly fronting her, with folded arms
    —then to throng continues.*]

Lo! do I here defy her to lift up
Her voice and say that Jucklet speaks a lie.

[*At sign of* Queen, Officers, *unperceived by* JUCK-
    LET, *close warily behind him.*]

And, further—I pronounce the document
That craven Herald there holds in his hand
A forgery—a trick—and dare the Queen,
Here in my listening presence, to command
Its further utterance!

CRESTILLOMEEM [*Wildly rising*]

                    Hold, hireling!—Fool!—
The Queen thou dost in thy mad boasts insult
Shall utter first thy doom!

[JUCKLET, *seized from behind by* Guards, *is hurled
    face upward on the dais at her feet, while a
    minion, with drawn sword pressed close against
    his breast, stands over him.*]

                    —Ere we proceed
With graver matters, let this demon-knave
Be sent back home to hell.

[*With awful stress of ire, form quivering, eyes
    glittering and features twitched and ashen*]

                      Give *me* the sword,—
The insult hath been mine—so even shall
The vengeance be!

[*As* Crestillomeem *seizes sword and bends for-
    ward to strike,* Jucklet, *with superhuman ef-
    fort, frees his hand, and, with a sudden mo-
    tion and an incoherent muttering, flings object
    in his assailant's face,—*Crestillomeem *stag-
    gers backward, dropping sword, and, with arms
    tossed aloft, shrieks, totters and falls prone
    upon the pave. In confusion following* Juck-
    let *mysteriously vanishes; and as the bewil-
    dered* Courtiers *lift the fallen* Queen, *a clear,
    piercing voice of thrilling sweetness is heard
    singing.*]

                  Voice

    The pride of noon must wither soon—
      The dusk of death must fall;
    Yet out of darkest night the moon
      Shall blossom over all!

[*For an instant a dense cloud envelops empty throne
    —then gradually lifts, discovering therein*
    Krung *seated, in royal panoply and state, with*
    Jucklet *in act of presenting scepter to him.—
    Blare of trumpets, and chorus of* Courtiers,
    Ministers, Heralds, *etc.*]

CHORUS

All hail! Long live the King!

KRUNG [*To throng, with grave salutation*]

Through Æo's own great providence, and
      through
The intervention of an angel whom
I long had deemed forever lost to me,
Once more your favored Sovereign, do I greet
And tender you my blessing, O most good
And faith-abiding subjects of my realm!
In common, too, with your long-suffering King,
Have *ye* long suffered, blamelessly as he:
Now, therefore, know ye all what, until late,
He knew not of himself, and with him share
The rapturous assurance that is his,—
That, for all time to come, are we restored
To the old glory and most regal pride
And opulence and splendor of our realm.

[*Turning with pained features to the strangely
      stricken* Queen]

There have been, as ye needs must know,
      strange spells
And wicked sorceries at work within
The very dais boundaries of the Throne.
Lo! then, behold your harrier and mine,
And with me grieve for the self-ruined Queen

Who grovels at my feet, blind, speechless, and
So stricken with a curse herself designed
Should light upon Hope's fairest minister.

[*Motions attendants, who lead away* CRESTILLO-
MEEM—*the* King *gazing after her, overmas-
tered with stress of his emotions.—He leans
heavily on throne, as though oblivious to all
surroundings, and, shaping into speech his
varying thought, as in a trance, speaks as
though witless of both utterance and auditor.*]

I loved her.—Why? I never knew.—Perhaps
Because her face was fair; perhaps because
Her eyes were blue and wore a weary air;—
Perhaps . . . perhaps because her limpid face
Was eddied with a restless tide, wherein
The dimples found no place to anchor and
Abide: perhaps because her tresses beat
A froth of gold about her throat, and poured
In splendor to the feet that ever seemed
Afloat. Perhaps because of that wild way
Her sudden laughter overleapt propriety;
Or—who will say?—perhaps the way she wept.
Ho! have ye seen the swollen heart of summer
Tempest, o'er the plain, with throbs of thunder
Burst apart and drench the earth with rain? She
Wept like that.—And to recall, with one wild
          glance
Of memory, our last love-parting—tears

And all. . . . It thrills and maddens me! And
    yet
My dreams will hold her, flushed from lifted brow
To finger-tips, with passion's ripest kisses
Crushed and mangled on her lips. . . . O
    woman! while
Your face was fair, and heart was pure, and lips
Were true, and hope as golden as your hair,
I should have strangled you!

[*As* KRUNG, *ceasing to speak, piteously lifts his
face,* SPRAIVOLL *all suddenly appears, in space
left vacant by the* Queen, *and, kneeling, kisses
the* King's *hand.—He bends in tenderness,
kissing her brow—then lifts and seats her at
his side. Speaks then to throng.*]

                Good Subjects—Lords:
Behold in this sweet woman here my child,
Whom, years agone, the cold, despicable
Crestillomeem—by baleful, wicked arts
And gruesome spells and fearsome witcheries—
Did spirit off to some strange otherland,
Where, happily, a Wunkland Princess found
Her, and undid the spell by sorcery
More potent—ay, *Divine,* since it works naught
But *good*—the gift of Æo, to right wrong.
This magic dower the Wunkland Princess hath
Enlisted in our restoration here,
In secret service, till this joyful hour
Of our complete deliverance. Even thus.—
Lo, let the peerless Princess now appear!

[*He lifts scepter, and a gust of melody, divinely
    beautiful, sweeps through the court.—The star
    above the throne loosens and drops slowly
    downward, bursting like a bubble on the scep-
    ter-tip, and, issuing therefrom,* AMPHINE *and*
    DWAINIE, *hand in hand, kneel at the feet of*
    KRUNG, *who bends above them with his bless-
    ing, while* JUCKLET *capers wildly round the
    group.*]

JUCKLET

Ho! ho! but I could shriek for very joy!
And though my recent rival, fair Amphine,
Doth even now bend o'er a blossom, I,
Besprit me! have no lingering desire
To meddle with it, though with but one eye
I slept the while she backward walked around
Me in the garden.

[AMPHINE *dubiously smiles*—JUCKLET *blinks and
    leers*—*and* DWAINIE *bites her finger.*]

KRUNG

                    Peace! good Jucklet! Peace!
For this is not a time for any jest.—
Though the old order of our realm hath been
Restored, and though restored my very life—
Though I have found a daughter,—I have lost

A son—for Dwainie, with her sorcery,
Will, on the morrow, carry him away.
'Tis Æo's largess, as our love is His,
And our abiding trust and gratefulness.

CURTAIN

JAMES WHITCOMB RILEY—A SKETCH

JAMES WHITCOMB RILEY—A SKETCH

On an early day in a memorable October, Reuben
A. Riley and his wife, Elizabeth Marine Riley, re-
joiced over the birth of their second son. They
called him James Whitcomb. This was in a shady
little street in the shady little town of Greenfield,
which is in the county of Hancock and the state of
Indiana. The young James found a brother and a
sister waiting to greet him—John Andrew and Mar-
tha Celestia, and afterward came Elva May—Mrs.
Henry Eitel—Alexander Humbolt and Mary Elizabeth, who, of all, alone lives to see this collection of
her brother's poems.

James Whitcomb was a slender lad, with corn-silk
hair and wide blue eyes. He was shy and timid, not
strong physically, dreading the cold of winter, and
avoiding the rougher sports of his playmates. And
yet he was full of the spirit of youth, a spirit that
manifested itself in the performance of many in-
genious pranks. His every-day life was that of the
average boy in the average country town of that day,
but his home influences were exceptional. His
father, who became a captain of cavalry in the Civil
War, was a lawyer of ability and an orator of more

than local distinction. His mother was a woman of rare strength of character combined with deep sympathy and a clear understanding. Together, they made home a place to remember with thankful heart. When James was twenty years old, the death of his mother made a profound impression on him, an impression that has influenced much of his verse and has remained with him always.

At an early age he was sent to school and, "then sent back again," to use his own words. He was restive under what he called the "iron discipline." A number of years ago, he spoke of these early educational beginnings in phrases so picturesque and so characteristic that they are quoted in full:

"My first teacher was a little old woman, rosy and roly-poly, who looked as though she might have just come tumbling out of a fairy story, so lovable was she and so jolly and so amiable. She kept school in her little Dame-Trot kind of dwelling of three rooms, with a porch in the rear, like a bracket on the wall, which was part of the playground of her 'scholars,'—for in those days pupils were called 'scholars' by their affectionate teachers. Among the twelve or fifteen boys and girls who were there I remember particularly a little lame boy, who always got the first ride in the locust-tree swing during recess.

"This first teacher of mine was a mother to all her 'scholars,' and in every way looked after their comfort, especially when certain little ones grew

drowsy. I was often, with others, carried to the sit-
ting-room and left to slumber on a small made-down
pallet on the floor. She would sometimes take three
or four of us together; and I recall how a playmate
and I, having been admonished into silence, grew
deeply interested in watching a spare old man who
sat at a window with its shade drawn down. After
a while we became accustomed to this odd sight and
would laugh, and talk in whispers and give imita-
tions, as we sat in a low sewing-chair, of the little
old pendulating blind man at the window. Well, the
old man was the gentle teacher's charge, and for this
reason, possibly, her life had become an heroic one,
caring for her helpless husband who, quietly content, waited always at the window for his sight to
come back to him. And doubtless it is to-day, as
he sits at another casement and sees not only his
earthly friends, but all the friends of the Eternal
Home, with the smiling, loyal, loving little woman
forever at his side.

"She was the kindliest of souls even when con-
strained to punish us. After a whipping she invari-
ably took me into the little kitchen and gave me two
great white slabs of bread cemented together with
layers of butter and jam. As she always whipped me
with the same slender switch she used for a pointer,
and cried over every lick, you will have an idea how
much punishment I could stand. When I was old
enough to be lifted by the ears out of my seat that
office was performed by a pedagogue whom I prom-

ised to 'whip sure, if he'd just wait till I got big enough.' He is still waiting!

"There was but one book at school in which I found the slightest interest,—McGuffey's old leather-bound Reader. It was the tallest book known, and to the boys of my size it was a matter of eternal wonder how I could belong to 'the big class in that reader.' When we were to read the death of 'Little Nell,' I would run away, for I knew it would make me cry, that the other boys would laugh at me, and the whole thing would become ridiculous. I couldn't bear that. A later teacher, Captain Lee O. Harris, came to understand me with thorough sympathy, took compassion on my weaknesses and encouraged me to read the best literature. He understood that he couldn't get numbers into my head. You couldn't tamp them in! History I also disliked as a dry thing without juice, and dates melted out of my memory as speedily as tin-foil on a red-hot stove. But I always was ready to declaim and took natively to anything dramatic or theatrical. Captain Harris encouraged me in recitation and reading and had ever the sweet spirit of a companion rather than the manner of an instructor."

But if there was "only one book at school in which he found the slightest interest," he had before that time displayed an affection for a book—simply as such and not for any printed word it might contain. And this, after all, is the true book-lover's love. Speaking of this incident—and he likes to refer to it as his "first literary recollection," he says: "Long before I was old enough to read I remember buying a book at an old auctioneer's shop in Greenfield. I can not imagine what prophetic impulse took possession of me and made me forego the ginger cakes and the candy that usually took every cent of my youthful income. The slender little volume must have cost all of twenty-five cents! It was Francis Quarles' *Divine Emblems,*—a neat little affair about the size of a pocket Testament. I carried it around with me all day long, delighted with the very feel of it.

"'What have you got there, Bub?' some one would ask. 'A book,' I would reply. 'What kind of a book?' 'Poetry-book.' 'Poetry!' would be the amused exclamation. 'Can you read poetry?' and, embarrassed, I'd shake my head and make my escape, but I held on to the beloved little volume."

Every boy has an early determination—a first one —to follow some ennobling profession, once he has come to man's estate, such as being a policeman or a performer on the high trapeze. The poet would not have been the "People's Laureate," but the Greenfield baker, had his fairy godmother granted his boy-wish. For to his childish mind it "seemed the acme of delight," using again his own happy expression, "to manufacture those snowy loaves of bread, those delicious tarts, those toothsome bon-bons. And then to own them all, to keep them in store, to watch over and guardedly exhibit. The thought of getting

money for them was to me a sacrilege. Sell them?
No indeed. Eat 'em—eat 'em, by tray loads and
dray loads! It was a great wonder to me why the
pale-faced baker in our town did not eat all his good
things. This I determined to do when I became
owner of such a grand establishment. Yes, sir. I
would have a glorious feast. Maybe I'd have Tom
and Harry and perhaps little Kate and Florry in to
help us once in a while. The thought of these playmates as 'grown-up folks' didn't appeal to me. I
was but a child, with wide-open eyes, a healthy appetite and a wondering mind. That was all. But I
have the same sweet tooth to-day, and every time I
pass a confectioner's shop, I think of the big baker
of our town, and Tom and Harry and the youngsters
all."

As a child, he often went with his father to the
court-house where the lawyers and clerks playfully
called him "Judge Wick." Here as a privileged
character he met and mingled with the country folk
who came to sue and be sued, and thus early the
dialect, the native speech, the quaint expressions of
his "own people" were made familiar to him, and
took firm root in the fresh soil of his young memory.
At about this time, he made his first poetic attempt
in a valentine which he gave to his mother. Not
only did he write the verse, but he drew a sketch to
accompany it, greatly to his mother's delight, who,
according to the best authority, gave the young poet
"three big cookies and didn't spank me for two

weeks. This was my earliest literary encouragement."

Shortly after his sixteenth birthday, young Riley turned his back on the little schoolhouse and for a time wandered through the different fields of art, indulging a slender talent for painting until he thought he was destined for the brush and palette, and then making merry with various musical instruments, the banjo, the guitar, the violin, until finally he appeared as bass drummer in a brass band. "In a few weeks," he says, "I had beat myself into the more enviable position of snare drummer. Then I wanted to travel with a circus, and dangle my legs before admiring thousands over the back seat of a Golden Chariot. In a dearth of comic songs for the banjo and guitar, I had written two or three myself, and the idea took possession of me that I might be a clown, introduced as a character-song-man and the composer of my own ballads.

"My father was thinking of something else, however, and one day I found myself with a 'five-ought' paint brush under the eaves of an old frame house that drank paint by the bucketful, learning to be a painter. Finally, I graduated as a house, sign and ornamental painter, and for two summers traveled about with a small company of young fellows calling ourselves 'The Graphics,' who covered all the barns and fences in the state with advertisements."

At another time his young man's fancy saw attractive possibilities in the village print-shop, and later his ambition was diverted to acting, encouraged by the good times he had in the theatricals of the Adelphian Society of Greenfield. "In my dreamy way," he afterward said, "I did a little of a number of things fairly well—sang, played the guitar and violin, acted, painted signs and wrote poetry. My father did not encourage my verse-making for he thought it too visionary, and being a visionary himself, he believed he understood the dangers of following the promptings of the poetic temperament. I doubted if anything would come of the verse-writing myself. At this time it is easy to picture my father, a lawyer of ability, regarding me, nonplused, as the worst case he had ever had. He wanted me to do something practical, besides being ambitious for me to follow in his footsteps, and at last persuaded me to settle down and read law in his office. This I really tried to do conscientiously, but finding that political economy and Blackstone did not rhyme and that the study of law was unbearable, I slipped out of the office one summer afternoon, when all outdoors called imperiously, shook the last dusty premise from my head and was away.

"The immediate instigator of my flight was a traveling medicine man who appealed to me for this reason: My health was bad, very bad,—as bad as I was. Our doctor had advised me to travel, but how could I travel without money? The medicine man needed an assistant and I plucked up courage to ask

if I could join the party and paint advertisements
for him.

"I rode out of town with that glittering cavalcade
without saying good-by to any one, and though my
patron was not a diplomaed doctor, as I found out,
he was a man of excellent habits, and the whole company was made up of good straight boys, jolly
chirping vagabonds like myself. It was delightful
to bowl over the country in that way. I laughed
all the time. Miles and miles of somber landscape
were made bright with merry song, and when the
sun shone and all the golden summer lay spread out
before us, it was glorious just to drift on through
it like a wisp of thistle-down, careless of how, or
when, or where the wind should anchor us. 'There's
a tang of gipsy blood in my veins that pants for the
sun and the air.'

"My duty proper was the manipulation of two
blackboards, swung at the sides of the wagon during
our street lecture and concert. These boards were
alternately embellished with colored drawings illus-
trative of the manifold virtues of the nostrum
vended. Sometimes I assisted the musical olio with
dialect recitations and character sketches from the
back step of the wagon. These selections in the
main originated from incidents and experiences
along the route, and were composed on dull Sundays
in lonesome little towns where even the church bells
seemed to bark at us."

On his return to Greenfield after this delightful but profitless tour he became the local editor of his home paper and in a few months "strangled the little thing into a change of ownership." The new proprietor transferred him to the literary department and the latter, not knowing what else to put in the space allotted him, filled it with verse. But there was not room in his department for all he produced, so he began, timidly, to offer his poetic wares in foreign markets. The editor of *The Indianapolis Mirror* accepted two or three shorter verses but in doing so suggested that in the future he try prose. Being but an humble beginner, Riley harkened to the advice, whereupon the editor made a further suggestion; this time that he try poetry again. *The Danbury* (Connecticut) *News,* then at the height of its humorous reputation, accepted a contribution shortly after *The Mirror* episode and Mr. McGeechy, its managing editor, wrote the young poet a graceful note of congratulation. Commenting on these parlous times, Mr. Riley once wrote, "It is strange how little a thing sometimes makes or unmakes a fellow. In these dark days I should have been content with the twinkle of the tiniest star, but even this light was withheld from me. Just then came the letter from McGeechy; and about the same time, arrived my first check, a payment from *Hearth and Home* for a contribution called *A Destiny* (now *A Dreamer* in *A Child World*). The letter was signed, 'Editor' and unless

sent by an assistant it must have come from Ik
Marvel himself, God bless him! I thought my
fortune made. Almost immediately I sent off another contribution, whereupon to my dismay came
this reply: 'The management has decided to discon-
tinue the publication and hopes that you will find
a market for your worthy work elsewhere.' Then
followed dark days indeed, until finally, inspired by
my old teacher and comrade, Captain Lee O. Harris,
I sent some of my poems to Longfellow, who replied in his kind and gentle manner with the sub-
stantial encouragement for which I had long
thirsted."

Not long after this Mr. Riley formed a connection
with *The Anderson* (Indiana) *Democrat* and contributed verse and locals in more than generous
quantities. He was happy in this work and had begun to feel that at last he was making progress
when evil fortune knocked at his door and, conspiring with circumstances and a friend or two, induced the young poet to devise what afterward
seemed to him the gravest of mistakes,—the Poe-
poem hoax. He was then writing for an audience
of county papers and never dreamed that this
whimsical bit of fooling would be carried beyond
such boundaries. It was suggested by these circumstances. He was inwardly distressed by the belief
that his failure to get the magazines to accept his
verse was due to his obscurity, while outwardly he
was harrassed to desperation by the junior editor of

the rival paper who jeered daily at his poetical pretensions. So, to prove that editors would praise from a known source what they did not hesitate to condemn from one unknown, and to silence his nagging contemporary, he wrote *Leonainie* in the style of Poe, concocting a story, to accompany the poem, setting forth how Poe came to write it and how all these years it had been lost to view. In a few words Mr. Riley relates the incident and then dismisses it. "I studied Poe's methods. He seemed to have a theory, rather misty to be sure, about the use of "m's" and "n's" and mellifluous vowels and sonorous words. I remember that I was a long time in evolving the name *Leonainie,* but at length the verses were finished and ready for trial.

"A friend, the editor of *The Kokomo Dispatch,* undertook the launching of the hoax in his paper; he did this with great editorial gusto while, at the same time, I attacked the authenticity of the poem in *The Democrat.* That diverted all possible suspicion from me. The hoax succeeded far too well, for what had started as a boyish prank became a literary discussion nation-wide, and the necessary exposé had to be made. I was appalled at the result. The press assailed me furiously, and even my own paper dismissed me because I had given the 'discovery' to a rival."

Dreary and disheartening days followed this tragic event, days in which the young poet found no present help, nor future hope. But over in In-

dianapolis, twenty miles away, happier circumstances were shaping themselves. Judge E. B.
Martindale, editor and proprietor of *The Indianapolis Journal,* had been attracted by certain poems
in various papers over the state and at the very time
that the poet was ready to confess himself beaten,
the judge wrote: "Come over to Indianapolis and
we'll give you a place on *The Journal.*" Mr. Riley
went. That was the turning point, and though the
skies were not always clear, nor the way easy, still
from that time it was ever an ascending journey.
As soon as he was comfortably settled in his new
position, the first of the Benj. F. Johnson poems
made its appearance. These dialect verses were
introduced with editorial comment as coming from
an old Boone county farmer, and their reception
was so cordial, so enthusiastic, indeed, that the business manager of *The Journal,* Mr. George C. Hitt,
privately published them in pamphlet form and sold
the first edition of one thousand copies in local
bookstores and over *The Journal* office counter.
This marked an epoch in the young poet's progress
and was the beginning of a friendship between him
and Mr. Hitt that has never known interruption.
This first edition of *The Old Swimmin' Hole and
'Leven More Poems* has since become extremely
rare and now commands a high premium. A second edition was promptly issued by a local book
dealer, whose successors, The Bowen-Merrill Company—now The Bobbs-Merrill Company—have

continued, practically without interruption, to publish Mr. Riley's work.

The call to read from the public platform had by this time become so insistent that Mr. Riley could no longer resist it, although modesty and shyness fought the battle for privacy. He tells briefly and in his own inimitable fashion of these trying experiences. "In boyhood I had been vividly impressed with Dickens' success in reading from his own works and dreamed that some day I might follow his example. At first I read at Sunday-school entertainments and later, on special occasions such as Memorial Days and Fourth of Julys. At last I mustered up sufficient courage to read in a city theater, where, despite the conspiracy of a rainy night and a circus, I got encouragement enough to lead me to extend my efforts. And so, my native state and then the country at large were called upon to bear with me and I think I visited every sequestered spot north or south particularly distinguished for poor railroad connections. At different times, I shared the program with Mark Twain, Robert J. Burdette and George Cable, and for a while my gentlest and cheeriest of friends, Bill Nye, joined with me and made the dusty detested travel almost a delight. We were constantly playing practical jokes on each other or indulging in some mischievous banter before the audience. On one occasion, Mr. Nye, coming before the footlights for a word of general introduction, said,

'Ladies and gentlemen, the entertainment to-night is of a dual nature. Mr. Riley and I will speak alternately. First I come out and talk until I get tired, then Mr. Riley comes out and talks until *you* get tired!' And thus the trips went merrily enough at times and besides I learned to know in Bill Nye a man blessed with as noble and heroic a heart as ever beat. But the making of trains, which were all in conspiracy to outwit me, schedule or no schedule, and the rush and tyrannical pressure of inviolable engagements, some hundred to a season and from Boston to San Francisco, were a distress to my soul. I am glad that's over with. Imagine yourself on a crowded day-long excursion; imagine that you had to ride all the way on the platform of the car; then imagine that you had to ride all the way back on the same platform; and lastly, try to imagine how you would feel if you did that every day of your life, and you will then get a glimmer—a faint glimmer—of how one feels after traveling about on a reading or lecturing tour.

"All this time I had been writing whenever there was any strength left in me. I could not resist the inclination to write. It was what I most enjoyed doing. And so I wrote, laboriously ever, more often using the rubber end of the pencil than the point.

"In my readings I had an opportunity to study and find out for myself what the public wants, and afterward I would endeavor to use the knowledge

gained in my writing. The public desires nothing
but what is absolutely natural, and so perfectly natural as to be fairly artless. It can not tolerate af-
fectation, and it takes little interest in the classical
production. It demands simple sentiments that come
direct from the heart. While on the lecture platform I watched the effect that my readings had on
the audience very closely and whenever anybody left
the hall I knew that my recitation was at fault and
tried to find out why. Once a man and his wife
made an exit while I was giving *The Happy Little
Cripple*—a recitation I had prepared with particular enthusiasm and satisfaction. It fulfilled, as
few poems do, all the requirements of length, climax
and those many necessary features for a recitation.
The subject was a theme of real pathos, beautified
by the cheer and optimism of the little sufferer.
Consequently when this couple left the hall I was
very anxious to know the reason and asked a friend
to find out. He learned that they had a little hunch-
back child of their own. After this experience I
never used that recitation again. On the other
hand, it often required a long time for me to
realize that the public would enjoy a poem which,
because of some blind impulse, I thought unsuita-
ble. Once a man said to me, 'Why don't you re-
cite *When the Frost Is on the Punkin?*' The use
of it had never occurred to me for I thought it
'wouldn't go.' He persuaded me to try it and it
became one of my most favored recitations. Thus,
I learned to judge and value my verses by their

effect upon the public. Occasionally, at first, I had presumed to write 'over the heads' of the audience, consoling myself for the cool reception by thinking my auditors were not of sufficient intellectual height to appreciate my efforts. But after a time it came home to me that I myself was at fault in these failures, and then I disliked anything that did not appeal to the public and learned to discriminate between that which did not ring true to the hearts of my hearers and that which won them by virtue of its simple truthfulness."

As a reader of his own poems, as a teller of humorous stories, as a mimic, indeed as a finished actor, Mr. Riley's gifts are rare and beyond question. In a lecture on the Humorous Story, Mark Twain, referring to the story of the *One Legged Soldier* and the different ways of telling it, once said:

"It takes only a minute and a half to tell it in its comic form; and isn't worth telling after all. Put into the humorous-story form, it takes ten minutes, and is about the funniest thing I have ever listened to—as James Whitcomb Riley tells it.

"The simplicity and innocence and sincerity and unconsciousness of Riley's old farmer are perfectly simulated, and the result is a performance which is thoroughly charming and delicious. This is art —and fine and beautiful, and only a master can compass it."

It was in 1883 that *The Old Swimmin' Hole*

and 'Leven More Poems first appeared in volume form. Four years later, Mr. Riley made his initial appearance before a New York City audience. The entertainment was given in aid of an international copyright law, and the country's most distinguished men of letters took part in the program. It is probably true that no one appearing at that time was less known to the vast audience in Chickering Hall than James Whitcomb Riley, but so great and so spontaneous was the enthusiasm when he left the stage after his contribution to the first day's program, that the management immediately announced a place would be made for Mr. Riley on the second and last day's program. It was then that James Russell Lowell introduced him in the following words:

"Ladies and gentlemen: I have very great pleasure in presenting to you the next reader of this afternoon, Mr. James Whitcomb Riley, of Indiana. I confess, with no little chagrin and sense of my own loss, that when yesterday afternoon, from this platform, I presented him to a similar assemblage, I was almost completely a stranger to his poems. But since that time I have been looking into the volumes that have come from his pen, and in them I have discovered so much of high worth and tender quality that I deeply regret I had not long before made acquaintance with his work. To-day, in presenting Mr. Riley to you, I can say to you of my own knowledge, that you are to have the pleasure of listening to the voice of a true poet."

Two years later a selection from his poems was published in England under the title *Old Fashioned Roses* and his international reputation was established. In his own country the people had already conferred their highest degrees on him and now the colleges and universities—seats of conservatism—gave him scholastic recognition. Yale made him an Honorary Master of Arts in 1902; in 1903, Wabash and, a year later, the University of Pennsylvania conferred on him the degree of Doctor of Letters, and in 1907 Indiana University gave him his LL. D. Still more recently the Academy of Arts and Letters elected him to membership, and in 1912 awarded him the gold medal for poetry. About this time a yet dearer, more touching tribute came to him from school children. On October 7, 1911, the schools of Indiana and New York City celebrated his birthday by special exercises, and one year later, the school children of practically every section of the country had programs in his honor.

As these distinguished honors came they found him each time surprised anew and, though proud that they who dwell in the high places of learning should come in cap and gown to welcome him, yet gently and sincerely protesting his own unworthiness. And as they found him when they came so have they left him.

Mr. Riley has lived in Indianapolis ever since Judge Martindale invited him to join *The Journal's* forces, and no one of her citizens is more devoted,

while none is so universally loved and honored.
Everywhere he goes the tribute of quick recognition
and cheery greeting is paid him, and his home is the
shrine of every visiting Hoosier. High on a sward
of velvet grass stands a dignified middle-aged brick
house. A dwarfed stone wall, broken by an iron
gate, guards the front lawn, while in the rear an
old-fashioned garden revels in hollyhocks and wild
roses. Here among his books and his souvenirs
the poet spends his happy and contented days. To
reach this restful spot, the pilgrim must journey to
Lockerbie Street, a miniature thoroughfare half
hidden between two more commanding avenues. It
is little more than a lane, shaded, unpaved and from
end to end no longer than a five minutes' walk, but
its fame is for all time.

"Such a dear little street it is, nestled away
From the noise of the city and heat of the day,
In cool shady coverts of whispering trees,
With their leaves lifted up to shake hands with the
　　breeze
Which in all its wide wanderings never may meet
With a resting-place fairer than Lockerbie Street!"

Mr. Riley has never married. He lives with devoted, loyal and understanding friends, a part of
whose life he became many years ago. Kindly con-
sideration, gentle affection, peace and order,—all
that go to make home home, are found here blooming with the hollyhocks and the wild roses. Every

day some visitor knocks for admittance and is not denied; every day sees the poet calling for some companionable friend and driving with him through the city's shaded streets or far out into the surrounding country. While he writes but little still his days are full of activities and his life is ever rounded with a song—

"For no language could frame and no lips could repeat
My rhyme-haunted raptures of Lockerbie Street."

NOTES

"I have been false!" she moaned, "I am not ____
I am not worthy now,
Nor never can I be a wife to you—
For I have broke my vow"
And as she kneeled there, sobbing at his feet,
He calmly spoke—no sigh
Betrayed his inward agony—"I count you meet
To be a wife of mine"—

And raised her up, forgiven though untrue.
As fond he gazed on her
She sighed,—"So happy!" and she ne'er never knew
He was a Widower.

Jay White

NOTES

The earliest of Mr. Riley's poems are found in a small time-stained note-book where the penmanship contrasts sharply with the artistic neatness of his writing of later years. The book contains twenty-four poems, each one bearing its date of composition, and includes verses that he wrote when a mere boy. The following appear in the body of this volume: *A Backward Look, Philiper Flash* (hitherto unpublished), *To a Boy Whistling* (not hitherto printed), *An Old Friend, A Poet's Wooing, A Ballad.*

p. 1   A BACKWARD LOOK

In the early note-book with the title, *A Retrospect,* and the date August 7, 1870; shortly afterward printed in *The Greenfield Commercial* (exact date lost), and signed "Edyrn"; published in a prose sketch entitled *The Gilded Roll* in PIPES O' PAN AT ZEKESBURY—1888. The poem was revised prior to each publication. The fourth stanza originally ended with these four lines:

> They got me to climb for the bluebird's nest
>   By telling me they'd give me half the eggs,
> And I got to the limb by tuggin' my best
>   And fell to the ground and broke one of my legs.

The following stanza originally stood at the conclusion of the poem but has subsequently been discarded:

> Through the great thoroughfare of the phantom past
>   Went garnering here and there
> These brittle baubles, too frail to last,
> And which flying Time with its blighting blast
>   Is hurrying—God knows where!
> And Memory brought them all back again,
>   Slipped again in my mind, and leant down
> And knocked the cigar stump out of my hand.
>   So I got up and walked back to town.

The references in this poem are true to the author's own life. In it are mentioned two of his boyhood companions,—George Carr, later mayor of Greenfield, and Alexander Skinner, always called "Eck" because as a child he pronounced his nickname, "Alec," in this manner.

St. 4, l. 5: "Doin' sky-scrapers": a child's term for swinging very high; "whirlin' round": the result obtained by revolving the swing and then allowing it to unwind of its own accord.

The *nom de plume* "Edyrn," by which this poem and others were signed when first printed, is the name of a knight in *Geraint and Enid* in Tennyson's *Idyls of the King*. Mr. Riley fancied the name on account of its strangeness.

p. 4   PHILIPER FLASH

In the early note-book with the date August 14, 1870; printed in *The Greenfield Commercial*, September 8, 1870, signed "Edyrn" and dated August 29, 1870; hitherto unpublished in book form. These lines were written under the inspiration of

John G. Saxe, whose happy knack of artless rhyming Mr. Riley greatly admired, as

> Young Peter Pyramus,—I call him Peter,
> Not for the sake of the rhyme or the meter,
> But merely to make the name completer.

In accord with a once popular custom, a man's character was often symbolized by his name, as in this poem. Mr. Riley rejoices that such an irritating artificiality is no longer in fashion.

p. 8   THE SAME OLD STORY

Printed in *The Greenfield Commercial*, September 7, 1870, over the pen-name of "Edyrn"; hitherto unpublished in book form. This is doubtless the first of his verse that found its way into print. Lionel E. Rumrill accepted the contribution for the *Poet's Column* of his paper, and its appearance was a source of great satisfaction to Mr. Riley. Commenting upon its publication he says "I read it over and over again until the verses sounded strange to me despite the fact that there is involved a perfect wrangle of bad grammar."

Mr. Riley has allowed these early poems to stand with their youthful imperfections.

p. 10   TO A BOY WHISTLING

In the early note-book with the date September 14-23, 1870; not hitherto printed.

p. 11   AN OLD FRIEND

In the early note-book with the title, *Summer's Return*, dated March 22, 1871; later printed in *The*

Greenfield Commercial (exact date lost), signed "Edyrn"; published in Home Folks (Homestead Edition)—1902, His Pa's Romance (Greenfield Edition)—1903, Songs of Summer—1908, A Summer's Day and Other Poems—1911, The Lockerbie Book—1911.

p. 12   WHAT SMITH KNEW ABOUT FARMING

Dated April 15, 1871; not hitherto printed. Mr. Riley has made a deliberate use of both "o'" and "of" in this and other dialect poems. In this detail as in all others he has carefully followed the dictates of spoken dialect as he has heard it. Various considerations control the pronunciation of the preposition "of," among which are, the rapidity with which it is spoken, the familiarity of the phrase in which it occurs, and the stress given it.

p. 18   A POET'S WOOING

As indicated by a fragment of the first five lines in the early note-book, these verses were begun prior to July 20, 1870, and were completed before February 9, 1872, at which time they were enclosed in a letter to the author's brother, John A. Riley, and entitled *The Bard and the Modern Miss;* first printed in *The Danbury News* (Conn.), August 8, 1874; hitherto unpublished in book form. The letter, full of youth's enthusiasm, containing this poem and the next, *Man's Devotion,* follows:

Feb. 9th, 1872.
My dear Bro.
That little letter of yours came . . . and I reply with like brevity—*Come to think,* I don't believe you asked a *reply,* but a *comply*—for your letter only requested me to send "that literary effort," so of course you'll consider you

are answered when you take its *fragile support* carefully—
tenderly I may say—from its Sarcophagus—(its envelope,
you know, but I am used to soaring—) . . . You will
find I have sent you *two* "Literary efforts—" though the
newer may hardly be termed an *effort* for *I done it with
the greatest of ease and avidity* as "Young P—" would say.
Of late I am startlingly prolific in composing, and, as you
hinted "Who knows, &c, &c." I could dispose of them like
brick—so much per thousand. I think "The Bard and the
Modern Miss" contains pretty deep satire—wade in and
see.—

> And say, Dear bro. you will sign Jay Whit,
> Providing the papers will publish it.

And if they *should* refuse, let me down gently! I have
written with a pencil to make it as plain as possible to
you—don't let them see *my* manuscript—unless you sho'd
endeavor to publish it in an *illustrated* paper—you may
then submit *my illustration* to them—

Yours obscurely,
Jim.

It was the practise of the author's brother to re-
write the verses in his own neat hand, because they
were not very legibly or accurately spelled. Later,
Mr. Riley, in an effort to furnish copy that no
printer could mistake, and especially to insure the
perfect reproduction of his dialect, developed a
handwriting which resembles lettering and pos-
sesses an artistic neatness.

The quotation from Tennyson at the head of the
poem is from *Audley Court,* 51, 52.

p. 20   MAN'S DEVOTION

Enclosed in a letter to John A. Riley, February 9, 1872; printed in *The Indianapolis Mirror*
March 31, 1872, signed "Jay Whit"; hitherto unpublished in book form. The original MS. of these
verses, contained in the letter printed in the previous note, was humorously illustrated by the author. See facsimile at beginning of the Notes. He

wrote to his brother as follows when the latter, after almost two months of persistence, finally got the contribution accepted:

Saturday, [Apr. 6,] 1872.

Dear Bro.

You're a good fellow!—I tell you I was very agreeably surprised when I saw myself in The Mirror the other morning—I mean at that *startling proof* of "Man's Devotion" (A Complimentary pun this is *meant* for.) "When at first *you* don't succeed *you* try, try again"—now, had *I* been declined—I should have most certainly "wilted," bereft of power to even demand the return of MS.—I don't know that I would *now,* for I think I have learned a lesson—hope so at least! I, of course, was sorry that there were so many errors, but I console myself that they are magnified thro' my tears—"but pshaw! I am growing womanish!—I'll none of it!"

p. 23   A BALLAD

As indicated by a fragment of eight stanzas in the early note-book, these verses were begun between August 14 and 17, 1870; printed in *The Indianapolis Mirror,* May 11, 1872, signed "Jay Whit"; published in HOME FOLKS—1900. These verses were revised considerably before each publication. Prior to their first appearance in print, the writer sent them, with the following comment, to his brother John who was to submit them to the editor of *The Indianapolis Mirror:*

Home, Tuesday eve. [May 7, 1872.]

Dear Bro:

I have written this poem hastily—for I am so busy—but I guess you can read it—I will try and write the next in ink—and you may try the experiment whether printers will receive such obscure H-le-o-griphicks—(I don't know how to spell it).

If you *can't* get this on the *front page*—don't put it in— for *I* consider it *the best thing I have ever written* and I want to see it occupy a *front seat,*—or we'll let it *stand* till one can be procured. It *looks* rather *voluminous* but it's only *eight verses* longer than the last—It will be the more apt—on that *score*—(20) with two verses for *good measure!* to *fill the measure* of the *public eye*—

I'd like you to try it for *this week*—And *feel* 'em a little on a *prose* sketch—for instance—"He has written some sketches that *I* consider good—not tiresome &c &c— but racy—original—with now and then a little spice of poetry—humor—wit—and quite "pathetic" occasionally— etc &c."—understand? Try it—and send me the result in the inside pocket of my old new coat and I'll be yours muchly.   Jim.

P. S.—Use your best endeavors to send it this week, and, if published—the poem—I expect there will be some one from Greenfield who would like to hand his name down to posterity by having it said that he once bro't *me* from the Renovator's—a second-hand coat—when I was too poor to even *thank* him for his trouble! (Exit laughing.)
                                                         Jim.

In a letter to his brother, dated Greenfield, May 14, 1872, Mr. Riley referred to the "very unsatisfactory" printing of the ballad, which both his brother and the printer had altered:

. . . I believe you have been a little hasty in condemning *"somersault."* I quote Webster's unabridged:—

> "So′m′er-sault.
> Som′er-set."

He gives his preference, you see, to the above, tho' *either* is correct. That verse *is* weak, and I expect it makes me "sicker" than you, but no matter—"you can't make a silk purse of a pig's ear"— I do not expect "to beat a pathway on to wealth and fame," but let the explanation in next week's Mirror be given as you spoke of. I will enclose the poem corrected as I would have it—there is a ponderous array of errors (*typographical, I believe*). The repetition of *and* I was aware of but I had thought it of no consequence.

John, all the little articles, pronouns, etc., that have become changed, *were chief characteristics of ballad style:* I refer you to *any ballad* of Longfellow's, or any *good* poet's—It makes it simple, plain and natural, and I wouldn't have had it changed for *anything*, in that particular, excepting those *ands*—you were right *there*—I do not know whether you or the printer changed the other —I regret *that* more than anything else. It hurts me more that the poem was my favorite, and I had "built an airy castle for it!" Well! enough! . . .

p. 27   THE OLD TIMES WERE THE BEST

Composed about June, 1872; first printed in *The High School Budget,* Greenfield, June, 1899; hitherto unpublished in book form. These verses were written at Greenfield one evening during the course of a pleasant gathering of youthful friends. Mr. Riley absented himself from the party and returned with these lines, which he gave to Miss Angy Williams (Mrs. Charles Downing) proposing that she set them to music. Later Mr. Barclay Walker, of Indianapolis, followed the author's suggestion.

p. 28   A SUMMER AFTERNOON

Written previous to March, 1873; first printed in *The Danbury News,* July 11, 1874; signed "Jay Whit"; hitherto unpublished in book form. This poem was originally called *The Argonaut.* Dr. Silas B. McManus relates the following incident concerning it:

In the spring of 1873, when I was reading medicine in Warsaw, Riley was in town filling an engagement painting window signs. He was handy at this sort of thing and did some nice jobs. About this time *The Warsaw Indianian* printed some little things of mine, out of charity, I suppose, or to encourage me or get rid of me. One day Riley and I were talking about them while he was painting a sign of a jewelry store. In a mild friendly way he was a trifle envious of my success in getting into print, and I posed beside him as a person whose literary standing was assured.

When he had made a marine blue period he took off his apron and we went over to the hotel together to see a little bit of rhyme which he said he had there. He wanted my opinion and criticism on it, and as I had more opinion and criticism to give than anything else, I was willing to bestow it even on a sign painter. Riley read the poem. It was called *The Argonaut,* and, inexperienced as I was, I knew that only a poet and a genius could have written it. I was unstinted in my praise, and I knew the Hoosier poet was born and was only waiting the recognition of the public which in a few years it so magnificently gave. After this episode we became warm friends, and an abiding and deep-rooted friendship was the result. I have read about all he has ever written, but nothing ever pleased me as much, no "reading" that I have ever heard of his, pleased me as well as that little poem, *The Argonaut,* read one raw spring day, up in a cold room, by a curtainless window, in the Wright House.

p. 30 AT LAST

Printed in *The Danbury News,* February 25, 1874, signed "Jay Whit"; hitherto unpublished in book form.

p. 32 FARMER WHIPPLE—BACHELOR

First printed in *The Greenfield News,* February 28, 1874; published in GREEN FIELDS AND RUNNING BROOKS—1892, LOVE LYRICS—1899, Christy edition with the title, THE GIRL I LOVED —1910. This narrative poem originally was written for recitation with no thought of publication. The expression found in the last line, "a pair o' license," though unfamiliar to-day, was once, as Mr. Riley testifies, a phrase heard not infrequently in Hoosier dialect. The special edition of these verses, published in 1910, with the title, THE GIRL I LOVED, was dedicated to the author's friend, Mr. John J. Curtis.

AT NOEY'S HOUSE

This was the next poem to appear in print,—printed in part by *The Danbury News* (Conn.), April 8, 1874, with the title, *That Little Dorg*. It is included in *A Child World* in a later volume.

p. 40   MY JOLLY FRIEND'S SECRET

First printed in *The Danbury News,* May 23, 1874; hitherto unpublished in book form.

p. 43   THE SPEEDING OF THE KING'S SPITE

First printed in *The Danbury News,* July 18, 1874, with the title, *An Oriental Idyl;* published in THE FLYING ISLANDS OF THE NIGHT—1900, THE LOCKERBIE BOOK—1911. Originally the title was followed by this quotation from *Othello* (Act 1, Sc. 3, l. 160), " 'Twas strange, 'twas passing strange." The poem has been thoroughly revised since its first publication, and stanzas 9 and 10 have been added. The following stanza, inserted when the poem was printed in *The Indianapolis Journal,* December 26, 1877, was later omitted from the text:

> One bro't a bubble of molten pearls
> Atwirl of the gleaming wands
> Of a group of fairy dancing girls
> With moonbeams in their hands;
> And ever their eyes were upward flung,
> And ever their laughing lips
> Tangled the tune of the song they sung
> As they kissed their finger-tips.

p. 49   JOB WORK

First printed in *The Indianapolis People,* July 19, 1874; signed "Jay Whit"; hitherto unpublished in book form.

p. 51 PRIVATE THEATRICALS

First printed in *The Danbury News*, August 15, 1874, signed "Jay Whit"; hitherto unpublished in book form.

p. 53 PLAIN SERMONS

First printed in *The Danbury News*, August 22, 1874; signed "Jay Whit"; hitherto unpublished in book form.

THE BEAR STORY

This skit, which was recited by Mr. Riley at a social evening "for the little folks" in Roberts Park M. E. Church, Indianapolis, October 1, 1874, is included in *A Child World* in a later volume.

p. 54 "TRADIN' JOE"

First printed in *The Greenfield News*, December 2, 1874; published in POEMS HERE AT HOME— 1893. In *The Greenfield News* the following dedication was printed beneath the title: "To Will S. Otwell in token of genial friendship and mellow remembrances this is respectfully inscribed by the author." About this time Mr. Otwell and Mr. Riley were taking part together in small public entertainments. The poem was prepared for a recitation with no thought of later publication, and it was constructed to read as much like prose as possible. Since its first appearance many minor changes have been made.

In introducing this poem in his early lectures Mr. Riley said:

However dialectic expression may have been abused, cer-

tain it is that in no expression is there better opportunity
for the reproduction of pure nature. In artlessness of
construction the dialectic poem may attain even higher excellence than the more polished specimens of English. Its
great defect seems to be that as written or printed, the
real feeling it contains is overlooked by the reader in the
contemplation of its oddity That it is more widely copied
by the press than any other type of versification, I am inclined to think, is the result of a superficial regard for its
general abandon rather than a wholesome recognition of
its real worth, which, though always more than half buried
in the debris of rhetoric, is the more precious when un-
earthed. Hence it is that we are so tardy in admitting it
has any worth whatever, much less its very superior worth
of character and truthfulness to life.

And now, before leaving a theme which, to myself at
least, has for years been a source of infinite interest and
delight, I will ask you to bear with the narration of a story
from real life, in which I will depart from the original
form of the narration only as the rhythmical requirements
demand.

p. 59   DOT LEETLE BOY

Read at the Christmas entertainment of the Third
Presbyterian Church, Indianapolis, December 24,
1874; first printed in *The Indianapolis People,*
with the title, *Karl Schronzs' Christmas Story,*
January 1, 1876, signed "Jay Whit"; published in
GREEN FIELDS AND RUNNING BROOKS—1892. This
poem was one of Mr. Riley's earliest recitations
and from the first one of his most popular numbers.

p. 64   I SMOKE MY PIPE

First printed in *The Indianapolis Saturday Herald,* January 24, 1875, signed "Jay Whit"; published
in HIS PA'S ROMANCE (Homestead Edition)—1908,
THE LOCKERBIE BOOK—1911.

THE DREAMER

This was the next poem to appear in print, published in *Hearth and Home,* April 10, 1875. It is included in *A Child World* in a later volume.

p. 66 RED RIDING HOOD

First printed in *The Indianapolis Saturday Herald,* June 26, 1875, signed "Jay Whit"; published in HOME FOLKS—1900, THE LOCKERBIE BOOK—1911.

p. 67 IF I KNEW WHAT POETS KNOW

Composed about August, 1875; printed in *The Indianapolis Journal,* October 2, 1877; published in AFTERWHILES—1887, THE LOCKERBIE BOOK—1911. This is one of the very few poems which Mr. Riley composed rapidly. Ordinarily he worked late into the night and was satisfied if he finished a couple of lines that rang true. Often he continued the work enthusiastically, and wrote, and interlined, and erased, and rewrote, until at length perhaps a third or fourth satisfactory line was added, whereupon he became dimly conscious that the light of the morning sun was slanting through his window. *If I Knew What Poets Know* was not composed in the usual manner. "One forenoon when I was studying law in my father's office," says Mr. Riley, "I commenced writing this poem, but had great difficulty in getting it under way. While thrumming abstractedly with my pencil, the condition of my shoes attracted my attention, and I decided to go immediately and get them half-soled. So I got up, went to the door and down the stairway into the street, making directly for the shoemaker's across the way. I remember that the street was muddy, and how my feet sank into the yielding earth. When I reached the middle of the road, I stopped, turned about, retraced my steps to the office, sat down and then and there wrote the poem rapidly to its conclusion. Of course, I did have to labor at it. It didn't just make itself, and yet in a very short time it was finished—and I got the shoes fixed in the afternoon."

p. 68   AN OLD SWEETHEART OF MINE

Composed about August, 1875; printed in *The Indianapolis Journal,* March 12, 1877; published in PIPES O' PAN—1888, AN OLD SWEETHEART (lithographic edition)—1891, LOVE LYRICS—1899, AN OLD SWEETHEART OF MINE (Christy edition)— 1902, THE LOCKERBIE BOOK—1911. The special edition has the following dedication:

To GEORGE C. HITT

The beginning of whose steadfast friendship was marked by the first publication of these verses which now, expanded by writer, honored by publisher and masterfully graced by artist, seem to be a worthier symbol of the author's grateful and affectionate regard for his earliest friend.

The phrase "expanded by writer" refers to the fact that for the special edition Mr. Riley wrote seven new stanzas, numbers 1, 2, 3, 9, 10, 13 and 14.

St. 3, l. 3; the "churchwarden-stem" is a long white clay pipe, a tobacco fancier's delight.

This poem was written when Mr. Riley was supposedly reading law in the office of his father, who was ambitious that his son should follow the same profession. During Captain Riley's absence in court or elsewhere, while he thought the boy was studying law, the latter would open the desk drawer,

take out the unfinished manuscript and work over
it. He did not realize then that in *An Old Sweetheart of Mine* he had found a theme destined to
make an almost universal appeal. That these verses
were the result of the author's fancy and that he
had no particular person or instance in mind is the
answer Mr. Riley makes to a question very fre-
quently asked. Another interrogation often made,
whether he has ever married, is answered in the
negative. Again, and strange to say, the identity of
the wife with the sweetheart is sometimes doubted,
as in the case of a man who wrote that he and several friends were of opinion that the wife and
sweetheart were separate characters, whereas their
wives believed them to be the same, and accused
the men of "having no sentiment." On the lower
margin of this letter Mr. Riley wrote in reply:

> Dear Mister McGrew,
> I am sorry for you
>   Whilst I'm testifyin' agin you,—
> But the "wife" is wan part
> Wid the "Owld Sweetheart"—
>   An' ye have no sintiment in you!
>   Yours for the love o' love—an' glory be!
>   Jamesy O'Riley.
>
> Indianapolis, Ind.
> Aug. 13—an' bad luck to ye!—1903.

p. 73   SQUIRE HAWKINS'S STORY

Composed about August, 1875; printed in *The
Indianapolis Saturday Herald,* February 9, 1878;
published in POEMS HERE AT HOME—1893, special
edition entitled A HOOSIER ROMANCE—1910. When
Mr. Riley was studying law in his father's office,
this poem was composed with the advice and consul-
tation of his comrade, Jesse C. Millikan, to whom

the special edition was dedicated. It was prepared originally for a recitation. When he first read the verses in public, Mr. Riley did not claim them as his own but left it to be inferred that they were the work of another, since he thought the obscurity of his name would discredit them. On the title-page of the special edition of the poem the date "1868" follows the title, indicating that the story has its setting in the days immediately following the War. The country squire, at that period, was a character of kindly patriarchal influence in the community, rendering justice according to sound sense and often with a spice of humor. Mr. Riley knew several at Greenfield, such as Squire Joseph Wright, whom he says influenced him in developing the character of Squire Hawkins.

p. 85   A COUNTRY PATHWAY

Sent to Benj. S. Parker August 31, 1875; printed in *The Indianapolis Journal,* September 22, 1877; published in GREEN FIELDS AND RUNNING BROOKS —1892, FARM RHYMES—1901, SONGS OF SUMMER —1908, THE LOCKERBIE BOOK—1911. Stanzas 3 to 9, inclusive, do not appear in the early version, while the following stanza, not in the present text, formerly followed the fourth stanza from the last:

> And spreads a glowing landscape at my feet,—
>   An orchard and a vineyard, arm in arm,
> Drawn on a ground of green and gold—a sweet
>   Creation of a farm.

In addition to these alterations the body of the text has been thoroughly revised since its early composition.

p. 90 THE OLD GUITAR

Dated January 7, 1876; first printed in *The Indianapolis Sentinel,* January 9, 1876; published in HOME FOLKS—1900, SONGS OF HOME—1910, THE LOCKERBIE BOOK—1911.

p. 92 "FRIDAY AFTERNOON"

First printed in *The Indianapolis Sentinel,* January 30, 1876; published in HIS PA'S ROMANCE (Homestead Edition)—1908, special edition under the title, OLD SCHOOLDAY ROMANCES—1909, THE LOCKERBIE BOOK—1911. Stanzas 6, 7, 8, 10, 11 and 14 were added when the poem was published in book form. The body of the text has been revised throughout. Stanza 9 originally stood as follows:

> An "Essay of the Science
>   Of Trigonometry,"
> And "Cataline's Defiance,"
>   And may be two or three
> Short dialogues, and punny,
>   And a little boy in blue
> Winds up with something funny
>   Like "Cock-a-doodle-doo!"

When the verses were first written the following stanza, now omitted, closed the poem:

> O! happy hearts and faces,
>   On that great day's review,
> Will you all be in the places
>   That were assigned to you?
> Will you conquer life's disasters
>   And with golden harps atune,
> Wait the signal of the Master
>   On that Endless Afternoon?

These verses are true to the author's own experiences. Dr. William Morris Pierson, to whom the poem is dedicated, was a school comrade of the author during the years 1868-70. John Lacy was the "watchful master" of this period. The "Golden Wreath" song-book and the recitations were used time out of mind as described.

p. 97   "JOHNSON'S BOY"

Printed in *The Hancock Democrat* (Greenfield, Indiana), February 10, 1876, signed "Jay Whit"; hitherto unpublished in book form.

p. 99   HER BEAUTIFUL HANDS

First printed in *The Indianapolis Sentinel,* February 20, 1876, under the title, *Beautiful Hands;* published in a prose sketch, *The Gilded Roll,* in Pipes o' Pan—1888, His Pa's Romance—1903, Songs of Home—1910, The Lockerbie Book—1911.

p. 101   NATURAL PERVERSITIES

Printed in *The Indianapolis Sentinel,* March 26, 1876, with the title, *Lusus Naturae;* published in Armazindy—1894, Songs of Home—1910.

p. 104   THE SILENT VICTORS

Read May 30, 1876, at Newcastle, Indiana; last eight stanzas printed in *The Newcastle Mercury,* June 1, 1876; poem entire printed with the title, *The Bivouac of the Dead* in *The Anderson Democrat,* June 1, 1877; published in Armazindy—1894, The Lockerbie Book—1911. On May 30, 1878, the author read the poem at the Decoration Day ex-

ercises held at Crown Hill Cemetery, Indianapolis.
Since then, the dedication to his friend and literary
comrade, Major Charles L. Holstein, has been
added, and many changes made in the text. The
following stanza, which ended the first section in
the early version, is omitted from the later:

And lives that bound themselves in strongest chain
  Were severed, and the broken links of love
In fragments now must evermore remain
  Until rejoined above.

Stanza 4 of Section 2 formerly read as follows:

The noisy hum of industry and thrift
  That marks the newer day that peace has blessed,
Can give no hope the hero's head to lift
  Out of its dreamless rest.

Mr. Riley wrote this poem when studying law in
the office of his father, who had been a captain in
the Union Army. The stirring echoes of the Civil
War were still reverberating through the land at
that time, and Captain Riley, who was a natural
orator, was called for on repeated occasions to
make patriotic speeches. Doubtless the fervor of
this environment produced the poem.

The writer valued as an honor and encouragement the invitation to read the verses at the Newcastle Decoration Day exercises in 1876, extended
through his friends, Benj. S. Parker and Judge
Eugene Bundy. In this incident is shown Mr.
Parker's early recognition of Mr. Riley's poetic
gift, and the kind of encouragement he tendered.

p. 110   SCRAPS

First printed in *The Newcastle Mercury,* June
8, 1876; hitherto unpublished in book form. The

editor of this paper was the author's friend, Benj. S. Parker.

p. 112 AUGUST

Composed during August, 1876; first printed in *The Indianapolis Journal,* August 14, 1877; published in GREEN FIELDS AND RUNNING BROOKS —1892, SONGS OF SUMMER—1908, THE LOCKERBIE BOOK—1911. While writing this poem and several others, the author availed himself of the counsel of Captain Lee O. Harris, who had been his favorite teacher. The reference recalls a significant incident of the schoolroom, where Captain Harris once "caught" the boy Riley reading a dime novel during the study period. The latter had ingeniously fastened a rubber band to the book and this whisked it quickly out of sight when the book was released by his thumb. His teacher told him that if he was so determined to read he would select his reading for him, and promptly introduced him to his own library and interested him in Dickens, Longfellow, Tennyson and other standard authors. Captain Harris wrote poetry himself, and so the two came to have an intimate mutual interest.

p. 114 DEAD IN SIGHT OF FAME

Dated September 5, 1876, first printed in *The Hancock Democrat,* September 7, 1876; hitherto unpublished in book form. These lines were written on the death of Hamilton J. Dunbar, a member of the law firm of Dunbar and New, of Greenfield, Indiana, who was a strong personality with keen literary perceptions and appreciations. He was one of the first to give Mr. Riley real encouragement in his work, and the latter held him as an ideal. Judge J. W. Lowe, of Kansas City, says of him: "I believe he had the most brilliant intellect I ever met. He was one of those rare creatures so seldom encountered who walks tenderly by our side, reciprocates our regards, and seems to comprehend and understand us thoroughly, and makes us feel that his soul was created in the same mould. He was a brilliant force in politics and was one of the most ready and inspired orators to be found anywhere. I believed, when I knew him, and believe still, that if he had lived, by this time he would have been one of the great leaders in our national life." Following his death, a memorial meeting of the Hancock County Bar Association was held in his honor, at which time addresses were made by various members and by visiting attorneys of distinction from the Indianapolis bar. On this occasion Mr. Riley read the poem.

p. 116   IN THE DARK

Composed prior to November, 1876; first printed in *The Indianapolis Journal,* March 16, 1877; published in PIPES O' PAN—1888, THE LOCKERBIE BOOK—1911. The following stanzas completed the poem in the original version but have since been omitted:

> I moan with a passionate yearning,
>   And a flood of hopes and fears
> Flows o'er the troubled spirit,
>   And ebbs in a tide of tears.
>
> The gleam of a star through the window
>   Falls like a soothing touch;
> And darkness wears to the dawning
>   For which I long so much.
>
> The dawn when the sun shall ripen
>   The soul in its genial light,
> And banish the tears like the dewdrops
>   That cling to the fruit at night.

In the fall of 1876, when Mr. Riley was much discouraged in his literary ambitions and felt that after all there might be no success or recognition for his poetry, he wrote to Longfellow and enclosed several of his poems, including this one written in a style reminiscent of Longfellow's. The letter of encouragement which he received in reply proved a turning point in his life. He describes the effect upon him in the following letter to Benj. S. Parker:

Greenfield, Ind., Nov. 6, 1876.

Dear Parker:

I'm in a perfect hurricane of delight, and must erupt to you, "O gentlest of my friends." I sent you a postal recently stating my intention of addressing Longfellow—well—his response to my letter lies open before me, and as it is brief, I will quote it verbatim:—

"Cambridge, Nov. 3d, 1876.

My dear Sir:

Not being in the habit of criticising the production of others, I can not enter into any minute discussion of the merits of the poems you send me.

I can only say in general terms, that I have read them with great pleasure, and think they show the true poetic faculty and insight.

The only criticism I shall make is on your use of the word *prone* in the thirteenth line of "Destiny." Prone means face-downward. You meant to say *supine* as the context shows.

I return the printed pieces as you may want them for future use, and am, My dear Sir,

With all good wishes,
Yours very truly
Henry W. Longfellow."

SHAKE! And let me thank *you* for the very great encouragement I have received from you, and your genial friendship from our first acquaintance. . . .

J. W. Riley.

The poem *Destiny* mentioned by Longfellow appears in A CHILD-WORLD with the title of *The*

Dreamer. Other poems sent to Longfellow at this time were *If I Knew What Poets Know* and *The Iron Horse.* He returned the verses clipped from newspapers, but retained the manuscript of *In the Dark.*

p. 118 THE IRON HORSE

Written prior to November, 1876; dated July 11, 1878, first printed in *The Indianapolis Journal,* July 13, 1878; published in GREEN FIELDS AND RUNNING BROOKS—1892, THE LOCKERBIE BOOK—1911. This poem was enclosed in the letter to Longfellow, mentioned in the previous note. It was always a favorite of Mr. Riley.

p. 121 DEAD LEAVES

First printed in *The Newcastle Mercury,* November 16, 1876, under the caption *Three Sonnets to Autumn,* subtitled *Morning, Evening, Night; Morning* (now entitled *Dawn*) and *Night,* hitherto unpublished in book form; *Evening* (now entitled *Dusk*) published in AFTERWHILES—1887, OLD-FASHIONED ROSES—1888, THE LOCKERBIE BOOK—1911.

p. 123 OVER THE EYES OF GLADNESS

Dated November 20, 1876, printed in *The Hancock Democrat,* November 23, 1876; hitherto unpublished in book form. Katie Beecher, infant daughter of Frederick and California Beecher, died at Greenfield, November 18, 1876. The public announcement read:

She was a bright and promising child, and her loss will be felt the keener that she was one of twin daughters,

414 *NOTES*

upon whom was lavished the love and interest of the
fondest of parents.

p. 125 ONLY A DREAM

Dated November 23, 1876; hitherto unpublished.

p. 127 OUR LITTLE GIRL

First printed in *The Hancock Democrat,* December 7, 1876; published in Morning—1907, The
Lockerbie Book—1911. *The Hancock Democrat*
of December 7, 1876, contained the following notice:—"DIED.—Minnie, infant daughter of William
and Catherine Crider, Tuesday, Dec. 5, 1876, at
Franklin, Ind. In her last moments she said: 'O,
Dod, I tan't stan' dis.'" The tragic incident suggested a poem which Mr. Riley called *Minnie.*
Later, giving it the present title, he rearranged it,
placing the second stanza first and writing an entirely new stanza in place of the last, which was:

> And yet she failed and faltered;
>   And though tears are in our eyes,
> We smile to think her spirit
>   Went lisping to the skies;
> For we know—in Christ believing—
>   Lips are ripest for His kiss,
> When in simplest faith they murmur,
>   "O, Dod, I tan't stan' dis."

p. 128 THE FUNNY LITTLE FELLOW

Quoted in Mr. Riley's letter of December 12,
1876, to Benj. S. Parker; printed in *The Indianapolis Journal,* April 13, 1877; published in
Rhymes of Childhood—1890, Child Rhymes—
1898, The Lockerbie Book—1911. The poem was

originally entitled *The Funny Fellow*. Lines 5 to
8, inclusive, of the second stanza were:

> And to hear him snap the trigger
> Of a pun, or crack a joke,
> Would make you laugh and snigger
> Till every button broke.

In the early version the following lines were inserted between stanzas 1 and 2:

> He was meek as any Quaker—
> When it furthered fun's desire—
> Solemn as an undertaker
> If occasion should require:
> He could wreathe his rosy features
> With a sorrowful belief,
> And lead all weeping creatures
> To the very tomb of Grief.

Mr. Riley's letter to Benj. S. Parker referring to
this poem is quoted in part as follows:

Greenfield, Ind. - - Dec. 12, '76.

My dear Parker:
. . . I have illustrated a *serio-humorous* poem, and sent,
for inspection, to Scribner's. I'm certain my illustrations
are as good as the average, found in Bric-a-Brac of that
Monthly—both in design and drawing, and I tho't 'twould
be a good idea to combine both poet and artist—as such
an article will be the more likely to attract the Editor's
attention—don't you think so? I have heard nothing in
reply as yet. I addressed them, asking their patronage,
and backing my ability with my Longfellow letter—so you
can imagine how anxiously I am awaiting their reply. In
the poem I sent are several little touches *you* would like I
am sure—yet the poem as a whole is not deep by any
means. I quote the first two verses that you may see the
style.

[Quotation]

Well! you must pardon my brevity, for I am very busy—
sign painting—I wonder am I destined to succeed T. Bu-

chanan Reid in that title "The Painter Poet." Ha! Ha! Ha! I'm sorry, too, I cannot come to you during the Holidays—nothing would please better, and as to *pay*—I wouldn't want it—only your *companionship*.

Your friend,
J. W. Riley.

Scribner's Magazine did not publish the poem.

p. 131   SONG OF THE NEW YEAR

Dated January 1, 1877, printed in *The Indianapolis Journal,* January 10, 1877; hitherto unpublished in book form.

p. 133   A LETTER TO A FRIEND

Dated Greenfield, January 11, 1877; hitherto unpublished. The letter was addressed to Mrs. Nellie Millikan Cooley, an old friend, who had moved from Greenfield to Illinois. She and her brother, Jesse Millikan, were among Mr. Riley's earliest literary comrades and advisers, and from the first had a firm faith in his ultimate success.

p. 134   LINES FOR AN ALBUM

These lines are found in an album belonging to Miss Lizzie Harris, of Greenfield, Indiana, dated January, 1877; hitherto unpublished. They were written when Mr. Riley was visiting in the home of Miss Harris's father, Captain Lee O. Harris.

Line 8: The quotation is from Longfellow's *The Rainy Day.*

p. 135   TO ANNIE

Written in Miss Annie Harris's album January 21, 1877; not hitherto printed. See preceding note, referring to the inscription in her sister's album.

p. 136   FAME

First printed in *The Earlhamite,* the magazine
of Earlham College, February, 1877; published in
THE BOSS GIRL—1885, AFTERWHILES—1887, OLD-
FASHIONED ROSES—1888, SKETCHES IN PROSE—
1891, THE LOCKERBIE BOOK—1911. Of all his
poems, this was the favorite of the writer's father.
It won this significant public comment in *The Richmond Telegram:*

The February number of *The Earlhamite* is out, with
a table of contents of unusual excellence. The initial
paper is a poem by J. W. Riley (a Hoosier poet unknown
to fame), which betrays the touch of genius in every line.

p. 139   AN EMPTY NEST

Dated Greenfield, February 5, 1877, first printed
in *The Indianapolis Journal,* February 7, 1877;
published in MORNING—1907. The original version
of the poem ended in the following stanza which
was later omitted:

> O weary, palpitating breast!
> The friends we think are ours alone,
> And cherish most, and love the best,
> Will fly as soon as wings have grown,
> And leave the heart an empty nest.

p. 140   MY FATHER'S HALLS

First printed in *The Indianapolis Journal,* Feb-
ruary 16, 1877, in the prose sketch, *A Remarkable
Man;* published in SKETCHES IN PROSE—1891.
An imitation of Cervantes.

p. 141   THE HARP OF THE MINSTREL

First printed in *The Indianapolis Journal,* February 16, 1877, in the prose sketch, *A Remarkable*

Man; published in SKETCHES IN PROSE—1891. An imitation of Thomas Moore.

p. 143 HONEY DRIPPING FROM THE COMB

First printed in *The Indianapolis Journal* with the title, *A Whisper,* February 22, 1877; published in RHYMES OF CHILDHOOD—1890, SONGS OF HOME—1910, THE LOCKERBIE BOOK—1911. As indicated by a torn manuscript, the first two stanzas given below, and at least one other, preceded stanzas 1 and 2 in the original form of this poem, and the remaining stanzas given below and two others, too mutilated to read, completed it:

> And gaily spangled days of shade and shine,
>   With evenings in costume
> Of dusk and diamonds—under veils divine
>   Of moonlight, with perfume
>
> Of Locust blossoms dowering the sigh
>   Of drowsy breezes with a wealth that brings
> So deft a memory its ghost flits by
>   Me now on odorous wings.
>
> .   .   .   .   .   .   pictures creep
>   Past the proscenium Remembrance:—
> Two barefoot boys, on Mischief's Mission, leap
>   Over an orchard fence—
>
> And here a study from a summer noon,—
>   Are clinging in a swinging tree-top's crown
> Two hatless boys, drunk with the air of June,
>   Drawn on a golden ground;
>
> And here another—of an old schoolroom,—
>   A rueful urchin cowers 'neath the rod—
> Could we rehearse it and enjoy the doom?—
>   Give back my paper wad!
>
> Ah! Schoolboy chum, *your* victory it was
>   When deepest in disgrace, enthroned "the
>   Dunce"—

Compelled to "stay in" two whole weeks because
  You flogged, at recess, once,

The preacher's boy—I loved you all the more,

            °   •   °

If they be foolish, why this old heart warms
  With holy fire the while with upturned gaze,
Grasping at Heaven with poor, palsied arms,
  I bless the Good old Days.—

Aye! bless these memories of ours, old Chum!
  God keep them ever green while spared us, and
Like little children suffer us to come
  Into the Perfect Land!

p. 144   JOHN WALSH

This poem was printed on the funeral announcement of John Walsh and dated Greenfield, February 23, 1877; hitherto unpublished in book form. John Walsh was born in Limerick County, Ireland, in the twenties of the last century and came to America when a youth. When he reached Greenfield he had just money enough to buy a maul to use in splitting timber. He was lucky at everything he undertook, and was by turns a stock-buyer, a butcher and finally a saloon-keeper. He was conspicuous for the kindness of his heart and for his open generosity. He died February 23, 1877. The verses were written to comfort his son James, a friend of the author.

p. 146   ORLIE WILDE

Dated Anderson, April 18, 1877, first printed in *The Indianapolis Journal*, April 19, 1877; published in ARMAZINDY—1894, THE LOCKERBIE BOOK —1911. Since its first appearance the poem has been revised throughout. The following lines, which formerly ended the poem, have been omitted:

> He sadly smiled, and raised his head,
> And in this vein continued:
> "I said 'her voice's music'—well
> 'Twas that indeed that broke the spell
> Of my strange love, for listening—Lo!
> She spoke bad grammar, don't you know—
> As fisher maidens always do,
> With golden hair and eyes of blue.

p. 154   THAT OTHER MAUD MULLER

First printed in *The Anderson Democrat,* April 27, 1877; hitherto unpublished in book form. *The Cincinnati Commercial* of December 26, 1877, printed the verses in an article entitled *The Literary Doings of the Stuffed Club,* a humorous sketch of the first and only meeting of an organization composed of "Larry, Jack and the Jaywhoop" (Captain Lee O. Harris, Mr. J. M. Anderson and Mr. Riley):

The name was given by the Jay-whoop, who says, "Since the public is to be the helpless victim of our atrocities, it behooves us to employ a weapon that will buffet but not bruise—belt but not mangle—knock down, but with a certain modesty that produces annihilation—"

As an encouragement to the venerated "John G. Whittaker" the Jay-whoop read the following little ballad. . . . . [The verses follow.]

After listening to the poem that had fallen like a blight upon the circle, the club next took up the pernicious habit of pie eating, and Larry read an original poem, *Joseph Brown and the Mince Pie.*

Then they rose, joined hands, sang a hymn, pronounced a sad and solemn benison upon each other and folded their ears like the members of other clubs,

"And silently stole away."

p. 156   A MAN OF MANY PARTS

Printed in *The Anderson Democrat,* May 7, 1877; hitherto unpublished in book form.

p. 158   THE FROG

First printed in *The Anderson Democrat,* May 18, 1877; published in ARMAZINDY—1894, THE LOCKERBIE BOOK—1911. In ARMAZINDY these verses introduce a section called *Make-Believe and Child-Play.*

p. 160   DEAD SELVES

Dated Anderson, May 21, 1877, first printed in *The Indianapolis Journal,* May 22, 1877; published in POEMS HERE AT HOME—1893, THE LOCKERBIE BOOK—1911.

p. 163   A DREAM OF LONG AGO

Dated Anderson, May 28, 1877, first printed in *The Indianapolis Journal,* June 1, 1877; hitherto unpublished in book form. The fact that the melody is reminiscent of Poe is significant, as it indicates what the writer was reading at the time. See the note on *Leonainie* referring to p. 194.

p. 166   CRAQUEODOOM

First printed in *The Anderson Democrat,* June 1, 1877; published in NYE AND RILEY'S RAILWAY GUIDE—1888, THE FLYING ISLANDS OF THE NIGHT —1900. In the latter book the verses are entitled *Spirk Troll-Derisive* and appear in a section called *Spirk and Wunk Rhymes, Rounds and Catches.* The second stanza is there omitted and the lines altered by several curious repetitions to enhance the weirdness of the effect.

A questioning newspaper criticism of this poem and Mr. Riley's reply are as follows:

The weird lines by the gifted J. W. Riley, of *The Anderson Democrat,* contain a mystery that we have tried in vain for one solid hour to solve. What do they mean? Will the author be kind enough to favor us with an explanation? He calls it *Craqueodoom,* but the meaning of the title itself is as obscure as that of the poetry that supplements it. We have read and reread it a score of times and for the life of us we can't get an idea out of it, only that it is the most weird piece of poetic thought we have ever read. It reads like an effusion of some poetic genius of the fabled age, in which "Mother Goose" wrote her melodies.—*Kokomo Dispatch.*

———

Although in endeavoring to reply to the above query I feel that I place myself in rather a peculiar position, I can but trust, in so doing, to escape the incessant storm of inquiries hailed so piteously upon me since the appearance of the above mentioned poem—or whatever it is.

As to its meaning—if it has any—I am as much in the dark, and as badly worried over its incomprehensibility as any one who may have inflicted himself with a reading of it; in fact, more so, for I have in my possession now not less than a dozen of similar character; and when I say they were only composed mechanically, and without apparent exercise of my own thought, I find myself at the threshold of a fact over which I can not pass.

I can only surmise that such effusions emanate from long and arduous application—a sort of poetic fungus that springs from the decay of better effort. It bursts into being of itself, and in that alone do I find consolation.

The process of such composition may furnish a curious fact to many, yet I am assured every writer of either poetry or music will confirm the experience I am about to relate.

After long labor at verse, you will find there comes a time when everything you see or hear, touch, taste, or smell, resolves itself into rhyme, and rattles away till you can't rest. I mean this literally. The people you meet upon the streets are so many disarranged rhymes, and only need proper coupling. The boulders in the sidewalks are jangled words. The crowd of corner loungers is a mangled sonnet with a few lines lacking; the farmer and his team an idyl of the road, perfected and complete when he stops at the picture of a grocery and hitches to an exclamation point.

This is my experience and at times the effect upon both mind and body is exhausting in the extreme. I have passed as many as three nights in succession without sleep —or at least without mental respite from this tireless something which

> "Beats time to nothing in my head
> From some odd corner of the brain."

I walk, I run, I writhe and wrestle with it, but I can not shake it off. I lie down to sleep, and all night long it haunts me. Whole cantos of incoherent rhymes dance before me, and so vividly at last, I seem to read them as from a book. All this is without will power of my own to guide or check; and then occurs a stage of repetition— when the matter becomes rhythmically tangible at least, and shapes itself into a whole of sometimes a dozen stanzas, and goes on repeating itself over and over till it is printed indelibly on my mind.

This stage heralds sleep at last, from which I wake refreshed and free from the toils of my strange persecutor; but as I have just said, some senseless piece of rhyme is printed on my mind and I go about repeating it as though I had committed it from the pages of some book. I often write these jingles afterward, though I believe I never could forget a word of them.

This is the history of the *Craqueodoom*. This is the history of the poem I give below [*A Wrangdillion*]. I have theorized in vain. I went gravely to a doctor on one occasion, and asked him seriously if he didn't think I was crazy. His laconic reply that he "never saw a poet that wasn't!" is not without its consolations.

p. 168 **JUNE**

Composed probably during June, 1877, as shown by a note-book in the handwriting of Mr. Riley's sister, Elva Riley Eitel; published in AFTER-

WHILES — 1887, OLD-FASHIONED ROSES — 1888,
FARM RHYMES—1901, SONGS OF SUMMER—1908,
DOWN AROUND THE RIVER AND OTHER POEMS—
1911, THE LOCKERBIE BOOK—1911.

p. 169   WASH LOWRY'S REMINISCENCE

Printed in *The Anderson Democrat,* June 15,
1877; hitherto unpublished in book form.

p. 173   THE ANCIENT PRINTERMAN

Printed in *The Anderson Democrat,* June 22 or
July 6, 1877, the issues of which dates have been
destroyed; hitherto unpublished in book form.

p. 175   PRIOR TO MISS BELLE'S APPEARANCE

First printed in *The Anderson Democrat,* June
22 or July 6, 1877, the issues of which dates have
been destroyed, entitled *Willie;* published in
RHYMES OF CHILDHOOD—1890. Stanzas 2, 3, 4 and
6 composed the early version; stanza 4 originally
read:

> Baby's a funnies' feller!
>   Naint no hair on her head—
> Is they, Charley?—it's meller
> Wite up there! I'd sell her,
>   An' buy one 'at wasn't so red—
> Wouldn't you, Charley? Nen we could play
> An' have most fun with him every day—
> Couldn't we, Charley?—an' have most fun.
> Wisht they'd a buyed a purtier one!

p. 178   WHEN MOTHER COMBED MY HAIR

Printed in *The Anderson Democrat,* June 22 or
July 6, 1877, the issues of which dates have been
destroyed; hitherto unpublished in book form.

p. 180   A WRANGDILLION

First printed in *The Anderson Democrat,* July
6, 1877; published in THE FLYING ISLANDS OF THE
NIGHT—1900. In the latter the lines appear in a
section entitled *Spirk and Wunk Rhymes, Rounds
and Catches,* where the third stanza is omitted and
this chorus added:

Nay, nothing—Nay, nothing affects him the least!
They may say he sings less like a bird than a beast—
They may say that his song is both patchy and pieced—
That its worst may be his, but the best he has fleeced
From old dinky masters not only deceased
But damn'd ere their dying,—Yet nothing the least—
        Nothing affects him the least!

See preceding note on *Craqueodoom* for comment
by Mr. Riley.

p. 182   GEORGE MULLEN'S CONFESSION

First printed in *The Anderson Democrat,* July
13, 1877; hitherto unpublished in book form.

p. 191   "TIRED OUT"

First printed in *The Anderson Democrat,* July
20, 1877; hitherto unpublished in book form. Beneath the title originally appeared this quotation
from a newspaper:

Pinned to the shawl of the drowned woman was a scrap
of paper on which was written simply the words, "Tired
Out." There was nothing else found upon the body that
might promise to lead to its identity.

p. 192   HARLIE

First printed in *The Anderson Democrat,* July

20, 1877; hitherto unpublished in book form. Harlie was the infant son of Samuel and Louise Richards and died July 17, 1877. Mrs. Richards, in an article on Mr. Riley's days at Anderson published in *The Bookman,* September, 1904, writes as fol·· lows about the composition of this poem:

The death of Richards' boy made upon Riley one of the deep impressions of his life. For the first time he found himself one of the bearers of a funeral bier; for the first time he could not speak to his friend of what was in his heart. But a few days later these lines, dedicated to a child and simply signed "R," appeared in the town paper.

p. 193   SAY SOMETHING TO ME

Dated Anderson, August 1, 1877, first printed in *The Indianapolis Journal,* August 5, 1877; published in Home Folks—1900, The Lockerbie Book—1911. The last three lines of the poem formerly were:

> And the whole world from above
> I could fling down like the crown of a king
> To nestle away in your love.

p. 194   LEONAINIE

First printed in *The Kokomo Dispatch,* August 2, 1877, signed "E. A. P."; published in Armazindy— 1894, Love Lyrics—1899, The Lockerbie Book— 1911. The occasion of this poem was a county newspaper hoax which to the astonishment and discomfort of its author grew to national proportions and met with such success as to deceive the best critics in America. Its perpetration was suggested by the criticism of an editor on *The Anderson Herald,* who rather heartlessly advised Mr. Riley to give up poetry and spoke disparagingly in the

paper and to him personally of his serious verse.
Annoyed by this man's criticism and by the return of manuscripts from magazines, a circum-
stance this editor cited to back up his opinion, Mr.
Riley devised a plan to win recognition in disguise.
This was to write a poem in imitation of a well-
known author and submit it to his unthinking critics
as a newly discovered manuscript. A friend, the
editor of *The Kokomo Dispatch,* undertook to
launch the hoax in his paper. Mr. Riley had prepared after much thought an elaborate introduction
which, however, the editor altered to make it the
more real. The original introductory story as re-
produced by Mrs. Samuel Richards, wife of Mr.
Riley's artist comrade in Anderson, was as follows:

In the woods of Howard County, Indiana, a belated
hunter, whom the editor was to represent as himself, had
lost his way. A terrific storm broke forth, and as he
wandered about in the drenching rain and pitchy darkness, a faint light suddenly appeared in the distance.
Guided by its flickering, he made his way toward it, which
brought him to a cave-like opening in the side of a hill.
(The Kokomo editor claims there isn't a hill in Howard
County big enough for a prairie-dog to hide in.)
Upon peering into the cavern, he saw a misshapen,
hunchbacked dwarf preparing his evening meal over
some coals heaped together on the earth floor. The hunter
asked for shelter from the storm, which the gnome-like
creature only half granted.
In this hermit's room there was a three-legged stool and
a rickety table upon which was an old book. The hunter,
curiously turning over the leaves, espied on a fly-leaf the
lines of a poem, evidently written a long while ago, and
signed E. A. P. On being questioned, the little figure of
a man, hitherto as uncommunicative as a sphinx, suddenly became alert, and told how it came to be written in
his grandfather's inn in Virginia.

The editor of *The Kokomo Dispatch* changed this
romantic introduction but left the remainder of the

story substantially as written by Mr. Riley, printing it with the poem in his issue of August 2, 1877, as follows:

POSTHUMOUS POETRY

A HITHERTO UNPUBLISHED POEM OF THE LAMENTED EDGAR
ALLAN POE—WRITTEN ON THE FLY-LEAF OF AN
OLD BOOK NOW IN POSSESSION OF A
GENTLEMEN OF THIS CITY

The following beautiful posthumous poem from the gifted pen of the erratic poet, Edgar Allan Poe, we believe has never before been published in any form, either in any published collection of Poe's poems now extant, or in any magazine or newspaper of any description; and until the critics shall show conclusively to the contrary, *The Dispatch* shall claim the honor of giving it to the world.

That the poem has never before been published, and that it is a genuine production of the poet whom we claim to be its author, we are satisfied from the circumstances under which it came into our possession, after a thorough investigation. Calling at the house of a gentleman of this city the other day, on a business errand, our attention was called to a poem written on the blank fly-leaf of an old book. Handing us the book he observed that it (the poem) might be good enough to publish, and that if we thought so, to take it along. Noticing the initials E. A. P. at the bottom of the poem, it struck us that possibly we had run across a "bonanza," so to speak, and after reading it, we asked who its author was, when he related the following bit of interesting reminiscence: He said he did not know who the author was, only that he was a young man, that is, he was a young man when he wrote the lines referred to. He had never seen him himself, but heard his grandfather, who gave him the book containing the verses, tell of the circumstances and the occasion by which he, the grandfather, came into possession of the book. His grandparents kept a country hotel, a sort of a wayside inn, in a small village called Chesterfield, near Richmond, Va. One night, just before bedtime, a young man, who showed plainly the marks of dissipation, rapped at the door and asked if he could stay all night, and was shown to a room. This was the last they saw of him. When they went to his room the next morning to call him to breakfast he had gone away and left the book, on the fly-leaf of which he had written the lines given below.

Further than this our informant knew nothing, and being an uneducated, illiterate man, it was quite natural that he should allow the great literary treasure to go for so many years unpublished.

That the above statement is true, and our discovery no canard, we will take pleasure in satisfying any one who cares to investigate the matter. The poem is written in Roman characters, and is almost as legible as print itself, although somewhat faded by the lapse of time. Another peculiarity in the manuscript which we notice is that it contains not the least sign of erasure or a single interlineated word. We give the poem verbatim—just as it appears in the original.

The editor of *The Anderson Herald* fell an easy victim to the hoax, and copying *Leonainie* from *The Kokomo Dispatch* commented as follows:

We expect a rhapsody of jealous censure from the jingling editor of the sheet across the way, and shall wait with the first anxiety ever experienced for the appearance of *The Democrat*. We look for an exhausting and damning criticism from Riley, who will doubtless fail to see "Leonainie's" apocryphal merit, and discover its obvious faults. As it is, we are led to believe *Leonainie*, to quote from Riley, is a "superior quality of the poetical fungus, which springs from the decay of better thoughts."

The "jingling editor," of course, rose to the occasion by reproducing the poem with copious comment, containing this "jealous censure":

We frankly admit that upon first reading the article, we inwardly resolved not to be startled; in fact we inwardly resolved to ignore it entirely; but a sense of justice due—if not to Poe, to the poem—has induced us to let slip a few remarks.

We have given the matter not a little thought; and in what we shall have to say regarding it, we will say with purpose far superior to prejudicial motives, and with the earnest effort of beating through the gloom a pathway to the light of truth.

Passing the many assailable points of the story regarding the birth and late discovery of the poem, we will briefly consider first—*Is Poe the author of it?*

That a poem contains some literary excellence is no assurance that its author is a genius known to fame, for how many waifs of richest worth are now afloat upon the literary sea whose authors are unknown, and whose nameless names have never marked the graves that hid their value from the world; and in the present instance we have no right to say,—"This is *Poe's* work—for who but Poe could mold a name like *Leonainie?* and all that sort of flighty flummery. Let us look deeper down, and pierce below the glare and gurgle of the surface, and analyze it at its real worth.

Now we are ready to consider,—Is the *theme* of the poem one that Poe would have been likely to select? We think not; for we have good authority showing that Poe had a positive aversion to children, and especially to babies. And then again, the thought embodied in the very opening line is not new—or at least the poet has before expressed it where he speaks of that "rare and radiant maiden whom the angels name Lenore," and a careful analysis of the remainder of the stanza fails to discover a single quality above mere change of form or transposition.

The second verse will be a more difficult matter to contest; for we find in it throughout not only Poe's peculiar bent of thought, but new features of that weird facility of attractively combining with the delicate and beautiful, the dread and repulsive—a power most rarely manifest, and quite beyond the bounds of *imitation*. In fact, the only flaw we find at which to pick, is the strange omission of capitals beginning the personified words "joy" and "doom." This, however, may be an error of the compositor's, but not probably.

The third stanza drops again. True, it gives us some new thoughts, but of very secondary worth compared with the foregoing, and in such commonplace diction the Poe-characteristic is almost directly lost.

The first line of the concluding stanza, although embodying a highly poetical idea, is not at all like Poe; but rather so *unlike,* and for such weighty reasons we are almost assured that the thought could not have emanated with him.

It is a fact less known than remarkable that Poe avoided the name of the Deity. Although he never tires of angels and the heavenly cherubim, the word God seems strangely ostracized. That this is true, one has but to search his poems; and we feel we are safe in the assertion that in all that he has ever written the word God is not mentioned twenty times. In further evidence of this peculiar aversion of the poet's we quote his utterance,—

"Oh, Heaven! oh, God!

How my heart beats in coupling these two words!"
The remainder of the concluding verse is mediocre till the few lines that complete it—and there again the Poe-element is strongly marked.

To sum the poem as a whole we are at some loss. It most certainly contains rare attributes of grace and beauty; and although we have not the temerity to accuse the gifted Poe of its authorship, for equal strength of reason we can not deny that it is his production; but as for the enthusiastic editor of *The Dispatch,* we are not inclined, as yet, to the belief that he is wholly impervious to the wiles of deception.

Thereupon the editor of *The Herald* congratulated himself on his predictions fulfilled. "True to our prognostication of last week," he said, "J. W. Riley, editor of *The Democrat,* slashes into *Leonainie* in a jealous manner." An entire column was devoted to Mr. Riley's reception of the poem.

The author's own account of the writing of the verses is contained in a letter, dated November 22, 1886, to C. B. Foote, a book collector, who had come into possession of the old Ainsworth dictionary in which the poem had been transcribed in facsimile of Poe's handwriting. Both the letter and the dictionary are now in the possession of Mr. Paul Lemperly, of Cleveland, Ohio.

Regarding the authorship of the poem, "Leonainie," I can claim the poem only—the autographic copy which your letter describes—its original, at least—was executed (at my instigation, and with equally boyish unconsciousness of guilt) by an artist friend of mine, now wearing first honors in the Art Schools of Munich [Samuel Richards]. He did his work well, and was thus the author of the best part of the poem. He worked then as he works now; —straight from the heart. He had only a line or two of Poe-facsimile to "inspire" from but some way the fellow caught the spirit of the whole vocabulary from it, furnishing a result that many notable and most exacting critics were bewildered by, as I myself saw tested many times.

It is but just to all concerned, for the better understanding of the real facts of the case, to speak further, though with you now I will be as brief as possible:—The poem was written about twelve years ago in the town of Anderson, Ind., while I was a very callow writer on The Democrat, of that place; and, being rallied to desperation over the weekly appearance of my namby-pamby verses, by the editor of a rival sheet, I devised the Poe-poem fraud simply to prove, if possible, that like critics of verse would praise, from a notable source what they did not hesitate to condemn, from an emanation opposite. By correspondence (still preserved) the friendly editor of a paper (The Kokomo, Ind., Dispatch—still conducted by same Ed.) assisted me in foisting the hoax on the public through his columns—this for reasons obvious; while to still further conceal the real authorship of the poem, as soon as published with its editorial hurrah, I attacked its claimed worth and authenticity in my paper. Then every one who knew me, knew, of course, I didn't write a rhyme of it. And so it went—and went—and kept on going—till at last the necessary exposé. Papers everywhere lit into me—friends read all this, and stood aside—went round the other way. The paper upon which I gained the meager living that was mine excused me—and no other paper wanted such a man—and wouldn't even let me print a card of explanation—not for weeks, while I stood outside alone, and walked around the Court House square at night, and through the drizzle and the rain peered longingly at the dim light in the office where I used to sleep, with a heart as hard and dark and obdurate as the towel in the composing-room. All of which is smiling material now, but then it was pathos from a-way back!

p. 196   A TEST OF LOVE

First printed in *The Anderson Democrat,* August 3, 1877; hitherto unpublished in book form.

p. 198   FATHER WILLIAM

First printed in *The Indianapolis Saturday Herald,* September 22, 1877, dated Greenfield, September, 1877, signed "Harrison Driley"; hitherto unpublished in book form. In this parody Mr. Riley wrote the questions and Captain Lee O. Harris the answers. The verses suggest the days when the former visited the latter at his home in Lewisville, near Greenfield, and discussed literature and read with him until far into the night. Lewis Carroll was a favorite author on these evenings.

p. 200   WHAT THE WIND SAID

First printed in *The Kokomo Dispatch* a few days prior to October 5, 1877; published in HOME FOLKS —1900, THE LOCKERBIE BOOK—1911.

p. 207   MORTON

First printed in *The Indianapolis Journal,* November 2, 1877, dated Indianapolis, November 1; hitherto unpublished in book form. Oliver Perry Morton, the "War Governor" of Indiana, was born at Saulsbury, Indiana, August 4, 1823. In 1867 he became a United States senator, and was appointed minister to England in 1870, but declined the office. He died in Indianapolis, November 1, 1877. Mr. Riley admired him exceedingly and was moved by his speeches.

p. 209   AN AUTUMNAL EXTRAVAGANZA

Dated Greenfield, November 1, 1877, first printed in *The Indianapolis Saturday Herald,* November 3, 1877; hitherto unpublished in book form.

p. 211   THE ROSE

Dated Greenfield, November 13, 1877, first printed in *The Newcastle Mercury,* December 6, 1877, with the title, *My Rose;* published in GREEN FIELDS AND RUNNING BROOKS—1892, LOVE LYRICS—1899, RILEY ROSES—1909, THE LOCKERBIE BOOK—1911, THE ROSE—1913.

p. 213   THE MERMAN

First printed in *The Indianapolis Saturday Herald,* November 17, 1877; hitherto unpublished in book form. The following comment appeared with the publication of the poem:

A literary club is now wielding above the ducked head of the community. Among the most extinguished members are the names of Alex. Black and J. W. Riley. At the next meeting the former will read an original paper of *Floridian Lagoons, or the Wrecker's Roost;* and the latter will whet his voice on the following plagiarism from Tennyson. [Cf. Tennyson's *The Merman.*]

p. 215   THE RAINY MORNING

Dated Marion, Indiana, November 22, 1877, first printed in *The Indianapolis Journal,* November 24, 1877; published in MORNING—1907, SONGS OF HOME—1910, THE LOCKERBIE BOOK—1911. The following stanza originally stood in place of the fourth:

I do not know that the sermon
Was meant for me alone,
Tho' it seemed to me God spoke it
In the faintest undertone.
Yet this I know: when the spirit
Is draped in the gloom of sin,
That only the hand of the Master
Can let the sunshine in.

p. 216
WE ARE NOT ALWAYS GLAD WHEN WE SMILE

Dated December 7, 1877; first printed in *The Indianapolis Journal,* December 14, 1877; published in THE FLYING ISLANDS OF THE NIGHT—1900, SONGS OF HOME—1910, THE LOCKERBIE BOOK—1911. The poem has been revised throughout: the second stanza of the present version was the first in the original; the second stanza in the original read:

We are not always glad when we smile,
For the world is so heedless and gay
That our doubts and our fears, and our griefs and
our tears
Are lighter when hidden away.
And the touch of a frivolous hand
May oftener wound than caress,
And kisses that drip from the reveler's lip,
May oftener blister than bless.

p. 218   A SUMMER SUNRISE

Dated Greenfield, December 12, 1877, first printed in *The Indianapolis Journal,* December 21, 1877; hitherto unpublished in book form. These lines accompanied the poem: "After Lee O. Harris. As a simple tribute to my early teacher and my truest friend, this humble imitation is inscribed."

p. 220   DAS KRIST KINDEL

First printed with the title, *A Dream of Christ-mas* in *The Indianapolis Journal,* December 25, 1877; published in AFTERWHILES — 1887, OLD-FASHIONED ROSES—1888, THE LOCKERBIE BOOK—1911. The poem has been revised in minor details since its early publication.

p. 225   AN OLD YEAR'S ADDRESS

Dated 1878; hitherto unpublished. This bizarre and extravagant nonsense verse was written for Frank S. Hereth, Samuel B. Moffit and Ed Yoe, passing acquaintances, who had it inscribed and illustrated on cards to present to friends on New-year's day.

p. 227   A NEW YEAR'S PLAINT

First printed in *The Indianapolis Journal,* January 1, 1878; hitherto unpublished in book form. The quotation at the beginning of the poem is from *In Memoriam,* V, 9-12.

p. 230   LUTHER BENSON

First printed in *The Kokomo Tribune,* January 5, 1878; hitherto unpublished in book form. Luther Benson, the famous temperance orator, was very greatly admired by Mr. Riley for his oratorical gifts and original force of expression. They were lifelong friends. The subtitle of these verses, *After Reading His Autobiography,* refers to his book, *Fifteen Years in Hell.*

p. 232   DREAM

Dated February 15, 1878, in the note-book of Mr. Riley's sister, Elva Riley Eitel; published in THE

Flying Islands of the Night—1891, Love Lyrics—1899, The Lockerbie Book—1911.

p. 234   WHEN EVENING SHADOWS FALL

Enclosed in a letter, dated Greenfield, February 25, 1878, to Miss Sarah G. Smith, of Kokomo, now Mrs. W. D. Pratt, of Indianapolis; hitherto unpublished. Mr. Riley met Miss Smith in February, 1878, when he was visiting in the home of Charles H. Philips, editor of *The Kokomo Tribune*. After his initial appearance on the lecture platform at Kokomo, February 14, 1878, she wrote a very complimentary press notice. It was in appreciation of this article in *The Kokomo Tribune* and in pleasant memory of his visit to the Philips' home that he wrote *When Evening Shadows Fall*.

p. 236   YLLADMAR

Dated Greenfield March 15, 1878, first printed in *The Indianapolis Journal*, March 16, 1878; published in His Pa's Romance (Homestead Edition) —1908, The Lockerbie Book—1911. The name was coined by Mr. Riley.

p. 238   A FANTASY

Dated April 20, 1878, first printed in the prose sketch, *An Adjustable Lunatic*, in *The Indianapolis Journal*, April 23, 1878; published in Sketches in Prose—1891.

p. 242   A DREAM

First printed in *The Indianapolis Saturday Herald*, May 11, 1878; hitherto unpublished.

p. 244 DREAMER, SAY

First printed with the title *Alkazar,* in *The Indianapolis Saturday Herald,* May 11, 1878; published in ARMAZINDY—1894, SONGS OF HOME—1910, THE LOCKERBIE BOOK—1911. The early version contained two more lines at the end of each stanza.

Stanza 1:
> Dreamer, say, will you dream for me
> Of a land like this, and a foaming sea?

Stanza 2:
> Dreamer, say, will you dream a dream
> Of a tropic land of gloom and gleam?

Stanza 3:
> Dreamer, dream of a land of love
> When hearts grow ripe for the world above.

p. 246 BRYANT

Dated June 12, 1878, first printed in *The Indianapolis Journal,* June 14, 1878; hitherto unpublished in book form. At the time of his death, William Cullen Bryant was the first of American poets. Mr. Riley has always been fond of Bryant's verse, and to-day one of his favorite poems is *The Planting of the Apple Tree.*

p. 247 BABYHOOD

First printed in *The Indianapolis Saturday Herald,* June 15, 1878; published in PIPES O' PAN—1888, RHYMES OF CHILDHOOD—1890, SONGS O' CHEER—1905, THE LOCKERBIE BOOK—1911. This poem has always held a special place in the author's affections and appeared on his business stationery in the early eighties.

MAYMIE'S STORY OF RED RIDING HOOD

These lines were the next to appear in print,—printed in *The Indianapolis Saturday Herald,* June 15, 1878. The poem is included in *A Child World,* in a later volume.

p. 249   LIBERTY

Read at a Fourth of July celebration at Newcastle, Indiana, in 1878; first printed in *The Newcastle Mercury,* July 6, 1878; hitherto unpublished in book form except the section referring to the Independence Bell, which was converted into *The Voice of Peace,* and published in MORNING—1907, THE LOCKERBIE BOOK—1911.

p. 259   TOM VAN ARDEN

First printed in *The Indianapolis Saturday Herald,* July 6, 1878; published in GREEN FIELDS AND RUNNING BROOKS—1892, LOVE LYRICS—1899, THE LOCKERBIE BOOK—1911. The author had no definite person in mind.

p. 263   T. C. PHILIPS

Dated Greenfield, July 8, 1878; first printed in *The Kokomo Tribune,* July 20, 1878; hitherto unpublished in book form. Mr. Riley composed this sonnet four days after the death of his venerable friend and mentor, T. C. Philips, an editor of statewide name and influence. As proprietor of *The Kokomo Tribune,* he had welcomed Mr. Riley's contributions for *The Home Department* of that paper, and on February 14 of the same year in which he died, had introduced him to his first Kokomo audience.

p. 264 **A DREAM UNFINISHED**

Dated Greenfield, Indiana, July 30, 1878, first printed in *The Hancock Democrat*, August 1, 1878; hitherto unpublished in book form. Miss Nellie Millikan, later Mrs. George B. Cooley, was one of Mr. Riley's early friends and among the very first to express faith in the ultimate success of his poetry. She died at Belleville, Illinois, July 27, 1878, and was buried at Greenfield. These verses were written in her memory.

p. 267 **A CHILD'S HOME LONG AGO**

Prepared for an Old Settlers' Meeting at Oakland, near Indianapolis, August 3, 1878; read also at the first meeting of the Indiana Pioneer Society at the old Indiana State Fair Grounds, October 2, 1878; first printed in *The Indianapolis Saturday Herald,* August 10, 1878; with the title of *The Old Cabin;* the section from l. 27, p. 270, through the last line, p. 272, published under the title of *A Child's Home Long Ago,* in RHYMES OF CHILDHOOD —1890, THE LOCKERBIE BOOK—1911; the remainder of the poem hitherto unpublished in book form. The section of this poem used in RHYMES OF CHILDHOOD is introduced by the following lines, now omitted:

Even as the gas flames flicker to and fro,
The Old Man's wavering fancies leap and glow,—

"Each man rewarded as his works shall be," was a favorite sentiment of Mr. Riley's father.

"The description of the interior of a pioneer log cabin," Mr. Riley once said in commenting on this poem, "is as true to life as I could make it. I was born in a log house, weather-boarded, and remember it well, as also numerous other log houses. I can not claim to be a pioneer, only that I knew many in my youth, and from actuality I can testify to the nobility of the type."

p. 275   THE FLYING ISLANDS OF THE NIGHT

First printed in the *Indianapolis Saturday Herald,* August 24, 1878; published in THE FLYING ISLANDS OF THE NIGHT—1891, THE LOCKERBIE BOOK—1911, THE FLYING ISLANDS OF THE NIGHT (Franklin Booth edition)—1913. *The Herald* printed this poem in the fourth number of the *Respectfully Declined Papers of the Buzz Club,* a series of six prose sketches interspersed with poetry, which Mr. Riley contributed at this period. The poem was revised for the 1891 edition and again for a later edition published in 1898. When it appeared in book form in 1891, the introductory poem *For the Song's Sake,* p. 277, and the *Songs of the Seven Faces,* pp. 279-283, were first included. The latter of these originally appeared in *The Indianapolis Journal,* February 4, 1879, under the title, *Of the Whole World Mine.* It was greatly altered to meet the requirements of the larger poem. The early version read:

OF THE WHOLE WORLD MINE

I KNEW you long and long before
God sprinkled stars upon the floor
Of Heaven, and swept this soul of mine
So far beyond the reach of thine.
Ere day was born I saw your face
Hid in some starry hiding-place,
Where our old moon was kneeling while
You lit its features with your smile.
I knew you while the earth was yet
  A baby—ere the helpless thing
  Could cry, or crawl, or anything;

Nor ever will my soul forget
How drowsy time, low murmuring
　　A lullaby above it, kept
　　A-nodding, till he dozed, and slept,
And knew it not, till wakening,
The morning stars began to sing.
I knew you even as the hands
　　Of angels set your sculptured form
　　Upon a pedestal of storm,
And lowered you to earth with strands
Of twisted lightning. And I heard
Your voice—ere you could speak a word
　　Of any but the angel tongue—
I listened, and I heard you say—
　　"Though Heaven sows our lives among
The worlds a million miles away
　　Each from the other, they will lean
Their tendrils nearer, day by day;
　　Till all the lands that intervene
Shall dwindle slowly—till the space
Shall see them, vine-like, interlace
　　Caressingly, and climb, and twine,
　　Up trellises of summer-shine;
　　And bud and burst in bloom divine."
You spoke and vanished; and a stream
　　Of some strange rapture overran
My laughing lips, as in my dream
　　I sang as only angels can.

SONG

I follow you forever on!
Through darkest night and dimmest dawn;
Through storm and calm, through shower and
　　　　shine,
I hear your soul call back to mine.
　　I follow through the dusk—the dew;
　　Through gleam and gloom I follow you.
　　I follow, follow, follow you.

I follow ever on and on,
O'er hill and hollow, brake and lawn;
Through rocky pass, and deep ravine
Where light of day is never seen.
　　I waver not—my heart is true:
　　Unfaltering I follow you;
　　I follow, follow, follow you.

I follow ever on and on!
The cloak of night around me drawn
Though wet with mist, is all besprent
With stars to light the way you went.
   The moon smiles brighter on me through
   The darkness as I follow you;
   I follow, follow, follow you.

I follow ever on and on!
The pilgrim staff I lean upon
Is wrought of love, and it will lend
Me strength to journey to the end.
   Though all the world I wander through
   In empty quest,—I follow you—
   I follow, follow, follow you.

I follow ever on and on:
I know the ways your feet have gone,—
The grass is greener, and the bloom
Of roses richer in perfume.
   And all the birds I listen to
   Sing sweeter as I follow you,
   I follow, follow, follow you.

I follow ever on and on:
For as the night fades into dawn,
So shall my vigil fade away,
And I will kiss your lips, and say:
   Through life and death, and Heaven, too,
   My eager feet will follow you—
   Will follow, follow, follow you

In Act I, the following did not appear until the 1891 edition: the apparition of the counter-self of Crestillomeem and Jucklet, showing these two conspirators as they might have been, with their remarks preceding the following, p. 290 l. 2 to p. 293 l. 16; the description of Crestillomeem's method of disposing of the princess and her lover, p. 294 l. 12 to p. 295 l. 18, p. 295 ll. 20-22, and p. 296 ll. 10-13; Jucklet's description of Spraivoll, p. 298 ll. 7-11, 14, 15, 19, p. 299 ll. 2-6, p. 301 ll. 1-7; and the last six lines of Spraivoll's song, p. 300 ll. 7-12.

Crestillomeem's conversation with Spraivoll, in which she unfolds her plot against the King, p. 303 l. 3 to p. 304 l. 20 and p. 305 l. 13 to p. 306 l. 19, was amplified for the 1891 edition, when Spraivoll's weird crooning, p. 304 l. 21 to p. 305 l. 12, and the Queen's remarks on Dwainie, p. 307 ll. 3-13, were first used.

The introductory lines to the song, *A Lovely Husband,* p. 286 l. 18 to p. 287 l. 2, and the song itself, p. 287 ll. 3-14, p. 302 l. 15 to p. 303 l. 2, were not included until the final edition.

In the 1891 edition the description of the King's garden at the beginning of Act II, p. 309, was expanded and a new improvised song by Amphine, p. 309 l. 1 to p. 310 l. 4, p. 310 ll. 13-21, p. 311 ll. 9-22, introduced.

The next song by Amphine, sung after he has discovered Dwainie near him in the garden, p. 313 l. 1 to p. 314 l. 8, also appeared as a part of this poem for the first time in the 1891 edition, having been printed separately under the title, *Song,* in *The Indianapolis Journal,* June 21, 1885. In this original form, before it became a part of *The Flying Islands,* "Lady" stood in place of "Dwainie" throughout the poem. The earliest version is given:—

SONG

Linger, my Lady! Lady lily-fair,
Stay yet thy step upon the casement-stair—
Poised be thy slipper-tip as is the time
Of some still star.—Ah, Lady!—lady mine,
      Yet linger—linger there!

Thy face, O Lady, lily-pure and fair,
Gleams i' the dusk as in thy dusky hair
The snowy blossom glimmers, or the shine
Of thy swift smile.—Ah, Lady!—lady mine!
      Yet linger—linger there!

With lifted wrist where round the laughing air
Hath blown a mist of lawn and claspt it there,
Waft finger-tipt adieus that spray the wine
Of thy waste kisses to'rd me, lady mine!
    Yet linger—linger there!

What unloosed splendor is there may compare
With thy hand's unfurled glory anywhere!
What glint of sun, or dew, or jewel fine
May mate thine eyes?—Ah, Lady—lady mine,
    Yet linger—linger there!

My soul confronts thee; on thy brow and hair
It lays its gentleness like palms of prayer;
It touches sacredly those lips of thine
And swoons across thy spirit, lady mine,
    The while thou lingerest there.

Part of Amphine's conversation with Dwainie, p. 315 ll. 7-15, was added to the 1891 edition; but instead of the latter part of Dwainie's reply and Amphine's answer, p. 316 ll. 7-20, the original text contained only the following:—

    When love lay like a baby in my arms
    And life was like a tinkling toy.

In the 1891 edition appeared for the first time: Dwainie's laudatory description of Wunkland, p. 317 ll. 10-14, p. 318 ll. 13-24, p. 319 ll. 9-14; Amphine's account of his lost sister, p. 323 ll. 13-16, p. 324 ll. 9-11; their discussion about the change in the King, including Dwainie's "asides" in which she reveals to the reader her supernatural powers, p. 325 ll. 3-13, p. 326 ll. 7-11, p. 326 l. 22 to p. 327 l. 4, p. 328 ll. 9-12, p. 329 ll. 6-9; and Jucklet's grotesque remarks after arriving in the garden, p. 338 ll. 5-10, p. 340 ll. 6-20, p. 341 ll. 1-13; though p. 320 ll. 12-26 and p. 331 l. 5 to p. 334 l. 7, including Jucklet's

song, *Fold Me Away in Your Arms, O Night,* were
not added until the final revision.

July 5, 1879, p. 331 l. 18 to p. 332 l. 8, p. 332 l. 13
to p. 333 l. 5 were printed separately in *The Indianapolis Saturday Herald,* as follows:—

GLIMPSE

". . . *My pen fell—*
My hands struck sharp together. as hands do
Which hold at nothing."

O, but a flash of some sweet light
Has smitten the eyes of my soul to-night!
Groping here in the garden-land,
I felt my fancy's out-held hand
Touch the rim of a realm that seems
Like an isle of bloom in a sea of dreams.
I stand here dazed and alone—alone
My heart beats on in an undertone,
And I hold my breath as I hear from far
  Away the voice of a dead guitar,
    And the wraith of an old love song,
And my cheeks are as red as the roses are
  Where the dews of night belong.
Low to myself I am whispering,
  I am glad, and the night knows why—
  I am glad that the dream came by
    And found me here as of old when I
Was a ruler and a king.

It was an age ago—an age
Turned down in life like a folded page—
See, where the volume falls apart,
And the faded book-mark—'tis my heart—
Nor mine alone, but another knit
So cunningly in the love of it,
That you must look with a shaking head
Nor know the living from the dead.
Ah! what a broad and a sea-like lawn
Is the field of love they bloom upon:
Hazy reaches of velvet grass
Billowing with the winds that pass,

And breaking in a snow-white foam
Of lily-crests on the shores of home.
Only a flash of some sweet light
Smiting the eyes of my soul to-night,
With my face upturned to a crescent moon
Atilt like the bowl of a silver spoon,
Skimming the sky of the rich white cream
Of the clouds still drifting o'er my dream.

The act originally ended with the last line of p. 347, when the Nightmares leap on the comet and disappear, omitting until the 1891 edition Jucklet's prayer to Æo, which was first printed in *The Indianapolis Journal*, December 28, 1884, with the title, *What Shall We Pray For*. An old manuscript indicates that its original form was as follows:—

What shall we pray for?—
　　Shall we pray
　　For health to-day—
　　We who so yearn
　　For health's return,
And laughing hours so long away?
　　Or shall we pray
　　The long delay
'Of Fortune shall have end,
　　And wealth be ours, as when
　　Each silver night and golden day
Of youth was ours, my friend?

What shall we pray for? What?—
That the sweet clusters of forget-me-nots
　　And mignonette
　　And violet
Be out of Childhood brought
　　And in our old hearts set
　　　A-blooming now, as then?
　　Or shall we pray
　　The love long flown
　　Return again
　　　Unto its own,
　　No more to fly away?

What shall we pray for?
  Shall it be
  The mother-faces we
Have missed for years
  So bitterly—
  Whose eyelids would
  Not lift, nor could
 Be melted open with our tears?
How we would greet them now—nay—nay!—
For what then shall we pray?

For what then shall we pray?
Pray—pray all self to pass away—
  Forgetful of all needs
    Thine own—
  Neglectful of all creeds,
    Alone
  Stand facing Heaven, and say:
    To Thee,
  O Infinite, I pray
    Bless thou mine Enemy!

In Act III, pp. 351-353, including the stage directions in regard to the disappearance of Spraivoll's apparition, p. 354, were omitted from the first rendering of the poem but included in the second in 1891; meanwhile the *Wraith-Song of Spraivoll*, p. 352 l. 3 to p. 353 l. 24, was printed in the *Indianapolis Journal,* March 24, 1883, with the title, *Sweet Bells Jangled.*

Krung's speech, in the original version, lacked p. 359 ll. 7-20, p. 360 l. 4 to p. 361 l. 7, p. 361 ll. 16-20, and the last two lines of the play.

The quotation at the beginning of the poem, "A thynge of wychencreft, an idle dreme," is from Aella, in the Rowley Poems of Thomas Chatterton, line 421. The original version contained the subtitle, *A Twintorette,* in place of this quotation.

The poem called forth both decided criticism and

praise from the first. Mr. Madison Cawein, to whom the poem is dedicated, writes about it as follows:

Thomas Bailey Aldrich said to me at dinner, on an Easter Sunday, a little while after *The Flying Islands* appeared, that he considered *that* book worthy of a place by the side of Shakespeare's *Midsummer Night's Dream*, and that if everything else Mr. Riley ever wrote were forgotten, this play would establish his reputation to posterity.

Mr. Riley, in replying to a letter from Benj. S. Parker, September 13, 1878, speaks thus of it:

That "Thing-um-me-jig rhyme" is the supposed production of a wild, eccentric character of mine who figures in a mythical club whose only ambition is to please itself— fully conscious that the public is too engrossed with matters of importance to listen to its jargon. Therefore I think you err in attacking me, ignoring, as you do, all allowance for the proprieties the production calls into use; . . . and I am startled and chagrined that you, a careful reader and an author as well, should find such serious fault with what is simply nothing more than my good nature,— for *The Flying Islands* is but, at best, a smile.